Preaching John

Other Titles in
Fortress Resources for Preaching

~

~

FORTHCOMING

Preaching John

Robert Kysar

Fortress Press
Minneapolis

PREACHING JOHN

Library of Congress Cataloging-in-Publication Data
Kysar, Robert.
        Preaching John / Robert Kysar
        p. cm.—(Fortress resources for preaching)
        Includes bibliographical references and index.
        ISBN 0-8006-3226-5 (alk. paper)
        1. Bible. 2. N.T. 3. John—Commentaries I. Title II. Fortress resources for preaching

BS2615.3 .K98 2002
226.'5/06—dc21   2002019881

⊖ The paper used in this publication meets the minimum requirements of American National Standard for Information Sciences—Permanence of Paper for Printed Library Materials, ANSI Z329.48–1984.

Manufactured in the U.S.A.
07   06   05   04   03   02   1   2   3   4   5   6   7   8   9   10

For
RAYMOND E. BROWN, S.S.
with gratitude

Contents

Abbreviations

AB	Anchor Bible
ABD	*Anchor Bible Dictionary.* Edited by D. N. Freedman. 6 vols. New York, 1992.
ACNT	Augsburg Commentary on the New Testament
ANTC	Abingdon New Testament Commentaries
BibIntSer	Biblical Interpretation Series
CurTM	*Currents in Theology and Mission*
FRLANT	Forschungen zur Religion und Literatur des Alten und Neuen Testaments
FRP	Fortress Resources for Preaching
GBS	Guides to Biblical Scholarship
ICC	International Critical Commentary
JBL	*Journal of Biblical Literature*
JSOT	*Journal for the Study of the Old Testament*
LXX	Septuagint
NCB	New Century Bible
NIB	*The New Interpreter's Bible*
NTS	*New Testament Studies*
NTT	New Testament Theology
RCL	Revised Common Lectionary
Semeia	*Semeia*
SBLDS	Society of Biblical Literature Dissertation Series
SBLMS	Society of Biblical Literature Monograph Series
SNTSMS	Society for New Testament Studies Monograph Series
SP	Sacra pagina
StABH	Studies in American Biblical Hermeneutics
WBC	Word Biblical Commentary

Preface

THIS BOOK IS THE CULMINATION of my whole career as a pastor and teacher. My interest in preaching roots way back to my seminary days (1956–59) and has continued through all these years. When I did my doctoral dissertation, I worked on the prologue to the Gospel of John and subsequently became captivated by this Gospel. Since that time, my career has straddled the church and academia, sometimes pleasantly and sometimes not so pleasantly. There were periods when I didn't know whether my place was in the parish or in a college or seminary. I left a tenured position as a full professor of religion at a small liberal arts college to return to parish ministry with my partner, Myrna. I had wearied of teaching introductory courses to college students. Not long after starting parish ministry, however, I began teaching part-time at the two Lutheran theological seminaries in Pennsylvania.

During this period of part-time seminary teaching, I was invited to team-teach several introductory preaching courses. I was hooked! I loved helping students discover their own preaching voices, and teaching preaching gave expression to my devotion to parish ministry. I spent the last decade of my career teaching both preaching and New Testament.

This book brings together what I know and love about the two major interests in my career—the Gospel of John and preaching. Such a book as this has been in my mind for the last ten years or so, but until now I did not feel ready to write it. With my retirement, I decided now was the *(kairotic?)* time for me to think and write my way through what would best help pastors and seminarians deal with John in their preaching ministries.

Naturally I am indebted to far more people than I can name there. At the top of my list is my wife, the Reverend Dr. Myrna B. C. Kysar. Not only has her love sustained me through a lot of difficulties, but her own skill as a parish pastor has been a constant resource for my thoughts about preaching. She helps me keep my feet on the ground in the congregation and to remember the preachers who struggle each week to interpret texts faithfully and with pertinence. More specifically, because Myrna is such a fine preacher, I have sought and received her permission to include some of her sermons along with my own as examples in this book.

Over the years, a number of opportunities to teach and lecture on preaching the Gospel of John have helped me hone the essentials for this study. Most especially, I am grateful to the Episcopal Preaching Foundation for the opportunity to give two lectures for its Preaching Excellence Program. Those lectures were rewritten and published as "Preaching John—Word and Words" in *Preaching through the Year of Luke*, vol. 9, in the series *Sermons That Work*, edited by Roger Alling and David J. Schlafer (Harrisburg: Morehouse, 2000, 87–97). My thanks to David J. Schlafer for this opportunity and for his guidance. The dialogue with pastors in a continuing education workshop at Candler School of Theology, Emory University, also sharpened some of my ideas, as well as my participation in a workshop sponsored by the Institute for Jewish-Christian Understanding, Muhlenberg College, Allentown, Pennsylvania. My retirement lecture at Candler forced me to think about "Preaching John in a Pluralistic Society," and a lay study on "Easter with John" made me think in new ways about John's Easter stories. For all these occasions I am most thankful.

This is an opportunity, too, for me to express my gratitude to Father Raymond E. Brown, S.S. Father Brown stimulated my study of John and afforded me several opportunities to write on the Gospel for publication. His untimely death in 1998 deprived both the church and the scholarly world of an extraordinary gift. His dual commitment to Christ and to scholarship is a model that influenced a great many of us. Although Father Brown might not agree with everything I say in this book, I nonetheless dedicate it to his memory in thanksgiving for his life.

1

Introduction:
The Problem and Promise
of Preaching John

SOME YEARS AGO, the Fifth Sunday of Easter, Year A, loomed ahead of me and with it a gospel lesson in the lectionary from John 14:1-14. For most of the week I struggled with the thick language of this passage. Finally in some desperation I settled on the old and familiar words of Jesus in verse 6: "Jesus said to him [Thomas], 'I am the way, and the truth, and the life.'" In the sermon I spoke of each of the three predicates—way, truth, and life. The sermon was a classic three pointer with time spent on each of the three terms by which Jesus identifies himself. (I seldom resort to three-point sermons anymore, but theoretically I maintain they are still useful at times with certain texts.) Regarding the term "way," my sermon discussed Christ as a means to eternal life. Under "truth," I argued that Jesus is all the truth we really need to know. With the third point, I asserted that true life is what Christ offers us. As any good preacher would, I tried as best I could to explicate the meaning of these terms and thereby clarify what the passage means today. It really was not a bad sermon. But as I look at it now, I realize that I diluted the saying of all ambiguity. In ten minutes I pretended to solve the problem that students of the fourth Gospel have wrestled with for years!

Most of us preachers have struggled long into the night with such a passage as this. Getting the Gospel of John to speak clearly is often a tiresome task. The sections of the fourth Gospel in which Jesus speaks are especially dense. There seems to be no connection between bits and pieces of his discourse. We often stumble over individual words that seem to mean so much and yet are hard to pin down with precision. What exactly does Jesus mean by spirit, for instance? Or, in the lesson discussed above, what meaning should we attach to those three words by which Jesus identifies himself?

The narratives about Jesus are not much easier. There are hints that certain actions attributed to Jesus reach beyond the context of a particular story to mean something more. But, again, how do we discern where they reach? Sometimes it looks like Jesus' words comment on something he has done, which appears to be the case in chapter 6. The long discourse of the "bread of life" seems to comment on the feeding of the crowd that begins the chapter. Often Jesus' words reach back or forward in the plot to some narrative; other times it looks as if a discourse has nothing to do with the narratives surrounding it.

The theological ideas of this Gospel, too, are profound—there is little doubt about that. Yet, so much of what Jesus says at one point is explicitly or implicitly denied, contradicted, or at least made more complicated elsewhere. What are we to make, for instance, of the fact that Jesus claims he judges no one (8:15), yet elsewhere asserts that he does judge and his judgment is just (5:30)? Thick language, dense discourses, tantalizing relationships between discourse and narratives, and puzzling theology are all part of the struggle we have with preaching on the Gospel of John.

That sermon on John 14:6 exemplifies our dilemma. We want to grasp the meaning of a Johannine passage and carry it over into the sermon so that it speaks to our congregation. We want to file the meaning of Johannine words, phrases, and narratives in our personal theological dictionaries, to package them for simple understanding, and to blow away the fog that creeps into our listeners' minds every time a passage from the Gospel of John is read. More often than not, however, the meaning of passages in John resists packaging. Often there appears to be a kind of unyielding ambiguity in the language of this Gospel, both in narratives but especially in Jesus' discourses. Words point in a number of directions at the same time, teasing us with which direction we should take in nailing meaning down. The texture of the language is such that the threads are not woven in neat discernible patterns but often in what strikes us as chaotic designs.

Doing exegesis of the kind we all learned in seminary involves studying how a word is used in a text, comparing its usage elsewhere in the same document, and discovering how it appears in other New Testament writers. When we have done this, we can proceed with our interpretative task. "Word studies" we call them. In the fourth Gospel, however, such a method seldom works very well. We are left with language that has possibility of multiple meanings with few clues about how Jesus or the evangelist is using it in a particular case. Like Nicodemus, we are utterly at a loss, and I, at least, sound like I am asking a dumb question comparable to the ruler's words, "How can anyone be born after having grown old? Can one enter a second time into the mother's womb and be born?" (3:4). Yet the very richness of Johannine language lies hidden in the problem of such ambiguous language.

The Gospel of John is filled with both promises and problems for preaching. In fact, the promises seem concealed in the very problems that plague us, much like a tasty walnut comes hidden in a rough shell. When we sense that is true, we struggle all the more to get a handle on those problems—to crack the shell—as indeed we should. The richness of John for preaching usually entails cutting through the problematic character of its language, narratives, the relationship between narratives and discourse, and theology. As the cross both reveals and conceals God, the Gospel of John both reveals and conceals its promise for proclamation.

This book is designed to enable preachers to understand better the Gospel of John in order that they might tap its resources for proclamation. The journey on which I invite you is not an easy one. It entails diving deep into the problems to find the promises lying on the murky and muddy bottom. Our journey involves, first, coming to some comprehension of scholarly proposals for the Gospel of John. I promise you this chapter will not yield to the temptation simply to become a purely intellectual exercise (chapter 1). With an understanding of what scholars are saying about John as a background, our trek moves successively through three topics: The Gospel's theology (chapter 2), its language (chapter 3), and its narratives and their relationship with Jesus' discourses (chapter 4). Since the Johannine Passion story is unique among the four Gospels, chapter 5 is devoted exclusively to it. Along the way I hope to demonstrate something of the power of selected Lectionary Johannine passages for preaching.

Finally, our journey should travel through the passages from John scattered throughout the RCL and note in passing what is excluded from the list of assigned readings (chapter 6). In the conclusion we will explore the promises of preaching John in the form of new movements in homiletics.

Each major section includes "Homiletical Implications," in which I will ask you to think about what the discussion means for our preaching. These implications will include an example of a sermon. But beyond such an example, I am concerned not only with *how* we preach but *why* we preach and our *understanding of preaching*. In other words, the implications for our preaching will include some theoretical matters that I hope will deepen your own reflections on preaching.

After chapter 1, at the conclusion of each subsection dealing with homiletical implications, I will offer a sermon or a fragment of a sermon that is intended to make explicit how a preacher might treat or be aided by the subject under discussion. My hope is that these homiletical insertions will make the discussions more easily applicable to preaching ministry. These fragments will vary in length and in quality as well. My wife Myrna has graciously allowed me to include several of her sermons, each of which provides a female perspective in a way I cannot. Of course, the task is not to write sermons for you, nor do I offer these as model sermons.

What I hope they do is stimulate your homiletical thinking with concrete examples.

These sermons and sermon fragments, however, will betray something of my understanding of preaching. For the most part, I am committed to narrative preaching, which does not mean that my sermons are filled with stories but that they are structured like narrative plots rather than rational arguments. Most often (but not always), when studying a text in preparation for preaching it, I look for a problem in the passage under study, some inconsistency, some outrageous claim most of us find hard to believe, or some strange feature. This is what Eugene Lowry has called the "conflict," the "peculiar," or the "felt difficulty" the text causes in us, when we are "looking for trouble."[1] It is that which upsets the equilibrium, scrambles our easy sense of order and logic, and sends us searching for some clue as to how to bring the pieces together again.[2] Moreover, I remain firmly convinced that the sermon is an oral event and any effort to reproduce that event on paper for reading is futile and ultimately distorts the event itself. Because I think of the oral event when putting a sermon together, I deliberately try to write in my own version of an oral style. That means, among other things, that I write in short sentences and sometimes only pieces of sentences, all of which works when they are heard but may offend when they are read. Use these sermon fragments in any way they are useful to you.

Before going further, a brief exploration of some of the issues at stake in the preacher's handling of a Johannine passage is in order. The major issues are left for later chapters and more extensive treatment; however, three preliminary matters concern us more briefly at this beginning juncture because each addresses a problem in interpreting John for preaching. The first is the question of the gospel genre as it is found in John; the second is the distinctive picture of Jesus presented in this Gospel, which is not always easy to preach; and the third entails interpreting John on its own without a Pauline theological framework.

The Gospel Genre

The Gospel Genre in the New Testament

The New Testament treats us to a particular form of literature that continues to stir debate among scholars. The term "gospel" seems to have arisen from the story of Jesus attributed to Mark, although it doubtless owes its peculiarly Christian use to the early church's preaching in the years before the writing of the Gospels. "The beginning of the good news (*euangelion*, gospel) of Jesus Christ, the Son of God" (Mark 1:1). The word, of course, means the announcement of a bit of good news; however, Mark attaches the word to an extended narrative about Jesus of Nazareth and even titles this narrative "gospel." If the scholarly consensus is correct, Mark's Gospel was the first written of those that have survived as independent documents. Speculation and research abound on several fronts. Were there earlier gospels, such as a narrative of Jesus' passion, a document that comprised a collection of his wonders, or even an anthology of his sayings (such as the hypothetical "Q" or "Sayings Source," which many supposed was behind the Gospels of Matthew and Luke)? What previous literary model, if any, was used in shaping the form and content of the gospel genre? Did the early Christians use ancient Greco-Roman biographical stories as models for the Gospels? Did other such contemporary literature influence the shaping of the Gospels? Or, did the evangelist we call Mark or early Christian preachers before the evangelist invent this new genre?

These are all important and fascinating questions. What interests us, however, is only the question of what it means to read a Gospel and what expectations we might have of it. The issue really boils down to this, if you will allow an oversimplification: How are the stories of Jesus' ministry and reports of his words, on the one hand, and the preaching of the early church regarding the meaning of Jesus' life and ministry, on the other hand, related in the gospel genre? To put the question even more simply, how are fact and faith interwoven in the stories of Jesus that we call Gospels? Any way we express this issue, we run the danger of reducing a very complex question to a formula. For the earliest Christians, there probably was no distinction between the historical Jesus and the living Christ. The distinction is ours, not theirs. Faith and fact can never be isolated, since faith always entails some factual experience, and fact already presumes a perspective that involves faith of some sort. At another level, however, we have to ask what is a pure "fact" that is not influenced by the faith (or assumptions) of the observer? Actually, as contemporary historians have concluded, there probably is no such thing as pure fact. Still, we ask the same question the laity raise for us: Which is reporting and which is preaching? Like it or not, we must deal with the modern distinction between the two.

The following conclusions are relatively safe to make. The earliest Christian communities experienced a new power and meaning in their lives as a result of Jesus' life, death, and resurrection. They began sharing that experience, as the early sermons in Acts suggest. Their witness entailed both the fact of Jesus' ministry and what that ministry means (especially his death and resurrection) for humans. So, the earliest creeds we can discern in the New Testament blend both the facts of Jesus and their meaning for Christian life. In 1 Cor. 15:3-8, Paul itemizes the essentials of Jesus' death, burial, resurrection, and appearances. Still, even in his rehearsal of the tradition that was handed on to him, Paul betrays the interweaving of the reality of Jesus' ministry and its meaning for Christians. Christ's death was "for our sins" (v. 3), which suggests that the community responsible for this creed attached extraordinary significance to the execution of one thought to be a criminal of the state. Jesus' death and resurrection (and burial as well, perhaps), according to Paul, were all "in accordance with the scriptures" (vv. 3-4), implying that the early Christians laid some kind of interpretative framework, derived from Hebrew scriptures, over these events in order to discern their meaning. The givenness of the past is fused with the community's experience to produce its creedal statement.

That fusion eventually produced the extended narratives we have in the first four books of our New Testament. Any attempt to pry that fusion apart is doomed to destroy its ingredients in the process and distort the fundamental purpose of the Gospels. The gospel genre was a particular way of articulating the synthesis of what happened and what significance it has for the benefit of the first readers. It was a form of Christian procla- mation, intended to nourish particular communities of believers and, per- haps, in some cases to convert unbelievers. The communities expressed their faith in stories, which were part of a larger story.

The Gospels are first of all stories. They are, if you will, the good news of God's redemptive activity in Christ told in narrative form. With all of the differences among the four Gospels, they share a common literary form. The plot of the gospel story moves through the stages of any good narrative to reach the same climax in the trial, crucifixion, and resurrec- tion of Jesus. Those of us who use stories in sermons know how natural and powerful the process of proclamation through story is. Story engages humans at a fundamental level for reasons that, in this discussion, must remain unexplored.[3] Each of the four Gospels tells its story of Jesus in order to allow readers themselves, first, to enter into that story and, second, eventually to claim it as their own story. The earliest Christians communi- ties gathered around this story of Jesus because they believed it articulated their own experience and their own being in the world.

Preachers of the Gospel lessons are more than content with this view of the Gospels, for we, in effect, restore the Gospel pericopes to their original and intended purpose, namely, the proclamation of the good news of what God has done for us in Christ. The historians may excavate the Gospels in search for that basic stratum where just the "facts" are found. Our interest in these documents, however, is precisely their proclamation of faith, that is, the meaning of one human life for others. In their role as proclaimers, preachers have no business in dabbling in the historians' task (but see chapter 1). The gospel genre molds its story with a clay fashioned of both historical fact (whatever that may be) and communal faith. This is not to exclude the possibility of a teaching sermon that addresses the way in which faith and historical fact are fused in Christian experience. Indeed, this may be a crucial issue among some in our congregations, given the way in which the press has exploited contemporary efforts to discern the "real historical Jesus." But, if we are to raise the issue at all in the pulpit, we ought to be careful to give it a full treatment.

Another important implication of this discussion of gospel genre for preaching is simple but vital: We preach a part of the story in the context of the full story. Suppose you want to tell a single episode of a movie in your sermon. You would need to frame the telling of one small part of the story with the whole story. You would sketch the plot up to the point of the episode and introduce the characters of the story who are involved in the segment you wish to tell. A separate incident makes sense only in the context of the larger story.

The same is true when we preach a separate pericope from any of the Gospels.[4] The primary difference is that we can assume our congregation is acquainted with the larger story, at least in a general way. That assumption, of course, depends entirely on a particular congregation. Still, we are wise to set the Gospel episode in its larger context, both in our interpretative efforts in preparing to preach and in the sermon itself for the sake of our congregation. The narrative context is vital to the process of understanding any single part of the story, because meaning is always derived from context, narrative or otherwise. While it is probably true that many, if not all, of the pericopes had a life of their own before they were incorporated into Gospel narratives, the four evangelists have given each of them fresh and deeper meaning by framing them within the larger story. (Good examples of this are found in a study of Jesus' parables in the Synoptic Gospels.)

The Genre of the Gospel of John

This discussion of the gospel genre is especially relevant when it comes to the fourth of our canonical Gospels. To begin, let us observe the simple and obvious fact that the writer or writers of this document chose the gospel genre as their medium. That tells us several things about the Gospel of John. It is an interpretation of a story—a faith report—of a human life. As D. Moody Smith has put it, in preaching John "we interpret an interpretation," that is, we interpret what was intended "to make the best sense of a history that has become the object of controversy and division."[5] We do well to honor the Gospel's own fusion of both history and interpretation.

We preachers frequently need to be reminded that the Gospels are an interpretation of an interpretation, if only that we might keep our congregation cognizant of that fact. Moreover, we are called to preach that interpretation as one that continues to bring purpose and meaning to human existence in another age. In the case of the Gospel of John, as well as the other Gospels, what happened (history) blends with interpretation of that (faith) for the sake of proclaiming its meaning.

John, however, seems to have a special homiletical quality. This Gospel begins with a hymn dedicated to the Word, *Logos,* and that Word is the subject of the narrative sermon that ends with the narrator telling us at 20:30-31: "Now Jesus did many other signs in the presence of his disciples, which are not written in this book. But these are written so that you may come to believe (or go on believing) that Jesus is the Messiah, the Son of God, and that through believing you may have life in his name." The narrative leads readers to an experience of the Life that is available in Christ.[6] With words the evangelist brings us to a confrontation with the Word, Christ. There is a kind of self-consciousness about the way the fourth evangelist proceeds. The Gospel of John is the only canonical Gospel (perhaps along with Luke) that states its purpose as clearly and completely as does John 20:30-31. The fourth evangelist writes with a special interest in conveying the Christian message to the readers.

The fact that the fourth evangelist employs the gospel genre suggests something more. The attempt is to tell a story that occurred within time and space in a world not unlike our own. The narrative world of John, then, is one we can imagine, even if that world sometimes seems strangely different from ours.[7] To us thunder is thunder, nothing more. Instead of thunder Jesus hears a heavenly voice confirming his destiny, while at least some of the bystanders recognize the sound only as thunder (12:28-29). The point is that the world this story implies is similar to our own world, even if it stretches our credulity. The originators of this Gospel could have produced a story of another world—the divine realm beyond the human world. Indeed, the fourth Gospel begins at such a point, "in the beginning" (1:1). But the Word that was in the beginning "became flesh and lived among us" (1:14). So, the story as a whole is one of a life lived in this realm we call the world.

Furthermore, the total narrative context of any single portion of John's Gospel is, if anything, even more important than it might be in the other three Gospels. Someone has said of the fourth Gospel that if you begin pulling on one of the individual threads of this document, soon you find that it is woven throughout the whole fabric of this document. There is a forward and a backward glance in nearly every individual Johannine pericope; every story and every discourse both build on what has come before and anticipate what is to come. Take, for instance, the story of the call of the first disciples in 1:35-51. Jesus asks of two of the disciples of John the Baptist, "What are you looking for?" ("looking" is the translation of *zēteō*, 1:38.) Let's pull on that thread. What comes up includes, among other things, the fact that John the Baptist has just declared that among the people is one they do not know (1:26), implying that they should look for this mysterious unknown person. Moreover, Jesus' question, "What are you looking for?" points ahead to seeking Jesus after he has "gone away" (8:21; 13:33; 16:19), seeking him for corrupt reasons (6:24-26; 18:4), and seeking the risen Lord (20:15). Interestingly, the Gospel uses "looking" as bookends for discipleship. The followers of John the Baptist look for Jesus in chapter 1, and Mary Magdalene looks for Jesus' body in chapter 20 and finds the risen Christ. A simple question in one story leads us through the whole Gospel linking other stories.

The Gospel of John is like a seamless garment, "woven in one piece" (19:23). In a sense, this is true of all the Gospels, but the weaving may be even tighter in John. This means for us preachers that the better we know the *whole* of the Gospel of John, the better we will understand its individual parts. In some of the discussions of later chapters, we will try to facilitate that comprehensive understanding even as we examine specific passages. For now, let's simply conclude that every specific passage is linked with the entirety of the narrative, even as every episode of a good novel is integral to the whole story.

Still another feature of John is relevant to the form of this story of Jesus. The fourth evangelist begins the story with a hymn concerning the Word. That hymn begins in a realm beyond history, outside of time and space, "In the beginning" (1:1). A story set within time and space begins beyond time and space. One of the clear purposes of the prologue to John is to identify the main character of the narrative that follows. Jesus is the Word made flesh, dwelling among us, and providing us glimpses of the presence ("glory") of God. By virtue of the prologue, readers know who this Jesus is, even though the characters in the story have yet to find it out.

Actually, this is a common feature of the Gospels, and hence perhaps of the gospel genre itself. Each of the four Gospels, in one way or another, states Jesus' true identity before beginning the story proper. Mark, for instance, declares that the second Gospel is "the gospel of Jesus Christ, *the Son of God*" (Mark 1:1). Like the Gospel of John, the whole of Mark's story is the gradual revelation of Jesus' true identity to the characters in the story, which is finally grasped by the centurion at the foot of the cross (Mark 15:39). I do not mean that the fourth evangelist necessarily knew any of the Synoptic Gospels; that question is saturated with difficulties of all kinds. What I do want to say is that in a unique and apparently deliberate way the fourth evangelist sets the gospel narrative in a transcendent context ("In the beginning," 1:1). That peculiar context appears again and again in the story, for instance, in Jesus' claim that he is from "above" (see 3:31; also 8:58).

To understand that the Gospel of John is a type—however unique—of the gospel genre designed to proclaim the Christian message is to have taken the first step toward preaching John for all its worth. With all this in mind, we turn our attention to another preliminary problem.

The Johannine Portrayal of Jesus

A Gallery of Portraits

Very early on the church declared its commitment to *four* Gospels, as opposed to a harmonization of them into one.[8] That commitment is both important and revealing. There is something of value in the diversity of the four Gospels, and one portrayal of Jesus formed out of an amalgamation of those found in the four Gospels loses something the church regarded as precious. Sustaining that commitment is not easy today, even as it troubled our ancestors in faith. Today there is a common desire to harmonize the four canonical stories of Jesus into one. Popular movies and television productions tell the Jesus story or a portion of it in ways that take a little from this Gospel and at little from another, and so on. Within the tradition of our congregations the harmonizing is no better illustrated than in the ubiquitous Sunday School Christmas pageant. There the Matthean wise men join the Lukan shepherds parading down the aisle to visit the manger, and the audience is content to accept this event as the biblical truth.

Years ago, watching the television movie *Jesus of Nazareth* for the first time, I was intrigued by how the writers had tried to merge separate accounts, even though the Gospel of Luke is given special preference. So, I was on the edge of my chair when the story came to the crucifixion, and in particular to the words that would be put into the mouth of the centurion at the foot of the cross—from Matt. 27:54 and Mark 15:39 or Luke 23:47? I confess that I laughed amid this somber scene when, without speaking a word, the centurion simply removed his helmet and held it over his heart!

Because our congregations are influenced as much (or more so) by these popular portrayals of Jesus as they are by their educational experiences in the church, many laity have their own personal portraits of Jesus that are most often a blending of the various Gospel pictures. In any sermon on a Gospel, we have to work with the fact that individuals have formed their own portrayal of Jesus, regardless of whether it has any basis in the four Gospels or not. Hence, it may be difficult to break through those beloved portraits with the peculiarities of any one Gospel's depiction of Jesus. Preaching necessitates our drawing an image specific to one of the four Gospels. To remember what we have said earlier, any single story about Jesus or his teachings inevitably references the whole of the Gospel in which the story is found. We are called on to remain faithful to those distinctive portraits in order to preach from any one pericope.

The four Gospels, of course, share certain common features of who Jesus is and what he did and said. The broad frameworks of the four are somewhat the same. But within that similar framework, each evangelist develops a peculiar portrayal of the story's main character. Mark's Jesus, for instance, engages in far less teaching than does the Jesus described in the other three. Mark paints Jesus in the bright colors of wondrous stories of healing and exorcism, toned with the ever-present command to silence. In bold strokes Matthew paints Jesus as the teacher par excellence. Luke concurs but stresses Jesus' associations with and teachings about the poor and outcast.[9] John adds a fourth distinctive picture to the assemblage. Each author has reason for their particular emphasis in their description of Jesus. When we preachers ignore this fact and collapse the four portrayals into one harmonious whole, we lose something of the subtleties of each of our Gospels. In effect, we violate our contract to preach the Scriptures faithfully and betray the church's commitment to the diversity of the Gospels.

Let one example of the general importance of attending to a Gospel's peculiar depiction of Jesus suffice before we turn to the Gospel of John. The preacher's text was the story of Jesus in the synagogue at Nazareth in Luke 4:14-21 (the Third Sunday after the Epiphany, C). He began by re-telling the story and drew an imaginative and engaging picture of Jesus *and his disciples* crowding into the synagogue until the little building was packed with guests. The problem was the preacher collapsed the comparable stories from Matthew (13:53-58) and Mark (6:1-6a) into the Lukan account. No matter how imaginative the retelling was, by reconciling the three accounts of this episode, the preacher missed a vital ingredient of Luke's placement of the story. For the third evangelist it was important to position this story as Jesus' *first* public appearance after his temptation (4:1-12) and before the call of the first disciples (5:1-11). The story functions in Luke as Jesus' programmatic declaration of the purpose of his ministry. The preacher's imaginative portrayal distorted the role Luke gives to this powerful tale.

The Johannine Portrait

The gallery exhibit is completed with a very difficult picture of Jesus. One of the classic scholarly problems with the fourth Gospel is the way this evangelist portrays its main character. The Johannine Jesus has been described, among other ways, as a docetic figure, that is, as one who only *appeared* (*dokeō*, "to appear," hence the word "docetic") to be human while actually consisting solely of pure spirit. First John leads us to believe that such an interpretation of the Gospel of John did in fact arise very early in the life of the church. In 4:2 this author declares, "every spirit that confesses that Jesus Christ has come in the *flesh* is from God" (emphasis mine). Apparently there were those in the community for which this letter was written who denied the fleshly incarnation and did so, perhaps, on the basis of their reading of the Gospel of John.[10] Moreover, a debate among Johannine scholars focuses on the precise meaning of John 1:14. Was the humanity of Jesus merely a thin disguise or a full participation in humanity? What is the relationship between "becoming flesh" and the "glory" perceived in Christ?[11]

There can be little debate over the fact that the Johannine portrait accentuates Jesus' extra-human capacities, even though 1:14 declares his humanity genuine. As compared with the other three pictures in the canonical gallery, John's presents a Jesus whose wonders exceed those reported in the Synoptics. An example is the raising of Lazarus in chapter 11. The narrator goes to considerable lengths to say that Lazarus is really dead. After three days, his spirit (his "life-breath"), which had hovered over his tomb, has departed. The body has begun to decay (v. 39). This is no resuscitation but a genuine resurrection (compare Mark 5:35-43, noting v. 39). Another case is the healing of the blind man in chapter 9 who has been blind since birth (v. 1). Jesus does not "restore" his vision as is the case in Mark's stories of comparable healings (8:25 and 10:51-52) but enables a capacity this man has never known. Add to this litany of highly wondrous actions, the story that Jesus passed through the crowd of opponents who sought to kill him without their ever laying a hand on him (John 7:44).

The accentuation on Jesus' extraordinary deeds is palatable, but less easy is the fact that Jesus seldom appears in the fourth Gospel as a compassionate and approachable friend. The Synoptics attribute compassion and pity to Jesus (for example, Matt. 9:36; 14:14; 15:32; and 20:34), and in the first three Gospels Jesus exhibits a friendliness, especially to those who have no friends. He is called a friend of sinners (Matt. 11:19), and he addresses others as "friend" (Matt. 26:50; see also 20:13 and 22:12). Of course, the Johannine Jesus is not devoid of such characteristics. The most vivid example is the relationship Jesus has with the Bethany family of

Mary, Martha, and Lazarus in chapters 11 and 12. Moreover, it is this Gospel alone in which Jesus names his disciples "friends" (15:15) and speaks of his death as laying down his life for his friends (15:13). Nowhere else in the Gospels is Jesus' love for his disciples stated more strongly than in John (13:1, 34; 15:9 and 12).

Yet the fact remains that the general impression one receives from reading John is that Jesus does not come across as a warm, caring, and compassionate person. Rather Jesus seems aloof and cold, reserving his love exclusively for his followers. It is not accidental that the citations of friendship and love mentioned above are confined to the final discussion Jesus has privately with his disciples just before the passion story. Compare Luke's story of Zacchaeus in 19:1-10 with John's story of the Samaritan woman (4:1-42). They are both stories of Jesus' acceptance of an outcast. The Johannine story, however, does not depict Jesus as a welcoming sort of fellow.

Such a portrayal as this fits the general theological perspective of the fourth Gospel, as can be seen in three clear foci. The first is the fact that in dealing with crowds, Jesus is often combative and stern. Christ is known to the world only as the occasion of division and offense. The second is that readers of John are never allowed to forget that this Jesus comes from "above" and is a foreigner in the world. Jesus' divine dignity is never compromised (see chapter 2). Finally, as we will discuss in the next chapter, John was probably written for a community separated from a society hostile to it. The fourth evangelist portrays Christ as one who comes from God's love for the world (3:16) but who stands with Christians against the general society.

The Johannine portrait reveals a number of other characteristics that fit into these three foci. Jesus' speeches are long and complicated. The Synoptic Gospels specialize in repeating Jesus' short, pithy sayings. Even when they are strung together into a larger teaching unit, as in Matthew's Sermon on the Mount (5:1—7:28) or Luke's version on the plain (6:17-49), one sees concise, brief sayings within the construction. Probably the parables attributed to Jesus represent his longest utterances in the Synoptics (see Luke 15). In contrast, John presents Jesus' discourses as extended orations, often rambling with themes interconnected only with catchwords that provide transitions between logically different subjects. Chapters 14–16 are exemplary of this feature. Moreover, Jesus is no parabler in the Gospel of John, and those beloved stories of the Synoptics are missing. The closest parallel we can identify in the fourth Gospel are those extended metaphors in which Jesus speaks of himself by means of a similarity with something else (for example, the shepherd and the sheepfold in 10:1-16, and the vine and branches in 15:1-11).[12]

What is a preacher to do with such a portrait of Jesus? Again, surely we do not want to blur the distinctions among the portraits. Our task is to let our congregations see the Johannine Jesus through our words. If the church is right in canonizing this Gospel, we may assume that there is value in such a radically different image of Christ. The Johannine Jesus as he is seen by the crowds is as valuable as the likeness the fourth evangelist projects of how Jesus made himself known to the disciples. The harsh and aloof Jesus who deals with his opponents is an integral part of the whole Johannine presentation of Christ. Let us not water down the aloof, foreign Jesus with the "friend" Jesus is to disciples.

Preachers have a double opportunity in showing their congregations the Johannine Jesus. On the one hand, it is the opportunity to develop friendship as a new model for understanding God's revelation in Christ and even as a means to understand the cross in new ways.[13] For Christians, Jesus reveals God's friendship with humans. On the other hand, we have an opportunity to preserve the "otherness of Christ." The alien character of the Johannine Jesus protects the transcendent quality of the Word that addresses us from beyond ourselves and our world.

The two attributes of friend and alien are remarkably combined in one particular text. In 16:29-33 (unfortunately not found in the RCL—see chapter 6), Jesus speaks his last words to the disciples before his passion. The disciples declare that "now [finally?] you are speaking plainly. . . . Now we know that you know all things, and do not need to have anyone question you" (vv. 29-30). They think they finally "get it," but Jesus has to correct them, for that which is the hardest to understand is about to happen, "when you shall all be scattered . . ." (v. 32). Here at once we have a Jesus who is understandable and intimate, and one who will yet go to the cross as a mocked "King of the Jews." The alien Jesus is coupled with the understandable Jesus. In preaching this text, we might have an opportunity to sketch the strangeness of having a Lord who is both a friend and yet always an "other" who encounters us from "above."

The Threat of Pauline Intrusions

In effect, the discussion above emphasizes the importance of preserving the integrity of the fourth Gospel from contamination by Synoptic intrusions. A different but equally threatening tendency is to interpret Johannine themes through Pauline eyes. In the case of the Synoptics, the problem arises when we force John's narratives and the words of Jesus to fit the pattern of the first three Gospels. Paul poses a similar kind of danger. We may be inclined to interpret Johannine theology in the light of the theologies of Matthew, Mark, and Luke, but it is perhaps an even greater temptation to read John in light of Paul. Our attention moves therefore to the integrity of the thought of the fourth Gospel independent of Pauline thought.

The New Revised Version of Pauline Theology

Surely Paul has been the most influential of the New Testament writers on Christian theology. He has been credited with being the first Christian theologian or blamed for introducing theology into the church, depending on how you evaluate his thought. Some think he spoiled the "pure religion" of Jesus. Paul certainly has provided the church with the basic ingredients for many of its central doctrines, not least of all justification by grace through faith. Because Paul corresponded with congregations he either knew or intended to visit, his language tends to be more theological than the Gospels. Many of us maintain that the narrative genre of the Gospels is as theological as Paul's letters, even though until recently our Western mentality led us to seek doctrinal basis in propositions rather than in narratives. Hence, Paul has been elevated to the position of master theologian of the first century.

Increasingly, however, the apostle Paul has been viewed in a different light. Without elaboration, the newer trends in Pauline studies have urged us to see Paul more as a practical than systematic theologian. He was much more what today we might call a mission developer than an analytic and abstract thinker determined to seek intellectual clarity for faith. In his letters, we most often see him trying to nurture congregations, to address their immediate and practical needs, and to empower them to deal with conflicts and threats both within and beyond the church. Such a perspective on Paul enables us to treat his writings with a greater accuracy and faithfulness than when we try to force his views into a systematic scheme of our own making.

The Pauline understanding of justification provides a key example of how the apostle's writings are being reinterpreted. While it had become commonplace to claim that God's justification of sinners was the axle of the Pauline wheel out of which all its spokes emerged, recent scholars have demonstrated this is simply not the case. Paul appeals to justification by faith in only two of the epistles among those commonly taken to be his own work, namely, Romans (for example, 3:21-26) and Galatians (see 2:15-21). Even in these two cases, justification is not offered as the true view in and of itself. In both cases, justification works as one argument by which Paul hopes to accomplish a more practical and less doctrinal purpose. In Romans, for instance, some of us are convinced that Paul's major goal is to reconcile Jewish and Gentile factions in the church by insisting on God's concern for all humans.[14] God's justification of believers in both groups provides part of the commonality the Roman Christians share. Much the same is true for Galatians, except there the disturbance seems to stem from certain Christian missionaries whose message divided the congregation Paul had established. The point is that the theological view of how we are brought into right relationships with God is not the primary substance of what Paul is trying to communicate but is a means along the way to his social goal—a Christian community comprised of a diversity of humans.[15] This does not mean that justification by grace through faith is not true; it only puts this view in proper perspective within the Pauline writings.

This newer understanding of Paul does not seek to diminish the importance of his thought nor to minimize his role as a resource for contemporary theological thought. It does, however, invite us to treat the Pauline writings with a greater honesty and faithfulness to the texts themselves. Recent scholarship has reopened the portals to Paul with promise of finding a newer and greater diversity of treasures stored in his epistles. The sense in which Pauline thought might intrude into our interpretation of the Gospel of John is significantly modified by taking this fresh approach to his writings, but it does not remove the threat entirely.

Pauline Encroachments

In the past and under the reign of Pauline influence on theology, it was far easier for us to read Johannine thought and transpose it into categories more compatible with Paul. This was due to several factors. First, many of our core Christian doctrines were shaped by Pauline ideas. So, naturally when we read passages from the Gospel of John and have trouble understanding them, we resolve our conflict with John by filtering ideas and language through a Pauline sieve. Second, our concern that the Bible speak with one voice and always in unity also led us to the same thing. Paul, the master theologian, became the norm by which we created unity within the diverse voices of the New Testament. These same dangers lurk in the shadows of our studies today when we have trouble making sense of John.

The classic example often occurs on the occasion of what Lutherans celebrate as Reformation Sunday. In the Lutheran Lectionary, the assigned Gospel lesson is John 8:31-36, paired with a second lesson from Rom. 3:19-28. John and Paul meet face to face. Guess who usually wins, especially among Lutherans who so treasure justification by grace through faith? The Johannine themes of freedom and slavery in the Gospel lesson are often treated in terms drawn from Pauline thought, and indeed the Johannine language here does have a Pauline ring about it, especially in verse 34. It is not uncommon to hear the preacher interpret the Johannine category "truth" *(alētheia)* as Paul's "justified by his grace as a gift, through the redemption that is in Christ Jesus . . . he justifies the one who has faith in Jesus" (Rom. 3:24, 26). Indeed, I have a number of Reformation Day sermons in my file using just such an interpretation—by a preacher who is supposed to know something about John. The weighty matter of what John means by "truth" must await further explorations. What matters here is that the Romans lesson is laid over the Gospel lesson, and the colors of that overlay make John into Paul's likeness. If you cherish the doctrine of justification by grace through faith half as much as I do, you are liable to do the same thing.

A Johannine passage, however, does not have to be paired with a Pauline passage in the lectionary for us to seek clarity of John through Paul. Most of us carry around the essentials of Pauline thought, at least as we learned them, within ourselves; and our own eyes provide the Pauline overlay that is simply more obvious when the second lesson is from Paul and the Gospel lesson is from John. For instance, when we try to figure out how it is John believed that the cross afforded humans salvation, we often resort to what we think is Paul's view of the cross. We almost instinctively read the fourth Gospel through the lens of some sort of "expiation atonement" that is mentioned once by Paul (Rom. 3:25) and two other New Testament writers (Heb. 9:5 and 1 John 2:21 and 4:10). Actually, this word *(hilasmos)* is rare in the New Testament and represents only one of several different ways in which the cross is understood. Despite this, it has become a popular view of atonement far beyond its role in the New Testament. Consequently, when we read John 13:24 or 15:13, we are liable to understand them in terms of Jesus' being some kind of sacrifice for sins. I believe that the Johannine understanding of the cross is very different than expiation, and I hope to explore that more fully later. For now, it is enough to point out that one of Paul's ideas is quickly and easily allowed to intrude into our reading of John.

Does the revision of scholarship on Paul free us from such temptation to read John through a Pauline lens? Not entirely. Whether or not Paul's theology was pragmatic, regardless of the apostle's goals in advocating certain views for the sake of congregational unity and growth, Paul still threatens to overrun the interpretation of the Gospel of John. Hermeneutics (here meaning only the science of interpretation) suggests that understanding often comes through associating the data we have before us with something we already know.[16] In other words, understanding is created out of associations we make among various ideas or even stimuli. There is, therefore, no such thing as a purely objective, unbiased, and untainted interpretation of a text. We always read in terms of what we know and what has shaped our understanding. So, for instance, if I read a novel about males in the New South, my interpretation of the story will invariably be influenced by my early preconceptions of southerners.

Consequently, none of us is able to read John purely in terms of what the text presents. We will always impose our own preunderstanding on the meaning of the text. Incidentally, this is precisely why we desperately need to read Scripture within the context of the community of faith. Only in doing so can we ever achieve anything other than our own narrow interpretations. So, Pauline intrusions are only one set of preconceptions that get in the way of understanding the Gospel of John, and perhaps in many cases the least dangerous, since it is a set of preconceptions fashioned out of another group of canonical writings. Of course, we can test our interpretations by consulting others (both lay people and scholars) to learn what meaning they have found in John. This is probably the best use preachers can make of commentaries. As you well know, commentaries seldom help much in the process of sermon preparation. Actually no reading can enable us to discern the message of a particular text for our congregation. That is our task within our own particular setting. What commentaries (and other assistance) can do, however, is provide us a source of different readings of a biblical document.

Therefore, Pauline intrusions are inescapable because intrusions into the interpretative process are inescapable. Let us turn this assertion upside down to view its positive side. Homiletical interpretation depends on what I have been calling "intrusions." Preachers do not want to read any text purely objectively (if we could) in order to preach it. Rather, we want our congregations to be a kind of overlay in at least some steps in our interpretative process. We want the concerns, needs, and conditions of our parishioners to come into play as we study a text in preparation for preaching it. We hope that the Spirit will enable us to see the text with new eyes—eyes that perceive meaning in terms of how the text might be the Word for our congregation this Sunday. Another way of saying this is that we pray for the Spirit's *intrusion* into our reading of the lessons for any given Sunday, including those from the Gospel of John.

Conclusion

The Gospel of John presents special problems for interpretation and especially interpretation for preaching. Among them are the Gospel's peculiar form of proclamation (genre), its unique portrait of Jesus, and its distinctive theology when compared with Paul and other New Testament writers.

Isolating these three is only a way to kickstart our investigation of preaching John. Much more remains to be said and many other avenues left to explore. Still, having lifted these three matters into consciousness, we may be better prepared to address the other aspects of the homiletical use of the fourth Gospel.

At this juncture, we should summarize the "payoff" inherent for preachers in the three preliminary matters we have discussed. What, if any, difference do these three make in preaching John? First of all, of course, I believe that a new sensitivity to these three matters—gospel genre, the portraits of Jesus, and Pauline intrusions—makes all of us more faithful interpreters and credible preachers of the Gospel message. The dividing line between the so-called theoretical and the practical is not as clear as some would have us believe. Understanding the issues at stake in reading John for itself as a unique Gospel has immediate and important practical results.

Nonetheless, there is still something more, and something more specific, to say about the implications of these matters for preachers. The question of gospel genre invites us to see that we preachers are asked to do precisely what the Gospels themselves attempt to do. When we preach from any of the Gospels, and most especially from John, we revive the text's own proclamation for our day. It is my conviction that the fourth evangelist is a preeminent preacher and that the fourth Gospel shows us not only *what* to preach but *how* to preach it. The evidence for that conviction must be forthcoming in the remainder of this book. For now, I invite you to contemplate the following parallel: We are trying to do with the text exactly what the text was trying to do in its original setting. This is all the more true when you remember that, like the other New Testament documents, the fourth Gospel was written, not for private reading, but for public hearing—just as our sermons are oral events.

Second, the Gospel of John offers preachers a refreshingly different Jesus whose words and works can be explored for themselves. The lectionary takes us systematically through a continuous reading of each of the three Synoptics, with one year devoted to each. The Johannine Jesus confronts us on only rare and sporadic occasions (see chapter 6). Those occasions invite us to consider jolting our listeners with the uniqueness of the Johannine picture. Rather than helping them feel comfortable with what many of them regard as the harmonious presentations of Jesus in the four Gospels, let them see another side of Jesus, a side that perhaps has been ignored all too often, such as the utterly alien character of God's Revealer.

Finally, the diversity of New Testament theologies represented in the Johannine corpus affords us an opportunity to encourage diversity and differences in unity. A good number of baby boomers, and perhaps later generations as well, believe they know what Christian faith is and are none too comfortable with it. John implies that there are different ways of construing the basic elements of Christian faith and life. When we are successful in articulating the uniqueness of Johannine thought, we implicitly suggest that there may be and should be a variety of thought even within the same congregation. North Americans are being challenged in this new century to rethink our posture toward those who are different from what used to be the dominant culture. Why not allow that rethinking to begin with another consideration of the variety of ways we can conceive of what God has done for us in Christ?

Notwithstanding the importance of the issues we have examined in this introduction, there is still another we ought to address as we begin this journey. Unlike the three that are explored above, this is not so much a danger as it is a promise. We really know little or nothing about the fourth evangelist, although in the next chapter we will explore scholarly efforts to understand the evangelist's setting. Of course, the Gospel seems almost to presuppose that whoever wrote it commanded some authority in the eyes of the first readers, whatever that authority might have been.

Moreover, the author of the fourth Gospel includes heartening words about the sending of the Paraclete, the Holy Spirit. Among those words is the promise that this mysterious Presence "will teach you everything, and remind you of all that I [Jesus] have said to you" (14:26). Still later, another Paraclete passage pledges, "he will guide you into all the truth" (16:13). Without excessive speculation, two important conclusions can be drawn from these passages. The first is that the evangelist regarded the Gospel itself as a result of the Spirit's guidance and an expression of how the Paraclete had taught the evangelist "all things." We can be fairly confident that the Paraclete passages subtly offer a rationale for the truthfulness of the Gospel as a whole. A second conclusion we might reach after studying these passages is that the evangelist believes the Paraclete will lead *readers* to understand the Gospel. The Paraclete "dwells with you and will be in you" (14:17), so that readers may be prodded to grasp the sense of the words of this document.

In other words, the Gospel was written under the influence of the Spirit to be read under that same influence. I do not pretend to understand all that this means for our study. I am convinced, however, that the evangelist believed our reading, studying, and preaching the fourth Gospel is part of the work of the Holy Spirit, in some way or another. That does not let us off the hook in any way. It does, however, provide us a promise that our homiletical work with John and any biblical book is done with the availability of divine guidance.

1

A Tangle of Theses:
Understanding Johannine Research

HAVE YOU EVER BEEN FRUSTRATED, as I have, trying to untangle a mess of rope, say twenty-five feet or so? Of course, I blame my age for quick frustration and my sheer clumsiness for making the task seem impossible. Still, it is no easy task to straighten out a rope that runs this way and that, crossing itself one way and then another. No matter which end you choose to start with, untangling the rope takes patience and a good deal of time.

The theories espoused in Johannine research are entangled with one another in complicated ways, like a mess of tangled rope. One thesis arises from another but goes off in a different direction and touches upon still a third proposal. No one proposal is self-contained, for each involves other theses. The complexities of research into the fourth Gospel are due to at least two different reasons.

To begin with, the Gospel of John has always troubled scholars and evoked a multitude of proposals. Within a decade or so of the Gospel's composition, a schism appears to have occurred in one congregation (or a cluster of congregations) concerning the Gospel's interpretation. First John seems to have been written for a situation in which different interpretations of John had produced two opposing groups. The author of 1 John insists that the true interpretation is that Christ had come in the flesh, while a group of schismatics maintained, apparently, that Christ was never fully human.[1] That difference of interpretation was very soon followed by conflicting interpretations of the fourth Gospel on the part of Gnostic Christians and so-called mainstream Christianity. This conflict is evidenced in the work of Irenaeus, who remains one of our sources for understanding early Christian Gnosticism.[2]

The early differences of interpretation of John continued through the centuries right up to the present. On almost every issue of critical study, there has seldom been a consensus of views. Authorship, date, occasion of the writing, locale, theology, and all the rest have been hotly debated by those who devoted their scholarly lives to this Gospel. An example of the tangle of theses is the matter of dating (to which we will not devote extended attention). Within the last several decades, the older theory that John was written very late, say 110 C.E., has been espoused, while others have argued that the fourth Gospel was possibly the first of the four canonical Gospels written, perhaps as early as 45 or 50 C.E.[3] What is it about the Gospel of John that accounts for the failure of scholarship to offer us clear and unequivocal views of it? In large part, it is the puzzling character of the Gospel itself that has resisted easy answers to our questions.

The task of understanding scholarly studies of the Gospel of John is made all the worse by the fact that biblical interpretation as a whole is today undergoing a massive expansion. In the last half of the twentieth century the number of interpretative methods and hermeneutical reflections has exploded. In my own training in the late fifties and early sixties, the historical-critical method was the only show in town—at least the only one worth considering. By the end of the century, the historical-critical method had come under severe criticism, and a number of newer methods had been espoused as either replacements of or significant supplements to the older method. All of these changes in biblical studies have influenced research on the fourth Gospel, with nearly all of the newer methods represented in some way within the total field of Johannine investigations.

Consequently, contemporary Johannine studies propose a vast array of theses and counter-theses. Many of the differences among these theses are unresolvable, and preachers must proceed without the assurance of scholarly consensus. Another example of the situation is the relationship between John and the Synoptic Gospels. Did the fourth evangelist know and use these other three in the composition of John? Or, are the similarities between the Synoptics and John accountable by means of a common tradition shared by both? Did the fourth evangelist know the Synoptic chronology of Jesus' ministry and intentionally move the cleansing of the Temple (2:13-22) to early in his ministry? Or, did this evangelist's tradition pass on through the church, have Jesus cleansing the Temple as one of his first public acts? Who knows? Every imaginable kind of answer to the relationship of the fourth Gospel and the Synoptics has been proposed.[4] Preachers cannot settle this dispute and must either avoid the issue entirely, or select one of the solutions and go with it in the absence of scholarly consensus.

This chapter tries to untangle some of the major issues that are vital to a sound and faithful preaching of John and to offer some insights into them. I will attempt to outline a reasonable view of the Gospel in light of contemporary research as a foundation for the preacher's study of Johannine texts. We will limit the discussion to three different areas where we can find some clarity of research and viable proposals. The first is the historical origin of the Gospel; the second, the sociological study of John; and the third, the literary character of the fourth Gospel. I have chosen only these three because I believe they provide preachers with rich possibilities for the homiletical task. For each of the three I will try to provide some examples of how contemporary scholarship aids the preacher. A basic assumption of this chapter as a whole is that preachers need to be informed about the major movements afoot in biblical scholarship, and in this case Johannine studies.[5]

The Historical Origin of the Fourth Gospel

The origin of this Gospel has puzzled critics for centuries, and hypotheses for its setting are numerous. The puzzle is only accentuated by the one place in the Gospel where the narrator states the purpose of the document (20:30-31). In some ways this statement is helpful. The narrator claims that the Gospel was written so as to provide readers with "life." Verse 31, however, blurs an answer to the question of whether the Gospel was written to win converts or strengthen the faith of those who already believed. The ancient manuscripts disagree as to the tense and mood of the verb that the NRSV translates "may come to believe" (*pisteuēte*, "may come to faith" [present subjunctive]; or *pisteusēte*, "may continue believing" [aorist subjunctive]). This leaves ambiguous whether the Gospel had an evangelical or a nurturing intent. Preachers might avail themselves of this ambiguity with a sermon that poses both possibilities and addresses the importance of *both* initial and continuing belief.

Left without an unequivocal statement of purpose in the Gospel itself, scholars scurry to find evidence elsewhere in the Gospel that might tip us off about the evangelist's purpose in writing. Some argue that it originated among Jewish Christians, others among Gentile Christians, and still others among Gnostic Christians. There have been countless proposals for the original purpose of the Gospel. These include the theories that the evangelist was trying to counter the influence of a group that claimed John the Baptist was the Messiah, or oppose an overly physical emphasis on the sacraments of Baptism and the Eucharist, or formulate the Christian faith in terms of Hellenistic philosophical thought. While there were swings in one direction or another throughout the twentieth century, there was no one proposal that won wide approval. Rudolf Bultmann's radical view of the Gospel of John occupied a great deal of discussion among scholars and even convinced some of its truthfulness, but on the whole the Bultmannian view was influential but not widely received with approval. In 1960 scholarship was at an impasse concerning the origin of the Gospel.

The Separation of the Synagogue

Yet in the last four decades a theory has emerged that has captured a great deal of attention and achieved considerable—even remarkable—consensus. In brief, the proposal suggests that the fourth Gospel was written for a group of Christian Jews soon after they were separated from the synagogue in which they had worshiped. The textual evidence for such a theory is found in the use of the word *aposynagōgos* ("expelled" or "put out of the synagogue") in 9:22; 12:42; and 16:2. Building on that evidence, scholars have proposed that those Christians who formed the Johannine Christian community were originally Jews, perhaps including some Hellenistic Jews. These Christians were convinced that Jesus was indeed the Messiah but saw no reason to leave the synagogue. Furthermore, the particular synagogue of which they were a part was, in all likelihood, a rather tolerant and pluralistic community, composed of a variety of forms of Judaism and—in the period between the destruction of the Jerusalem Temple (70 C.E.) and the formulation and spread of rabbinic Judaism in the second century—was trying to determine exactly what it meant to be a Jew. The presence of a "messianic" group within this synagogue was, at first, of little significance.

How and why the separation of the Johannine Christians from the synagogue occurred is debatable. The two major proponents of the theory that the Gospel was written soon after the community's separation from the synagogue each offer different reasons for the separation.[6] More than likely, the separation occurred only at a local level, that is, in one particular village and synagogue. The Gospel regards the separation as an "expulsion," but that may tell us more about how the Johannine Christians *felt* than what really happened. Of course, the division between the synagogue and the church was occurring gradually throughout locales where Christians could be found, as the Acts of the Apostles and the Gospel of Matthew both suggest.

More important than why or how the separation took place is the fact that after the separation of the messianic Jews from their sisters and brothers in the synagogue, the two groups engaged in a lively and sometimes vitriolic dialogue about their differences. J. Louis Martyn, one of the early proponents of this hypothesis, suggested that as a result of this dialogue between Christians and Jews, the Gospel is a two-level drama. At one level is the story of Jesus and his ministry, but an only slightly deeper level reveals the story of the Johannine church and its experience.[7] The story of the healing of the man born blind in chapter 9 is the easiest example. On the one hand, the story reads somewhat like many other stories of Jesus' healings. The cure is accomplished, but then there is a discussion with the religious officials about the event. On the other hand, in reading this chapter one very soon begins to feel that something else is going on. The man's parents are afraid to get involved because "the Jews had already agreed that anyone who confessed Jesus to be the Messiah would be put out of the synagogue" (9:22). That statement sounds anachronistic, imposing a later situation back to the time of Jesus. Then the formerly blind man must defend himself in an interrogation by the religious leaders (vv. 24-34)—something that may also reflect a situation of a later time rather than Jesus' ministry.

It appears that this is part of the evangelist's own homiletical style. Tell a story about Jesus, but in telling it bring it to bear on the situation of the first readers. The evangelist in effect does with the Jesus story something very much like what preachers set out to do each Sunday with the appointed passage(s). We elaborate the text but soon lead our listeners to consider another level at which the text intersects with our lives. For example, even in retelling a story of Jesus' encounter with the Pharisees, we hint that they had developed a system of laws and regulations not unlike those we find in some contemporary churches today. The Pharisees are scandalized by Jesus' association with gays and lesbians!

This theory for the origin of the Gospel of John has helped us to understand several things about the document. As a consequence of this situation at the time of the writing of the Gospel, the Johannine community was trying to determine its identity, separated from but still in continuity with Judaism. If this hypothesis is sound, the question at stake for both the Johannine church and its sister synagogue was "who are we?" Moreover, the theory enables us to comprehend the Gospel's view of Judaism and the Johannine sectarian insider/outsider ("us against them") language. Its preoccupation with Christ's identity also makes sense, since the major issue between the synagogue and the church was probably the question, "who is Jesus?"

The most important contribution this proposal for the Gospel's origin makes to preaching is the light it sheds on the tone with which the fourth evangelist speaks of Jews and Judaism. The issue of John and Judaism is complex and controversial beyond the scope of this discussion, but certainly "the Jews" *(hoi Ioudaioi)* are most often presented in this Gospel as Jesus' opponents.[8] Moreover, the evangelist clearly claims that Christianity is superior to Judaism (see, for example, 1:17). The most striking example of this anti-Jewish tone is 8:44, where Jesus declares that Jews are children of the devil and thereby demonizes them and their religion. The theory of the separation from the synagogue helps us recognize *the polemic quality of this language* (to which we will return in a later chapter).

If the Gospel originated out of a clash between Christians and Jews, it is no wonder that the story includes attacks on the church's opponents. Polemic language was common between different groups in the ancient world and was often designed less to destroy an opponent than to bolster the reader's confidence.[9]

A contemporary example of this kind of polemic is the language political candidates sometime use in primary elections of their opponents from the same party. Once candidates are defeated and out of the race, they speak glowingly of the candidate they had formerly attacked. Perhaps an even better example is the manner in which our national leaders will demonize another nation in order to unify the United States against that nation. The language is aimed more at bringing the American people together than providing a fair and accurate description of the other nation. Remember the U.S. president who called the Soviet Union an "evil empire" but before long established new and cordial relationships with the Soviet Union?

The fourth evangelist's proclamation of the Word in words is tainted with this polemical intent. Although not commendable, the polemic is understandable, since the proclamation of the gospel always takes seriously the context of the community to which it is addressed. In that sense, the preached Word in John has an occasional character, fashioned for a particular situation in the life of the church. The same is true of the Gospel's attempt to strengthen the embattled community, to emphasize their unity, and to build their confidence.

Homiletical Implications of the Gospel's Origin

With the observation that the fourth evangelist has customized the Gospel for a specific occasion, we have already passed beyond a description of the theory of the separation from the synagogue into preaching John. There are, however, more specific connections between this understanding of the origin of the Gospel and preaching.

The first has to do with the serious task of trying through preaching to neutralize the anti-Semitic sound of the fourth Gospel. The use of the expression "the Jews" in John surely offers fuel for the fires of anti-Semitism, smoldering in the hearts of some of our parishioners. We preachers have a responsibility to help our congregations understand the occasion for which the Gospel was written. In particular we need to offer reasons for the harsh treatment of the Jews in John. Sermons offer important opportunities for such explanation and for diminishing, insofar as possible, the use of the Gospel's language for anti-Semitic purposes today. Describing the situation of the Johannine community is not without its contemporary relevance. How often do churches tend to demonize their opponents? In our current times, Islam is likely to become a kind of scapegoat for our anger and frustration. When we do this sort of thing, we are mimicking one of the fourth Gospel's least desirable features.

In the Johannine community, the expression "the Jews" represents Jesus' opponents and the established religion of the time. Some have proposed that we ought to alter the translations of John and substitute a more neutral term for "the Jews."[10] Perhaps this is not the best course to take. Instead, in sermons we might speak always simply of "Jesus' opponents." And when the text describes the hostility of the religious leaders toward Jesus, as is the case in chapter 9, we need to make clear that they were trapped within the religious establishment of their day and intent on preserving the status quo (and their power). They are not alone in that entrapment, are they? The institution always tends to preserve itself against all those who attack it either from within or without. Who are the entrenched religious leaders of our own day?

A Sermon Example

The following is a fragment of a sermon in which the preacher is retelling the Gospel lesson, John 10:11-18 (the appointed Gospel in the RCL for the Fourth Sunday of Easter, Year B). (Unless otherwise indicated, I have written the sermons and sermon fragments.)

◯

Jesus continues the self-portrait that he began earlier in this chapter. He has spoken of himself as the shepherd of the sheep, who knows the flock. Then he compared himself with the door to the sheepfold. Now he invites us to imagine him to be like a good shepherd. A shepherd contrasted with a hired hand. Unlike the hired hand, the shepherd is willing to sacrifice his life for the sheep. When danger approaches, the hired hand runs like a frightened rabbit. Hired help doesn't care that much for the sheep.

Who do you suppose this hired hand is? Just whom does Jesus have in mind when he contrasts himself with the hired help? The answer is pretty clear. If we look back at the end of the previous chapter, we hear Jesus charging the religious leaders with blindness. He seems to be saying that the religious leadership of his day care very little for the people. They are not likely to defend the people against danger. Most certainly they will not sacrifice their lives for the people.

So, what's their problem? Why are the religious leaders like hired help? Are they simply afraid of the risks in caring for the sheep? Or, is it that they are too busy with administrative details to be concerned with the people? I'm inclined to think they like their power. They appreciate the way things are and don't want to see them change.

Sound familiar? It's easy for us to throw stones at the Pharisees of Jesus' time. But we aren't immune to their problems. In fact some of us are too often just like them. When we gain our power from the ways things are. When we are content with the status quo. Lots of us have succumbed to the temptations to cling to the establishment the way it is.

How many times have you said—I've said—"that's not the way we have done it"? When a new idea surfaces, how often have some of us not wanted things to change? Many of us like things the way they are and have been. Lots of us are tempted to care more about preserving the system than serving others.

Some of you may remember that old movie, *Mass Appeal*. A young seminarian priest comes to a large, prestigious congregation to serve his internship. The regular priest has served this congregation for years. And he is much loved and appreciated by the people. Above all, he wants to please everyone. Don't rock the boat! Don't disturb the peace! With his charm, he keeps things quiet in the congregation. He displeases no one.

But the seminarian has a different style. His sermons confront the people with who they are and challenge them. He charges them with caring more about their affluence and comfort than about the needy. He tells it like it is. And his supervisor is all aflutter . . . angry . . . enraged. He tries to get the young seminarian to change his style. Please the people; don't disturb them! Gradually, however, the two of them get to know one another. Finally, the elder priest has to confess that *he needs to be liked*. He needs to be in control. He needs to have the power his charm brings him. The elder priest realizes he has become a hired hand. This upstart of a seminarian is just trying to be a good shepherd.

Whenever we contemporary Christians resist the new in favor of the old, we are but hired help. Whenever we avoid conflict for the sake of a superficial peace, we act like a hired hand. The church needs above all to care for the sheep and to be willing to sacrifice the church's life for the sake of the sheep.

The hired hand, however, is only the contrasting color in this self-portrait. That figure only highlights the character of the "good shepherd." . . .

～

If we understand the (likely) historical setting of the Gospel of John, individual passages take on new meaning. This theory that the fourth Gospel was written to a community of Christians only recently separated from their synagogue is related to another major movement in Johannine studies.

The Social Scientific Study of John

Probably the most significant development in the classic historical-critical method of biblical studies has been the attempt to use social science in the analysis of the writings and the settings in which they were composed and read for the first time. Armed with a good deal of historical information, scholars have undertaken to apply the findings of the social sciences to the biblical world. This has entailed the use of categories and methods drawn from anthropology, sociology, and psychology (especially social psychology), so we are speaking of a vast new discipline in biblical studies—much too vast for us to discuss fully here.[11] There is, it seems to me, one underlying assumption in the social scientific studies of the New Testament, whatever specific discipline may be used. That assumption is simply that what the social sciences have learned to be true in more recent times in societies also functioned in some way in the ancient societies contemporaneous with the writing of the biblical document.[12] In the case of the anthropological studies of the Bible, however, it is often other ancient cultures that offer lenses through which to study the biblical cultures. Nonetheless, in every case these social-scientific methods operate cross-culturally.

One early example of this enterprise involved the study of adventist groups in the United States during the last century. These were groups that believed the parousia was about to occur, and that the final events of history were upon us. In particular, the groups that were studied had determined that, on a given date, Christ would reappear in glory. Of course, the anticipated parousia did not occur, and the group had to face the fact that their prediction was wrong. Logic would suggest that the group would be disillusioned, fall apart, and fade entirely out of existence. What sociologists of religion discovered, however, was that just the opposite was the case. The failure of their prediction bred even deeper conviction and determination in the adherents to the movement. The groups proved to be stronger *after* their prediction was proven wrong than before. Armed with this fact, some applied it to early Christianity. The earliest church, too, expected Christ's impending appearance in glory (see, for instance, 1 Corinthians 7). That obviously did not happen. But the failure of that expectation only strengthened the evangelistic zeal of the early church and deepened its commitment to its Lord.[13]

This social-scientific movement has ignited two closely related tasks. The first is to gather more information and data about the societies in which early Christianity took shape; the second is to use that data to apply social-scientific hypotheses to the biblical world.[14] A number of other movements have spun off the larger stream of social-science studies, including the socio-rhetorical method, which combines interest in the New Testament's use of classical rhetoric as it was practiced in the first century with social features of the time.[15]

The Social World of the Gospel of John

The proposal that the Johannine community had just separated from the synagogue and at the time of the writing of the Gospel was still engaged in an ongoing dialogue with the synagogue sparked new interest in that community, both in its history and its features.[16] This hypothesis for the Gospel's historical origin seemed to open a window through which we could finally see with more clarity the early Johannine church. In general, social-scientific criticism came to the study of John armed with this theory of its origin and worked from it. It was a sociologist's dream: A community uprooted from its home in the synagogue, under assault for its views, isolated from its society, and conceiving itself in a nearly sectarian manner. What fertile ground for investigation!

For our purposes, it will suffice to summarize the impact of the social-scientific biblical criticism on Johannine studies in only two categories: First, the nature and role of Johannine language, and, second, sectarian life and theology. These two will provide a basic but very rudimentary understanding of the contributions of social-scientific studies of the fourth Gospel.

The Language of the Fourth Gospel
from a Social-Scientific Perspective

The language of the Gospel of John has puzzled scholars for centuries, and we will later devote an entire chapter to the topic as it influences preaching. Social-science investigators became interested in the Gospel's language because of what it seemed to be accomplishing within the context of the community. Hence, the study of the social character of Johannine language offers us a rare glimpse into the Christians behind the Gospel.

The most striking thing about the language of the Gospel of John is that it seems to nurture an antisocial fervor. When one tries to imagine such language as the fourth Gospel uses over against, shall we say, the ordinary language of the time, it is clear that the fourth evangelist was fostering a different set of values through language. Much of that language is what has been called *antilanguage*, meaning that it uses the language of the culture in ways that undermine that very culture. Thus, ordinary language is employed in unfamiliar ways. Of this *deformational language*, Alan Culpepper wrote, "Images, concepts, and symbols common in its milieu are defamiliarized, given new meaning, and used idiosyncratically."[17] The Gospel's so-called symbolic use of "water" and "bread" are examples of such radical redefinitions.

In effect, the evangelist *relexicalizes* language, writing a new dictionary of the common language of the day and place. "Relexicalization refers to the practice of using new words for some reality that is not ordinarily referred to with those words."[18] Yet another feature of this massive redefinition of daily language is what has been called *overlexicalization*, which means little more than that the fourth Gospel uses a number of terms to mean the same thing.[19]

What did the evangelist seek to accomplish through the social impact of the Gospel's language? Simply put, the Gospel seeks to provide readers with an entirely new and different perspective on reality than the one propagated by the dominant society. The language is countercultural in the sense that it opposes the values of the readers' dominant society and offers another set of values in their place. The Gospel invites readers into a process of *resocialization*—becoming part of a new society at the center of which is a new religious perspective. This is far more important than it may appear to be on the surface. It means that the Gospel's goal is more social than individual or personal. While we may tend to think that the evangelist is trying to convince individual readers of the truth of the gospel message, in fact the goal is to structure a whole new subsociety or subculture. The importance of using such extraordinary language is at once both to disclaim the culture of the time and to foster a new society within the community of faith.

Sectarian Life and Theology

The social analysis of the Gospel's language actually builds upon and elucidates a view implicit in the theory that the Johannine community was a small group of messianic Jews separated from their synagogue, namely, that the community had features of what we today would call a sect. What we mean by labeling the Johannine community sectarian is simply that it was a minority group within a culture and regarded its own views as true as opposed to those fostered by a larger culture. The sectarian nature of the church implicit in the Gospel is clear in what appears as an "us-against-them" mentality (for example, see 15:18-25). The life and beliefs of such a Christian sect have been a rich field of investigation for social-science investigations.[20]

An example of the study of the Johannine community as sectarian, but one that tries to move beyond the category of sect, is the adaptation of a model developed by the anthropologist Mary Douglas. The model was used by Douglas to study social groupings in terms of the social pressure at work within a group and the degree to which the group resisted the symbol system of the prevailing culture. By analyzing specific areas of interest, such as ritual, she proposed stages in a group's development. In the 1980s Douglas's model was widely used in social-scientific investigations of Scripture.[21]

Applying Douglas's model to the Gospel of John scholars have attempted to assess the nature and growth of the Johannine community. In particular, the Christology of John has been studied in terms of the social nature of the group that produced and adhered to it. To oversimplify the complex studies of the sociological nature of Johannine theology, one might say that the group's social situation in relationship to the larger culture of its time shaped their view of Christ as an alien in the world, at odds with the world as a whole, and destined to return to his heavenly home with God. An unnecessarily harsh way of putting it is that the group imposed its own sense of social alienation and opposition to the larger culture on Christ and God's act in Christ. So, for instance, Christ says that the world hates him and will hate the disciples, but that Christ has chosen the disciples "out of the world" and they are no longer "of the world" (15:18-19). Christ is thought of as one who has descended from above into this world and will once again ascend, so that he is a stranger in this realm (see 3:13).

There is inevitably something very speculative about these studies of the Gospel of John, but they raise profound issues for the whole of Christian thought. To what degree, for instance, does our social situation influence what we believe? Even if we are not willing to say that our beliefs are simply a result of our relationship with a culture (which is far too reductionistic), we have to acknowledge that cultural positioning impacts faith and theology. A simple study of the differences among Christian denominations today in beliefs and practices and in social composition provides ample evidence of the role of social positioning on beliefs and practices.

The Homiletical Importance of Social-Scientific Methods

Our interest is not in the theoretical value of the social-scientific methods of interpreting John but what, if any, value these methods have for preaching John. Let us think about several of the possible contributions these methods might make and then suggest a sermon fragment that employs the results of such interpretative methods.

One of the clearest and most important contributions the social-scientific methods make to our preaching task is that they allow us to imagine a real community behind the text. That is to say, that the first readers of the Gospel of John were humans living in community with all of the hurts, struggles, and joys of their life together, much as we know them today in our churches. In particular, they help us to grasp what it meant for Christians to stand against or cooperate with their culture. In a day in North America when we are inclined to think that Christian faith and American patriotism are near-cousins, if not twins, it may be helpful for us to get inside the lives of the Johannine Christians, who felt constantly threatened by their culture.

If there is any truth to the studies we have summarized in this section, the Gospel of John may afford us precious glimpses into a Christian community's efforts to define its relationship with its culture. By preaching certain passages in the Gospel, we can dare to suggest that our congregations need to think hard and seriously about their relationship with culture. Are we merely mirrors of our culture? Or, is there something about the Christian faith that means communities of believers will always, of necessity, be suspicious of a too-easy identification of cultural values with Christian values?

Another related value of the social-scientific methods for our preaching concerns the liberating message of the Johannine Gospel. It is not difficult to imagine that the dominant culture of the time and area oppressed the Johannine community, socially ostracized it, and prevented their full participation in society. The fourth evangelist seems to want to empower the Gospel's readers with a new sense of freedom and dignity through Christ. The famous words, which have become nearly a cliché, "the truth shall make you free" (8:32), may well mean that the Christian gospel frees us from social oppression to become who God seeks us to be.[22] The liberating quality of the gospel message is not, however, limited to those who suffer the oppression of poverty, discrimination, and marginalization. In a real sense, the middle and upper classes of our nation are also oppressed by cultural values, even if the oppression is not as explicit or as tragic as that experienced by lower economic classes.

A Sermon Example

How might the use of the social-scientific perspective on John be expressed in an actual sermon? What follows is only a fragment of a sermon on John 17:6-19 for Easter 7, B. This portion of the sermon raises the question of our relationship with the world as it is expressed in 17:14 (see also chapter 6).

༈

Ah, come on now, Jesus—or John—or both! Isn't that a bit extreme? "the world has hated them (the disciples), because they do not belong to the world, just as I do not belong to the world." That seems an unnecessarily grim assessment of the world and our lives in the world.

After all, there's little evidence that the world we live in hates us. In the good old U.S.A., we Christians are actually appreciated. Christianity is still the dominant religion of our nation, or so we are told. Why, there's even a movement afoot to get the Ten Commandments displayed in every public school and all governmental offices. That seems hardly an expression of the world's antagonism toward us. On the contrary, some Christians feel that this nation actually favors our faith and protects our churches. So, what's this business of the world hating us? How can we not "belong to the world" while we live in it?

Of course, John's Gospel was written for a different situation than ours. The first readers of this Gospel were in some ways oppressed and ostracized by their culture. They were regarded as weirdos and freaks. The members of the village in which the first readers lived probably wished that the Christians would pack up and move to another locale entirely. Most important, the church's values were different from the culture's values. Christians thought there were more important things than what the society held were worthwhile. We don't know all the details about this. Just what were those differences? But this much is certain: The Christians to whom this Gospel was written *felt* hated, *felt* despised, and *felt* oppressed. The world was their opponent. It hated them just as it hated their Lord.

We can quickly dismiss all of this as irrelevant for us. But maybe we ought to think about it a bit before dismissing it. Are there ways in which we today stand at odds with the world in which we live? Are there values that Christians hold that are not appreciated in some other circles even in our own community?

Christians in business may sometimes have to question their company's values. Do we really want to import and sell at a profit items made in other countries *by means of child labor?* Children are forced to work to produce these goods? Do we want to endorse child labor for the sake of our company's profit line?

Christians may also need to challenge some decisions of our political leaders. Maybe it's at the national level, maybe the state, or maybe our city. When programs for the poor and needy are cut back. When they suffer so that we can continue to subsidize the tobacco industry or build new stadiums for our athletic teams, do our values clash with those of society? What about the values that are endorsed in an informal way among us? What about the feeling that it's alright to cheat on our taxes since everyone else does it? What about the practice of blaming working women for the decline of the family? Do we not sometimes find ourselves at odds with our society over matters such as these? And I am sure that you can add your own examples.

The Gospel of John invites us to think about our relationship with the world around us. Maybe "hate" is not the exact word we need. Maybe the evangelist's situation was more drastic than ours. This passage about the world's hatred makes us think again. What is our church's relationship with our culture, our society?

We can fall off the edge both ways. We can too easily go along with our culture. Claim as Christian whatever our culture proposes. Then we compromise the unique message we have to offer our world.

Or, we can fall the other way. We can disclaim our culture entirely, draw into our little shells, and let the world go to hell in a handbasket. If we do that, we deny our mission to the world. We surrender our efforts to be the leaven in society for goodness and righteousness. And we become the weirdos and freaks that no one listens to.

No, there is no easy answer to these questions. No easy solution to the way we live in the world without becoming only another part of it. And John's answer may not be ours. We cannot simply say that the world hates us, and we do not belong to the world. That may have been appropriate for John's situation. But ours is more complicated.

So, how do we live in this world without either endorsing it or leaving it to die? Maybe the language of this passage helps us more than we recognize. The word translated "belong" is a key. . . .

~

The Literary Features of John

The third major movement in Johannine scholarship, with which preachers could profitably be familiar, emphasizes the literary qualities of John. This interpretative trend is quite different from the first two we have studied. In each of those cases, history is a primary factor. The historical origin of the Gospel and the social-scientific study of it are both concerned to go back in history and get behind the Gospel to find information that will help us interpret it. This third movement takes a different approach—one that does not necessarily deny the importance of the historical setting of the Gospel but which focuses its attention elsewhere.

There is a new interest in the purely literary character of Scripture without (primary) reference to its historical origin. The whole of biblical studies has been influenced by what is sometimes called the "new literary criticism," and in the last few decades it has had an impact on Johannine studies. Generally this new literary concern concentrates on the text as we have it, without dependence on theories about the origins of the biblical documents or their historical settings. Most literary critics do not, however, propose that we abandon historical criticism all together but only that we pay more attention to the features of the text as it stands. This method looks for the way in which the text is designed, what impact it has on readers, and what literary techniques are used to facilitate that impact. The movement includes such interpretative methods as reader-response criticism and narrative criticism. Rather than to summarize the results of these separate but related critical methods, we will concentrate more generally on their features and contributions. There are an increasing number of very fruitful studies of the literary qualities of John. It will suffice here to mention only a few examples of these studies and their importance for a homiletical interpretation of John.[23]

The Narrative Structure of the Gospel of John

The first example of the success of literary criticism is the investigations of the way the Gospel plots its story of Jesus.[24] Investigations of narrative structure build on earlier and more historically oriented studies of the compositional skill of the evangelist. Each of our four Gospels molds its story of Jesus in a unique manner, showing relationships among different episodes and shaping a road toward the story's climax. The fourth Gospel, of course, has a rather different plot when compared to the Synoptics. Some of the characteristics of the plotting of the story include closures, the use of irony, characterization, and the narrative world of the story.

A number of scholars have identified *closures* in the whole of the Gospel. Closures are those passages that, when taken together, provide a kind of packaging of what comes between them. To discern closures within a narrative suggests that the material between them constitutes an identifiable unit. But more, what comprises closures (or bookends as they have been called) often provide readers with some clue as to the meaning of the enclosed section. Some examples of those include the following.

In the prologue, Christ (the *Logos*) is called God (1:1 and 18). That identification clues readers to the identity of the main character and thereby provides them information that the characters within the story do not have but—in the case of the Gospel stories—are trying to discover. Having named Christ God at the Gospel's beginning, the narrative proper then closes with Thomas's confession that Christ is both "Lord and God" (20:28). (Most scholars regard chapter 21 as an appendix to the Gospel.) The whole of the Gospel therefore is enclosed with affirmations of Jesus' identity, making it clear that this is the major theme of the story.

Another pair of closures around the whole Gospel has been proposed. The prologue claims that those who receive and believe in the *Logos* receive "power" (or authority, *exousia*) to become children of God" (1:12). Then in the crucifixion scene in John, Jesus entrusts his mother and the beloved disciple to one another as parent and child. This episode suggests, among other things, that in his crucifixion Christ creates a new family of God around these key characters—his mother and the unnamed disciple whom we are told Jesus loved (19:26-27).[25] These bookends hold the narrative together by leading readers to see that the purpose of Christ and even the retelling of the Jesus story is the formation of a new community around the central character. Both of these closures connected with the prologue and the Passion story provide readers with an indication of the major thrust of the message of all that is between them.

Lest I give the impression that closures occur only at the beginning and end of the story, literary critics have proposed the structuring of the sections of the story could be discerned in the light of closures. We have often marveled at the role of the Passover in John's story of Jesus and wondered about its significance. Among other possible meanings, one could argue that the allusions to Passover are markers in the plot. The mention of Passover occurs first at 2:13, then 6:4, and finally 11:55. Could it be that the two sections enclosed by reference to the Passover are skillful ways of dividing the story? Between 2:13 and 6:4 we find the initial ministry of Jesus. Between 6:4 and 11:55 Jesus' conflict with the religious leaders increases steadily, and the last allusion to the festival introduces the final section of the Gospel. References to time may comprise enclosures but geographical reference might also be understood in this way. The story of Jesus' ministry between 2:1 and 4:54 begins with Jesus in Cana and then cycles back to that region in 4:43-54.[26]

Closures indicate structure, point readers toward meaning, and frame the plot. Another example of the richness of the literary study of John is the work done on *irony*. There are many types of irony, of course, but in this case it is adequate to think of it as a situation in which characters say more than they realize they are saying. Paul Duke elaborates the different kinds of irony one finds in the Gospel of John and summarizes the meaning of the word in this way: "irony as a literary device is a double-leveled literary phenomenon in which two tiers of meaning stand in some opposition to each other and in which some degree of unawareness is expressed or implied."[27]

In John, irony often occurs when characters in the story do or say something that suggests more than they intend, while readers see and know something the characters do not. The Samaritan woman's question to Jesus in 4:12 ("Are you greater than our father Jacob, who gave us the well . . . ?") is fraught with irony, since we readers know that of course Jesus is greater. Pilate does not realize the full sense of the placard he has placed on Jesus' cross (19:19-22). Johannine irony has been studied with great care, with the result that we more fully appreciate the subtle skill with which the evangelist speaks to readers.

Irony is often found in the so-called misunderstanding theme in John. The story's characters, both opponents and disciples, often misinterpret Jesus' words, sometimes even in comical ways. For instance, when Jesus tells him that he must be born again from above, poor Nicodemus thinks Jesus is asking that he reenter his mother's womb and come out again (3:4). When Jesus speaks of "going away," the people think he is going to kill himself (8:22); when he suggests that people will seek him but not find him, they think he is going off to "the Dispersion among the Greeks" (7:35). The irony in the misunderstandings of Jesus is that there is a sense in which the speakers are both wrong and right. Jesus will indeed be taken out into the dispersion among the Greeks by the church, and—although he will not kill himself—he will voluntarily go to the cross.

Irony is important in all these ways but in still another. The whole Jesus story is told with an ironic twist. Revelation itself is ironic in the fourth Gospel.[28] The double meaning of the cross is the easiest example. Jesus' crucifixion is indeed his death, but it is also his glorification, as the fourth evangelist so often says (for example, 17:1). Death is his enthronement as king (see the next chapter). The meanings of the crucifixion stand in opposition to one another, and readers detect that something more than death is involved in this event. God reveals the divine self in ways that require humans to comprehend another level of meaning in the obvious and immediate one. We will touch on this subject again, when, in chapter 3, we deal with the multiple levels of meaning in Jesus' words in the fourth Gospel.

The new literary interest in John has also resulted in studies of the *characters* in the narrative.[29] Fascinating characterizations dot the pages of this Gospel. Disciples, for instance, express commitment and determination (see Peter's words in 6:68), but they never quite "get it." Even in the final section of the Gospel, they cannot understand Jesus (14:8). When they think they understand him, they are actually still totally confused (16:29-33).

This portrayal of the disciples is hardly unique to John (see Mark).

What perhaps is more peculiar to this Gospel is the way in which characters almost always seem to model one of two responses to Jesus—belief or unbelief. That is to say, the fourth evangelist seems generally to divide characters into the two realms of light and darkness (see chapter 2). For instance, "the Jews" model unbelief, while the Samaritan woman mirrors belief.

Not all the characters in the Gospel are so clear-cut and obvious in their roles. There are few characters in the Gospel, such as Nicodemus, who represent a position somewhere between belief and unbelief. He leaves us doubting whether or not he ever comes to believe in Jesus. He drops out of his discussion with Jesus utterly dumbfounded and lost (3:1-10), and we hear nothing more about him until chapter 7, when he seems to defend Jesus against the other chief priests and Pharisees (vv. 50-52). For his efforts, he is accused of being one of Jesus' followers (7:52). Then the narrative is again silent concerning Nicodemus until Jesus' burial, when he and Joseph of Arimathea take care of the preparations of the body and the acquisition of a tomb (19:38-42). In that story, we are told that Joseph was a "secret believer." Was Nicodemus? We are never informed, and the character remains ambiguous. Pilate may also fall into a category between belief and unbelief, although there is little doubt that the narrative condemns the Roman for his failure to oppose the crowd even when he thinks that Jesus is innocent.

The characters in the fourth Gospel leave us with only two alternatives—belief or unbelief—but never simplify the process. Coming to faith is not always easy; and, for those of us who find it difficult, there are characters with whom we can identify. A study of the paralyzed man in chapter 5 and the blind man in chapter 9 summarizes the dilemma in two seemingly contrasting characters. The title of one such study captures the struggle of both characters to grasp the light Christ brings: "Stumbling in the Dark, Reaching for the Light."[30]

Another feature of John's characterizations asks us to identify with the struggles of faith. A fascinating proposal concerns the role of the unnamed characters in the Gospel story (for example, the Samaritan woman and the beloved disciple). We might be inclined to think that leaving a character unnamed diminishes her or his importance. David Beck, however, persuasively argues that the fourth evangelist uses anonymous characters to foster the reader's identification with them. Since a character is without a name, we ourselves can more easily take that role in the story.[31] That proposal strengthens the impression that the evangelist leaves the beloved disciple unnamed in order to invite readers to think of themselves as such a disciple.[32]

A final example of the results of the new literary criticism in Johannine studies pertains to the *narrative world* of the Gospel. A narrative world is simply the world created by the storyteller and within which a story's characters live and the plot unfolds.[33] Authors invite readers into the world of their narratives—the environment of the story—and ask them to accept that world as believable and true for the duration of the story. Every story creates such a world. Sometimes it is very much like our own real world, like the novel *Primary Colors,* and sometimes very different, like the *Star Wars* movies. The narrative world of the fourth Gospel is unique because it ushers readers into a milieu that, among other things, has two quite distinct realms—the above and the below—and in which there is a clear and sharp distinction between truth and falsehood. Culpepper writes:

> The implicit purpose of the gospel narrative is to alter irrevocably the reader's perception of the real world. The narrative world of the gospel is therefore neither a window on the ministry of Jesus nor a window on the history of the Johannine community. Primarily at least, it is the literary creation of the evangelist, which is crafted with the purpose of leading readers to "see" the world as the evangelist sees it so that in reading the gospel they will be forced to test their perceptions and beliefs about the "real" world against the evangelist's perspective on the world they encountered in the gospel.[34]

Every story's world is distinct to that story, and we must take care not to dilute the narrative world of the fourth Gospel simply into one like those of the first three Gospels. The narrative world is carefully constructed, bit by bit, through every episode of the plot. Only by carefully reading the plot of John and allowing its world to embrace us can we participate fully in the story. That observation leads us naturally into the homiletical implications of the study of the literary features of the fourth Gospel.

Homiletical Implications of the Literary Criticism of John

Preachers want to do the very same thing with their listeners as the evangelist does with the readers of the Gospel. When we read the Gospel carefully and openly, it entices us into the story, lures us into being characters in its drama, and wraps us with its own distinctive narrative world. That is precisely what preachers seek to do with their listeners. We are, it seems to me, particularly interested in the story's world and leading our congregations into that world by means of particular texts. One could construct a whole view of biblical preaching around the supposition that our goal is to pull our listeners into the biblical story and invite them to take a role in that story.

We are interested in the concept of narrative world because the story's world is both like and unlike our own lived worlds—the worlds in which we perceive ourselves to be actors. When we ourselves enter the world of the text, it seems most likely that we first discern something about that world that is like our own. John's world is one in which people have to struggle with their faith, even as we have to struggle. Or else, perhaps what appeals to us about the Johannine world is that it is so radically different from ours that we become curious to learn more about it. For instance, I think the reason Disney movies work for me is not that the Disney world is often like my own, but that I really want my world to be as simple as that imaginary world in which the good always triumphs over the evil in a remarkably short span of time. Whether it is by the attraction of similarity or dissimilarity, we try to entice our listeners into the Johannine world (or more precisely, the world of the text on which we are preaching) and then demonstrate how that world may be like our own but also challenges our worlds. For this reason, I believe preachers could profit from developing a kind of sketch of the world that is visible in and behind the texts on which we preach.[35]

The new literary criticism also cultivates an appreciation for the text itself—something preachers have long treasured. The contributions this movement makes to preaching include at least two quite different matters. First, the new literary criticism of Scripture suggests that we can concentrate on the text without being overly worried about its historical background. This is not to say that literary criticism renders historical studies irrelevant, for that is clearly not the case. As preachers, however, we always bump up against historical questions that are not solved and which we cannot solve. We must go ahead and preach the text without that historical bit of knowledge. For instance, is the "disciple whom Jesus loved" a historical or purely literary character? Without always answering such questions, literary criticism allows us to attend to and preach the text as we find it and frees us to preach without historical certainty.

Second, and more important, we can identify literary techniques in the Gospel story and try to replicate them in our sermons. For instance, the evangelist's ironic presentation of Christ's kingship might fashion a sermon for Christ the King (or the Reign of Christ) Sunday. A sermon on the Samaritan woman might ask what her name was and invite listeners to name her with their own identity. Whatever literary quality of the Gospel one chooses, fashioning a sermon around that feature is biblical preaching at its best.[36] When we preach one of the "closure texts," we might show our congregations its relationship with its partner closure and the meaning that relationship yields. For instance, preaching the Johannine crucifixion scene provides us opportunity to explore the relationship of Jesus' commendation of his mother and the beloved disciple to one another with the reference to children of God in 1:12. The feature of irony leads us to both the language of the Gospel (chapter 3) and to its ambiguity[37] and paradox, which are important theological features (chapter 2).

A Sermon Example

An ambiguous feature of the Gospel gave birth to the following portion of a sermon on the Nicodemus passage (3:1-17), which is the assigned Gospel lesson for Trinity Sunday, B, and an alternate lesson for Second Sunday of Lent, A.

⌒

I must tell you, my sympathies are with Nicodemus. I mean, Jesus treats this poor guy like dirt. As if he wasn't worth the time of day. He comes to Jesus out of a sincere desire to learn. We have no evidence in the story to think otherwise. He obviously admires Jesus—calls him a "teacher." Says that no one could do what Jesus has been doing unless he came from God. I get the picture of a seeker, as we might call him today. One who is looking for some further relationship with Jesus in order that he might believe in him.

And it looks like he's taking a terrible risk in coming to see Jesus. He is a learned teacher in Judaism. His colleagues are dead set against this Galilean prophet figure. But Nicodemus is willing to risk it. That's why he comes under the cover of darkness to where Jesus is staying. If word gets out about his visit, he is liable to lose his job. He will be discredited. Booted out of the circle of the Pharisees before you can blink an eye. Yet he's willing to risk it all for the possibility that Jesus may be the one he's been looking for.

But look at how Jesus treats him! He speaks to Jesus with respect. But Jesus? No, there's no respect in his voice. Instead, Jesus makes this obscure claim: You are not going to enter God's kingdom unless you are born—born what? The Greek word can mean both "again" or "from above." Which did Jesus mean? Nicodemus is as puzzled as I am by Jesus' words, and he makes a stab with a question. How's he going to be reborn? But Jesus never really gives him an answer. He just starts talking about birth and the Spirit and the wind. Nicodemus asks, "How can this be?" And Jesus scolds him! "How can you be so stupid" seems the essence of what Jesus says to him.

And then . . . then Nicodemus disappears! *Disappears!* We are never told that he leaves. If he said anything more, we don't hear about it. He has made three statements—each one a bit shorter than the previous one. And then he is silenced. He just fades away. Does he go back into the darkness of the night any more informed than when he came? We are never told.

What becomes of Nicodemus? We would like to think that he sat through Jesus' rather long speech that follows his last question. We would like to think that he found Jesus' words helpful and even that he came to believe in Jesus. But we don't know. What became of Nicodemus? Did he become a follower of Jesus? Or, did he remain confused and puzzled by the Galilean?

We do have a couple of hints later on in John. In chapter 7 we learn about a meeting of the religious authorities about Jesus. They had sent out their officers to arrest Jesus, but they come back empty-handed. And the religious leaders are divided over Jesus. Some think he is from God. Others think that no one with any knowledge could possibly believe in him. And, then, lo and behold, Nicodemus speaks up. Here he is—in this meeting of the religious leaders. And he speaks up in Jesus' defense. In effect, he says that Jesus deserves a fair trial before being judged guilty. His colleagues only taunt him for this—"Are you too a Galilean, like this Jesus?"

Again Nicodemus disappears from the story, as quickly as he had reappeared. But he does come on stage one more time. Jesus has been crucified. Then Joseph of Arimathea and Nicodemus come, claim the body, and give Jesus a decent burial. Curious! Strange that Nicodemus should pop up on this occasion. The story-teller informs us that Joseph is a "secret believer" in Jesus. That is, he believes in Jesus but doesn't make his faith publicly known. Should we assume that Nicodemus is like Joseph in this matter? Is he too a "closet disciple"? We are never told. And once again Nicodemus disappears. This time for good—never again to appear in the Gospel.

Was Nicodemus one of Jesus' followers? Maybe a secret follower? What do you think? It sounds to me as if Nicodemus continued to struggle with his response to Jesus. Maybe he wanted to believe but was afraid to do so. Maybe he wanted to believe but found it hard to take that first step. Maybe he wanted to believe but found it just too costly.

Perhaps some of you can identify with Nicodemus's struggles. Perhaps some of you feel that you are stranded in between faith and unbelief. A perpetual seeker. A Nicodemus. I certainly can identify with him. I have had my moments of struggle with my faith. There have been times too that I assumed the role of "closet disciple"—afraid to make my faith public in some situations. Lots of us struggle to come to firm faith. Maybe that's okay. It's possible that God makes allowances for us Nicodemuses. God understands those who wrestle with Christ, sometimes believing, sometimes denying him. . . .

Conclusion

Yes, there is a tangle of theses surrounding the Gospel of John. A complex tangle that would give any thoughtful preacher a headache. There are so many theories that one is tempted to put the Gospel of John aside and preach on one of the other lessons—and in a pinch even on the psalm. There are, however, a couple of patterns in the tangle that are discernible and on which the preacher can depend at least for the time being. We certainly have not untangled the mess of hypotheses concerning this Gospel, but we have found some loose ends with which we can start.

Historically, it seems pretty clear that—at least for the time being—preachers can assume that the fourth Gospel was written soon after a small community of messianic Jews were separated from their synagogue but went on disputing the question of who Jesus is with their former colleagues in the synagogue. In that setting, some unnamed leader wrote this Gospel to strengthen the community of believers amid their sense of isolation and their uncertain identity. Historically, it also seems relatively certain that this community sought a social identity over against the dominant culture of their time and place and did so through the development of a peculiar language that nurtured their identity. As a small group, in opposition to the larger society, they developed their theology in ways that were relevant to their social situation. However, let's never forget that this is all hypothetical.[38]

From a literary perspective, whatever one may say about the historical origin and setting for the Gospel, this Gospel is a masterpiece of writing. Carefully structured, filled with irony, and dotted with a variety of characters, the Gospel paints a world that is both enticing and challenging. While these features are most certainly debatable, they do not dangle on threads of historical speculation, and so we can depend on them as the backbone of preaching John. We do not have to have degrees in literary criticism to understand and appreciate what the text of the Gospel does to and for readers. Nor do we have to be historians able to critique the theories for how the Gospel came about, since the text is there for us to preach. The tangle is still tangled. But we can use even a tangled rope when we need to.

The theological themes of the fourth Gospel are entwined with its literary features and its historical origin. In the tangle of theses, there is an entanglement of theological themes. In particular, the Gospel advocates theological themes through its use of language and its carefully crafted structure. Equipped with some sense of the scholarly treatments of the Gospel, we are now better prepared to enter the thought world of the Gospel of John.

2

Theological Themes:
The Heart of Johannine Thought

AFTER THE BRIEF DISCUSSION of the most important movements in research on the Gospel of John, we turn now to its theological nature.[1] This Gospel is saturated with theological thought and represents one of the major theologies of the entire New Testament. Probably no other single document in the New Testament (with the possible exception of Romans) has had more influence on Christian thought through the centuries than the Gospel of John. Its emergence in the literature of the second century was occasioned by the Gnostics interpretation of the Gospel and the response of other Christian thinkers. It was influential in the theological debates in the history of the church, especially with regard to Christology and pneumatology. Among its affirmations concerning the Holy Spirit, the Nicene Creed states that the Holy Spirit "proceeds from the Father and the Son." The creed bases this statement on the words of Jesus in the fourth Gospel about the Counselor or Advocate. In 14:16 and 25 Jesus promises that God will send the Counselor, but in 16:7 he claims that he will send the Counselor. The creed simply coalesces the two passages.

It is no wonder, then, that the Gospel of John remains at the eye of several of the theological hurricanes of our own time. The debate over the question of whether or not John teaches us the essence of the sacraments of the Lord's Supper and Baptism is a case in point, with scholars taking every possible position imaginable on the subject. The richness of Johannine theology has enabled many to find somewhere in the pages of this Gospel a view that suits them. We preachers know how theologically thick this Gospel is—if one chooses to preach on one theme in a passage, it is complicated with connections with other ideas.

I believe that we can preach John effectively only when we have a handle on the broad theological motifs of the Gospel. Interpreters in general, and not just preachers, run the danger of stressing one theme without knowing how it fits into the whole picture. Indeed, we might think of John as one large and complex painting, filled with brilliant colors and images. If we try to interpret the lower right-hand corner of the picture without understanding what role it plays in the total theme of the painting, we do violence to both the part and the whole.

For those reasons, we devote our attention in this second chapter to the theological heart of Johannine theology in the conviction that as preachers we can ground ourselves in a grasp of the whole in order to preach individual passages. This is not to say that we can solve all the puzzles of Johannine thought, or even that we need to do so, but only that we need a panoramic view of the thought world of the Gospel.

Before undertaking our introduction to Johannine thought, perhaps we should consider a prior question, namely, how do we discern a theological theme in this theologically rich Gospel? Several suggestions might help. First, we should keep the whole of the Gospel before us when working on any one passage. Perhaps we may need to reread the whole of John to get a fresh perspective on a passage. Second, it helps if we remember that the author of the Gospel is not a contemporary systematic theologian. The Gospel's purpose is to nurture faith not explicate theology. This means that we should not read John through the eyes of the church's creeds (for instance, what Christ's sonship means in John), for to do so may get us into more trouble than truth. Third, we ought to be aware that the Gospel is a community document, written for and out of a real Christian community—with hurts and fears and all the rest. The evangelist was writing on behalf of a community and addressing that community.

Finally, we do well to remember that the basic theme and claim of the Gospel is revelation. God has been revealed in Christ. Because of Christ, we know something about God we did not know before, since Christ "exegetes" the very heart of God (1:18). "Truth" in John probably means the truth of the revelation. The consistent theme of John is that in seeing and hearing Christ we see and hear God (see 5:24 and 14:9). We are probably wise to ask of every text we read and preach on, how does this passage in some sense make God known?

In what follows then we can only sketch some of the major theological ideas and show how they relate to one another. It is equally important in this chapter that we come to grips, too, with what one might call the evangelist's method of doing theology—how the text seems to think about ideas of theological importance. Some of the Gospel's major themes are sketched here, including Christology, eschatology, pneumatology, faith, salvation, and Christian hope. The sketch does not propose to be exhaustive but with economy offers major motifs and elucidates the ambiguity of thought (that is, paradox), which is intrinsic to Johannine theology. We will also make some suggestions about the homiletical implications of Johannine thought and way of thinking.

Johannine Christology

Few students of the fourth Gospel would deny that Christology is the core of Johannine theology. Every theological view arises from the question of who Christ is: pneumatology, eschatology, ecclesiology, soteriology, and all the rest. Even the understanding of God is Christocentric, since everything John says about God entails God's relationship with Christ. God is Christ's Father. God is the sending One, who sends Christ. You know God through knowing Christ. Like a hub of the wheel, all the theological spokes reach into Christology and find their center there.

A Variety of Christologies

When someone raises the topic of the Christology of John, most of us think immediately of the incarnational theme in the Gospel's prologue (1:1-18), and with good reason. That poem about the Word represents one of the central themes in John's teaching about Christ's identity and work. One of the amazing things about the Christology of the fourth Gospel, however, is that it is so very diverse. We really should speak of "Christologies."[2] The fourth evangelist describes Christ in many different ways, of which the incarnation of the Word is only one. Furthermore, the evangelist seemed unconcerned about consistency among the various views the Gospel offers.

The heart of the problem of the diversity of Johannine christological thought is 1:14, or at least we can take that as a beginning point to explore this diversity. On the one hand, "the Word became flesh" and, on the other hand, "we beheld his glory." How are we to reconcile human flesh and divine glory? How can flesh and glory reside in one person?[3] That kind of radical assertion of apparently contradictory ideas is typical of Johannine thought in general and Christology in particular.

Another good example is 5:19-25, where Jesus speaks of his dependence on God. "[T]he Son can do nothing on his own, but only what he sees the Father doing . . ." (v. 19). How might we reconcile this statement of utter dependence with the Christology of the Gospel's prologue where Christ is called God's Word and even God? Or, Christ claims to be one with God and yet says he is subordinate to the Father (14:28), or is "subordination" the right word in the complex nature of Christ's relationship with God? (See chapter 6.)

The evangelist weaves together a number of very different christological statements without harmonizing them. Christ is the Word, God's own self, the revealer of God, a prophet or messenger (the one sent), and an agent of God.[4] Actually, if we were to determine the major christological category in the Gospel of John in terms of the frequency of use of the various categories, it would not be the incarnational theme but the emissary theme that dominates. Christ speaks most often of being sent, of serving as an emissary representing God in the world. The text never offers a resolution to the collage of christological statements in the Gospel. John seems to say all these different views are helpful in some way and does not allow one to elbow the others out.

Another incident of christological diversity is found in the words of John the Baptist in 1:32: "I saw the Spirit descend as a dove from heaven, and it remained on him." The similarity with the Lukan view of John's baptism of Jesus (3:21-22) is striking. In Luke, however, the descent of the Spirit is appropriate to what we might call Luke's pneumatic Christology—Jesus is the Christ and Son of God by virtue of the Spirit's presence in his life. What does it mean in the Gospel of John that the Spirit descended on Jesus? First, we recognize that the fourth Gospel never records Jesus being baptized and that the Baptist's witness about the Spirit's descent is not in the context of baptism. Moreover, what would it mean for the Spirit to descend on one who has just been called God's own Word embodied and equated with God's own being? To put the question more coarsely, what need would Jesus have of the Spirit, if he is God's Word? Yet such a contradiction seems never to bother the author of this provocative story of Jesus.

In summary, the Christology of the Gospel of John is an amalgamation of images of Christ, or metaphors by which to express his identity and significance. To ask the question, what is John's Christology, necessitates the presentation of a number of different images and a discussion that attempts to make sense of the whole of the christological collage. Of course, we can never penetrate the author's mind to discover exactly how she or he thought of Christ. We can only observe the complexity and variety of the ideas floating around in the text.

Homiletical Implications

We can learn an important homiletical lesson from John's pluralistic Christology: Christ's identity is forever a mystery that we need not try to solve. There are a variety of ways of speaking of Christ's relationship with God, many of which are valid and need to be held together. There may be a tendency for us to lock onto certain christological themes and claim they are the whole truth. In doing so, we put ourselves in the position of having to diminish the importance of other themes and images, which the fourth evangelist never does. Therefore, John may teach us to respect diversity in our language and imagery for Christ and to treasure the richness of such a variety of ways of expressing our faith.

Moreover, while John never says so in just these words, the language to speak of Christ's identity is essentially metaphorical. In speaking of that identity, we have no option except to forge language based on our own experience. So, Christ is compared to a child in a close relationship with a parent (the Father-Son language), to an agent authorized to act on behalf of his or her sender, and to human self-expression (Word). The nature of christological language (and ultimately of theological language in general) encourages us to create our own contemporary metaphors for understanding Christ. Preachers ought not be shy about attempting that kind of contemporizing of language about the identity and work of Christ. The making of metaphors to articulate the Christian faith in Christ is endless, and we may need to continue the search for new and more appropriate metaphors for our day. Indeed, to do so may be frightening—who are we to invent language to speak of who Christ is—and is certainly difficult, but it may be a way of capturing the imaginations of our congregations and helping them find new meaning in Christ for themselves.

Furthermore, I propose that we preach the sacramental quality of John. I do not mean sacramental exclusively in the sense of Baptism and Eucharist, although they are, of course, equally important. I have in mind the fact that John suggests seeing and hearing a flesh-and-blood Jesus is our way of seeing and hearing God. God encounters us through the material world. This view cultivates a sacramental perspective on experience by taking the incarnational theology of the prologue seriously. It encourages our congregations to experience the consolation of the community as God's consolation and the Christian colleague as the risen Christ. It is not that God once became flesh and dwelt among us, but that God is always becoming enfleshed in the community and hence dwelling among us.

To look at the other side of the issue (as John would want us to), we might also consider preaching the otherness of Jesus (see the introduction.) The Gospel of John portrays Christ as radically other and not as the compassionate, warm, and gentle Jesus we would like. Except for the scene at Lazarus's tomb, Jesus never expresses any kind of emotion, compassion, or empathy with the distress and afflicted. In 11:33, 11:35, and 11:38 deep and troubling emotions are attributed to Jesus, as they are in 12:27 when he considered his destiny. In both chapters, the strong emotions pass quickly. Moreover, Jesus is portrayed as an extrahuman creature who knows what others are thinking before they speak (1:47 and 2:25). He walks through a hostile crowd without them laying a hand on him (7:30, 7:44; and 8:20). He has no need to pray or hear God's confirmation because his relationship with God is so close (11:42). Christ is from above (8:23), from where he descended and to which he will once again ascend (1:51; 3:13; 6:62; and 20:17). He is an alien, a foreigner in this world.

All of this implies the allusive Christ and suggests that in him we encounter mystery. Perhaps we need a stronger sense of mystery in Christian worship and life today. Preaching his otherness may help us avoid domesticating Jesus, making him fit into our systems and presuppositions.

A Sermon Example

The following fragment comes from a sermon that attempts to speak of the otherness of Jesus in the Christmas setting. The assigned Gospel for the Third Sunday of Christmas for all three years is the powerful poem in 1:1-14, fragments of which are also the lection for the Second Sunday of Christmas (1:[1-9], 10-18) and the Third Sunday of Advent, Year B (1:6-8).

⁓

> Christmas Eve is only a few weeks ago. On that occasion, many of us become wrapped up in the traditional stories of that birth in the Gospels of Matthew and Luke. There is a kind of joy and satisfaction that comes from living within these stories for a time. I don't know about you, but my Christmas would never be complete without those carols. In particular I think of the American folk song, "Away in a Manger." Remember those words?
>
> > The little Lord Jesus laid down his sweet head.
> > . . . the poor baby wakes,
> > but little Lord Jesus no crying he makes.
>
> The movie *Simon Birch* was inspired by John Irving's novel, *A Prayer for Owen Meany*. Simon Birch is a tiny boy, about twelve years old, but only three feet tall. Simon was born tiny and malformed. His body is still twisted and disfigured. But he is a proud boy. He pays little attention to what others think of him. Much to his chagrin, however, every year he is asked to play the role of the baby Jesus in the church's Christmas pageant. He really wishes that he could play Joseph or at least one of the shepherds. But he is the only child of his age who will fit into the cradle.
>
> This particular presentation of the pageant, however, proves to be disastrous. Simon is very attracted to the girl who is chosen to play Mary, the mother of Jesus. The time comes and Mary leans over the cradle and speaks lovingly to her child. Simon cannot restrain himself. He pulls Mary down into the cradle and kisses her. About the same time, the harness that suspends the overly large boy playing an angel breaks. He comes crashing down on the shepherds and wise men. The whole thing ends in chaos.

Maybe the simple Christmas story is always filled with surprises. Let's hope not ones like the Simon Birch story. But we cannot harness the story for our own desires. The sweet and tearless baby Jesus may be what we would like. But there's something else going on.

The lesson for today from the Gospel of John surprises us. This is John's way of introducing Jesus to us. No birth story. No sweet and cuddly baby Jesus. Rather John begins by taking us into another realm. "In the beginning." That mysterious time before all time. That place without space. And there John speaks of the *Word*. The Word who was with God and was God. The Word through which everything that is came into being. The Word who came to his own people but was rejected by them. *The Word that "became flesh full of grace and truth. And we saw his glory. . . ."*

These words shatter all our simple concepts of the baby Jesus. They claim that this Galilean prophet figure was none other than God's own being in human form. And John never lets us forget this through the whole Gospel. Jesus descends from above and belongs to another world. He is human like us. But what a human! He has a destiny in this world. And nothing can prevent his fulfilling that destiny. His opponents try to arrest him, but he walks through the crowd without another laying a single finger on him. He is a human. But a stranger in this world, an alien from another realm. Above all, he is the Word of God made flesh and blood.

This is not the kind of Jesus we would like. Not a tender, compassionate, warm fellow. Not one who hands out warm fuzzies wherever he goes. He doesn't fulfill our every expectation. He is not at our command. He is the Word of God made flesh and blood.

You see, I think the Gospel of John begins with these words for one clear reason. John wants to present us with a Jesus who remains a mystery. Indeed, his humanity is a mystery. This is a Jesus who cannot be harnessed and put to work in ways we would like. He is not one who is at our beck and call to do our will. He is rather the mysterious Word of God.

John's Jesus reminds us that in Christ we meet the divine. In Christ the almighty God of the universe faces us. And we cannot understand this mystery. We cannot make him in our image. For he is the Word of God! The awesome other. The stranger from above come into our world. . . .

∾

Paradox as a Theological Method

The relationship among the various christological categories employed by the fourth evangelist implies a theological method or a way of thinking theologically. In this case we are interested in the way the evangelist uses paradox as a means of elucidating doctrine. We will delay discussion of other theological themes in John until we have had a chance to understand how the evangelist uses paradox. Understanding that way of thinking, that manner of posing affirmations about the divine, will assist us in dealing with some of the other theological themes.

John's Christology is paradoxical. Paradox occurs when two or more apparently contradictory truth statements are maintained in spite of their opposition to one another. A classical Christian paradox is that believers are at the same time both sinners and saints.

Paradoxical Theology

The Gospel of John seems to say that truth is found not in one view but in several held together in tension with one another. Christ holds together the divine and the human without compromise (1:14), and claims to be one with God while still subservient to God (for example, 10:30, 38; and 14:28). The multiplicity of Johannine Christologies is indicative of the paradoxical or many-faceted nature of Johannine theology. Out of this paradoxical Christology, the fourth evangelist presents several sides to a number of other theological ideas. Below we will see how paradoxical tension is present in other theological themes, such as eschatology and freedom and determination.

John's paradoxical method of thinking theologically is revealed in general themes, but we also encounter paradox or double-sidedness in John's use of words with multiple meanings. This point anticipates what we should include in the discussion of Johannine language below, but merits consideration here. Sometimes paradoxical theological thought is encapsulated into single words or phrases. If you recognize the possibility that John's so-called double entendre is deliberate, then it illustrates the paradoxical quality we have been discussing. That is to say, if in an instance of multiple meanings in the same word or phrase all the meanings make equal sense in terms of the evangelist's style and thought, then paradox is packed into a single word or phrase.

John 3 contains several specimens of paradox in single words or phrases. The best known is Greek word *anōthen* in verses 3 and 7, which means at least three different things: Born "again," born "from above," and born "from the beginning." The word translated "wind" (*pneuma*—vv. 5, 6,

8) can mean both spirit and breath. "Lifted up" (*huspoō*—v. 14) refers to both the enthronement of a king and a crucifixion. In each of these cases, it is easy to argue that *both* or all the meanings are proper and need to be included in the reading of this passage.

An easy example of this is the use of "lifted up" *(huspoō)* in 3:14. In chapter 5, we will discuss the idea that for John Christ's death is also his enthronement as king. Moreover, Pilate's placard on the cross is ironically true. So, the fourth evangelist invites us to think of the death of God's beloved child as the means by which Christ takes his role as ruler and sovereign in the world. The revelation of Christ's kingship is achieved in an entirely unexpected way in which the opposite of what appears to be the case (Jesus is executed as a common criminal) is actually true. This example shows that paradox is closely related to irony. When understood in the context of theological thought, the literary device of irony (see chapter 1) becomes a means of articulating paradoxical truth.

Interpreters are often inclined to seek a resolution to the paradoxical expressions in the fourth Gospel. That is, they will sometimes conclude that one or the other of two truth statements set in paradoxical tension with one another is actually what the evangelist "intended." Then they will interpret the opposing idea in terms of the one they select as the "true" statement. For instance, in the paradox of the incarnation (1:14), scholars have argued how one ought to deal with the relations between the terms flesh *(sarx)* and glory *(doxa)*. Christ cannot be both, so which is the predominant feature of Jesus' character, divine glory or human flesh? For some the flesh is only a disguise; for others Jesus is genuinely human and is given glory only in the course of his ministry.[5] Perhaps we should not always assume the evangelist actually meant *one* of the two possible meanings and not the other. Instead we may need to let John be John and think in paradoxical terms. We will find Johannine theology even richer and more complicated than we first thought.

Homiletical Implications of Paradoxical Theology

Preaching the paradoxes of John makes a significant contribution to the life of any congregation. The church today, I believe, needs to take paradox more seriously, because we would profit from understanding that knowledge or truth is complex. Much to our dismay, there may not always be a single, simple answer. In our time, some try to reduce truth to easy singular, uncomplicated statements. Indeed, those churches that hold this view seem to be the ones growing the fastest. People yearn these days for simple truth, since our lives are so complex and absolutely nothing seems simple.

I think John invites us to take a more complicated view. Truth is many-sided, paradoxical, and evasive. While that may not be a popular view today—and certainly not one that solves our desire for certainty—it seems far more realistic. If modernity has taught us anything, it is that truth is never as simple as we would like it to be. Helping our congregations understand paradox and accept the fact that much of truth is paradoxical nurtures their readiness for what the future is likely to hold for North America in a postmodern age.[6]

A Sermon Example

The fourth evangelist presents the many-sidedness of large theological themes in tiny word pictures. What follows is an effort to demonstrate the paradoxical quality of the cross. This is one part of a sermon on John 12:20-33, prepared for the Fifth Sunday of Lent, B. With its attention to verse 32, the goal of this movement of the sermon is to show that we can never fully understand the cross.

~

This passage is confusing enough already. Greeks come but Jesus doesn't talk with them. When they appear he claims his "hour has come." But something else is also puzzling. Jesus declares, *"And I, when I am lifted up from the earth, will draw all people to myself"* (v. 32). What do you suppose Jesus meant by this statement? What does it mean for him to be "lifted up?"

The meaning of the cross has always puzzled us. We know that something very significant happened in Jesus' death. We know that his death brought us closer to God. Through his death we see God in an entirely new light. But how is it that his death accomplishes all this? Christian thinkers throughout the history of the church have pondered this question. And without any clear and conclusive answer. So, we are left adrift. Each of us tries as best we can to come to some conclusion about the cross.

The Gospel of John presents us with a very different picture of the meaning of Jesus' death. At least it is different from other views in the New Testament. We cannot easily impose some of our preconceptions on John. There is little or nothing about the healing power of Jesus' death. Very little about his death being a sacrifice for our sins. Instead, we have this strange saying about his being "lifted up." John has used this expression quite deliberately, or so it would seem. On three different occasions in John, Jesus speaks of his death as a "lifting up."

The Greek word that our text translates "lifted up" is an ambiguous one. It can indeed refer to a crucifixion. Lifting a victim up on a cross to leave him or her there to die. Yet, oddly enough, the word was also used of an enthronement of a king. Lifting one up to the position of king and ruler. We would say that the inauguration of a president is a lifting up. The candidate is installed as our leader.

So, which is it? Does Jesus mean by "lifted up" his crucifixion? Or, does he mean his enthronement as king of the universe? Or, *could it be that John wants us to answer yes to both these possibilities?* Could it be that Jesus' crucifixion is his enthronement?

Ah, but that can't be, can it? How can an execution make one a ruler? That would be like saying the death penalty honors a person! As if death could exalt one. John is playing tricks with language here. The phrase "lifted up" tries to get us to imagine the unimaginable. Jesus becomes our King by dying on the cross! In a way we cannot imagine, God makes Christ our Ruler and Leader. What appears to be his death is actually his enthronement. The cross means something quite the opposite of what it seems to mean.

We finally have to say: We simply don't understand how this could be! We have to confess that this idea of the cross goes beyond our logic. Never can we say with absolute clarity exactly what the cross means. We can only say that it rescues us from our meaningless lives.

Sometimes the experiences that do not make sense rescue us. A friend of mine confessed to me that he was trapped in a meaningless life. Nothing made sense to him anymore. A pastor who had served the church for some ten years suddenly found his life empty and void of meaning. We talked, but I couldn't help him. Later, he was on the verge of resigning his position as pastor of a large congregation. Then something happened. The most beloved of the saints of his congregation was diagnosed with cancer. She was only thirty-five years old. The most devout and sincere Christian my pastor friend had ever known. But he joined his life with hers, and together they traveled the road to the woman's eventual death.

It made absolutely no sense whatsoever that this woman should suffer and die. Her agony and struggle were utterly meaningless. She died a painful and lingering death. Through her senseless suffering, however, my friend saw something more. He saw the dignity and worth of human life. He saw the way in which

her love could not be smashed, even in the worst pains imaginable. He saw her spirit strengthen even as the end approached. As
he finally said to me, "Her suffering and death seemed to open a
window to truth for me." And in her death, my pastor friend
found new life—new meaning and purpose.

"And I, when I am lifted up from the earth, will draw all people
to myself."

~

Sin and Evil

While Christology is the center of the theology of the fourth Gospel, there
are numerous spokes reaching out from that hub, all of which are important for preaching John. I propose that we look at a number of topics
grouped under three larger categories: sin and evil, faith and salvation, and
Christian hope. In certain cases, we will see additional evidence of the
evangelist's paradoxical method of thinking theologically.

Polarities

One of the things for which the fourth Gospel is famous, or notorious,
depending on your point of view, is its dualism or use of opposites. The
Gospel consistently speaks as if there are two realms of reality and two
opposing forces. In the discussion of Christology above, we have already
alluded to the distinction between the above and below. This dualism is
interwoven with the use of the word "world" (kosmos), which seems in
most cases to be synonymous with the reality of the below. Consider again
the polarities in 8:23: "You are from below, I am from above; you are of this
world, I am not of this world." The opposition of "below" and "above" and
"of this world" and "not of this world" are in synonymous parallelism with
one another.

Understanding the polarity, "from above" and "from below" (ek tōn
katō and ek tōn anō), has been a tough nut to crack. Scholars have argued
that it represents a kind of Greek cosmic dualism, an apocalyptic dualism,
and an existential dualism. If it is a cosmic dualism, then the evangelist
would want us to conceive the whole of reality divided between these two
segments. The Gnostic dualism that we know from a later century seems to
have thought in these terms. If it is a pair of apocalyptic polarities, however, then we imagine time divided into two parts—what is known elsewhere as the present time and the time to come (for example, see Rom.
8:18). An existential dualism has to do with human self-understanding.

The polarity in this case is two ways of being, of living, and of self-identity. Our understanding of the above/below distinction requires that we grasp the meaning of John's enigmatic use of the term "world." In most cases, the world denotes the realm of unbelief and rejection of the revelation (for example, 7:4, 7; 12:31; 15:18-19; and 17:14-18). The word sometimes seems to be neutral however and only designates physical creation (see 1:10). Rudolf Bultmann suggests that human sin—delusion about who we are—"perverts the creation into the 'world.'"[7] To paraphrase Bultmann, humans have adopted a deluded understanding of themselves as independent of any Creator, as their own lords and as masters of their destiny. That mistaken self-understanding strips the physical creation of all indebtedness for its being and humanity of its true roots in God's creative act and thereby distorts the world into the realm of sin and evil. By definition that means that the essence of sin and evil is an erroneous self-understanding.

The language attributed to Jesus in the fourth Gospel seems to bear out this interpretative view. In the key passage 8:23, all four of the terms "above," "below," "of this world," and "not of this world" are prefaced with the Greek preposition *ek*. It is translated "from" in the first clause and "of" in the second. We might say that this use of the preposition marks origin, roots, or affiliation. Again, Bultmann wrote of this verse, "in John origin is synonymous with membership."[8] The expressions "above," "below," "of this world," and "not of this world" designate that from which we humans draw our understandings of ourselves. The options are limited to two: self-understanding that assumes absolute independence of any transcendent power or assumes absolute dependence on God. For better or worse, the fourth Gospels sees no middle option between these two—the matter is posed in an unqualified either/or.

There we have the Johannine definition of sin. Sin is an erroneous understanding of our origin and therefore of the character of our lives. Of course, with the advent of Christ, sin becomes the refusal to accept the revelation of God and the stubborn insistence that true life does not require belief in God. It is for this reason that we are mistaken when we try to give the word sin *(hamartia)* a moral denotation. To be sure, if one believes in the revelation offered in Christ, then we obey Christ's command to "love one another" (13:34). But beyond that limited and basic moral injunction, the fourth Gospel delineates no moral boundaries outside of which we sin.

Furthermore, with this understanding of sin in the fourth Gospel, we have a better understanding of the source of evil. John has little to say about Satan or the Devil. Satan is mentioned only once (13:27), and the title "devil" is used only three times (6:70; 8:44; and 13:2). It is interesting that all but one of these passages (8:44) refers to Judas, and that one (8:44) speaks of those who reject Christ. The most telling expression for some sort of source of this tendency for humans to misunderstand themselves is the expression "the ruler of this world" *(ho archōn tou kosmou)* found in 12:31 and 14:30. "The evil one" (or just "evil"—*ho ponēros*) mentioned in 17:15 is clearly related to the believers' life in this world. The fourth evangelist locates the power of evil in the atmosphere or ethos of a world that has misconstrued creation and human dependence.

Homiletical Reflections

Those who preach for a decision have often been fond of John's absolute dualism, with no fence-sitting possible, and that is not an entirely specious use of the fourth Gospel's message. The trouble with preaching to "believe in Christ or suffer dire consequences" is the fact that, in its treatment of faith, John does not put all the emphasis on human decision, as we will see in the next section on faith and salvation. Still, the insistence that one cannot live an uncommited life, that we cannot go on delaying some commitment, is a viable and powerful message.

We preachers, who know the lives of our parishioners and are honest about our own lives, know too that life is not as simple as the Johannine dualism might lead us to believe. Our lives are complex, and sometimes we are faithful and believing and sometimes we are not. If you believe that human sin continues to plague us, no matter how committed we are to God and Christ, then we cannot simply say, "choose the realm of the above and not of this world." As a matter of fact, much like a Ping-Pong ball in play, we keep bouncing back and forth between the two. Precisely this kind of sermon is possible from any one of the many passages in which the Johannine dualism appears. Let the preacher challenge the simplicity of that radical either/or with the realities of our life in the world. Thereby she or he might articulate the real situation in which many of our listeners feel they live. Having challenged its oversimplification of life, the preacher can then use the radical either/or to invite the congregation to deepen their commitment to the revelation of God's love in Christ.

Moreover, what is at stake in John's use of the polarities we have discussed is self-identity. One of the deep issues of human life today in our North American society is the matter of who we are. Identity is challenged on nearly every front. Men, for instance, who embrace the women's movement, struggle to find a new gender identity in a world in which the male role of protector, master, and leader of the family has finally—but not yet entirely—crumbled. Moreover, identity is up for grabs right now as we wrestle with the role of our occupations in the question of who we are. We have seen too many (usually men) fall apart after they have been forced to retire from their work; their identity was derived from their work, and when that work has been taken from them they don't know who they are. Or, conversely, in a society in which we change jobs numerous times in the course of a single career, our work seems an unreliable source of identity.

So who are we? John helps us preach a self-identity derived not from some worldly condition or status but from our role as children of God. We can use the "of this world/not of this world" dichotomy to speak of identity based on our relationships in this life—role or job, for instance—and one based on who we are by virtue of our creation by God.

A Sermon Example

The following is a major portion of a sermon entitled "To Melanie," which Myrna Kysar (the author's wife) preached on John 10:10 on the Fourth Sunday of Easter, A. It is used here with her permission.

∼

She is only eleven days old. She must be struggling still to understand this new life of hers—this new life outside of the security and warmth of the womb. She weighed only six pounds, four ounces at the time of her birth. But there she is—a tiny human. All the parts are there! I marveled as I looked at her fingers and witnessed this new life. I stared in near disbelief that tiny Melanie would one day live a full and abundant life.

The image of the tiny, new life captured my mind the other day. I drove back to the office, filled with joy and excitement. But as I did, other images began to creep into my mind. The image of those wind-swept flames devouring the Apocalypse Ranch in Waco, Texas. And I was forced to think of the lives cremated in those horrible flames. Then the image of the torn bodies and the hopeless refugees around the world. And I was forced to think of the lives cremated and disrupted in all the senseless wars. Next came the images of the Holocaust Museum in Washington, D.C. But alongside that was the image of anti-Semitic graffiti on the walls of our own local high school. Again, I was forced to think of those who live in constant fear of persecution and prejudice. Finally, my mind raced on to the images of personal and family crises, and I was compelled to picture the lives lived in the midst of pain and suffering of both a physical and emotional kind.

Within a few hours, I had moved from celebrating the marvels of God's creation to the depressing reality of human destruction, violence, and sin. What could I say to tiny Melanie about this world into which she has just been born? What promise could we give her that life outside of the warmth and security of the womb is worthwhile?

I would want to tell her about Jesus' promise in today's Gospel lesson. I would want her to know that Jesus came so that she might have life and have it abundantly. But there are thieves and bandits, too, Melanie. There are those who would abduct us away from that promise. There are those who would steal and kill and destroy. Those who would rob us of the abundance of life—even of life itself. But there is also another. One who is our shepherd, who knows us by name, and whose voice we know. There are thieves and bandits. But there is also a shepherd whom we can follow.

How can Melanie, or any of us, live abundant lives in a troubled world? How is it that Jesus' promise can lead us through the destructive flames of the world to true life? How is it that Jesus' claims empower us for life?

Jesus declares that we belong to him! We sheep have a shepherd! There is a gate through which we can pass and find pasture!

The issue with which Melanie will struggle is the one most of us know so well. It is the issue of belonging. We emerge from the womb in search for a new home. We emerge into this world, wondering to whom or what we belong. And much of life is spent in that search. Searching for a connection, a relationship, a sense of belonging that grounds us. It is as if we spend life looking for a new womb. Wandering about homeless, hoping to find a place, a relationship, a sense of belonging. In the words of that lovely song from *West Side Story,* we wander about believing, "There is a place for us, somewhere a place for us."

There are few sights more pitiful than that of a stray animal—one that has for some reason lost its owner, one that wanders about homeless. Homeless animals are hungry for both food and affection. They will attach themselves to the first person who shows them any kindness. And beware! If you do show them some kindness, they are yours forever. Beware! If you feed them once, you have a friend for life. . . .

Yet we humans are little different! In those stray, homeless creatures we see something of ourselves: Lost, wandering, hungry for affection and attention. We have a kinship with them for we too seek a home, an owner. Someone who will feed and love us.

But we have a home! We have an owner! This is the promise: Jesus is the one to whom we belong! Christ is the source of our food and our need for love and acceptance. Christ is the one who can provide our home and our need for belonging. In a world filled with threats and danger, in a world overpopulated with thieves and bandits, in a world that would block the gate to the pastures of life, there is Christ! There is still one who calls us by name! There is still one who invites us to follow him! There is still one who leads us to life in abundance.

Christ tells us who we are: *We are sheep who belong to him. We are sheep who recognize Christ as our shepherd and owner.* That's what I would like Melanie to understand. That's what I pray she and all of us will hear.

But the abundant life lived in Christ is not a warm, secure womb, is it? Belonging to Christ's flock is no panacea! As his sheep we cannot close our eyes to the world. We cannot ignore the thieves and the bandits! We cannot become blind and deaf to all the pains and the suffering. The fire at Waco burns us, too! Death and destruction any place in the world inflicts our hearts with pain, too! The anti-Semitism of the ignorant few threatens us as well as our Jewish brothers and sisters. The agony of personal and family crises disturbs our peace as well.

The abundant life is no panacea! To live abundantly doesn't mean we withdraw into a new womb! But it does mean that we have a source of power. The abundant life is an empowerment for facing the world! We belong to Christ! Belonging to Christ, we engage the world in all of its evil and destructiveness. Not hide away from it!

God has given us life in Christ. God has loved us without condition, without reservation, without restraint! God has fed us homeless creatures and brought us into the divine home.

Now we have the power, the determination, the courage to fight the thieves and bandits. In that home with Christ, we are ready to take on the forces that make for homelessness. With the food God offers us at this table, we are nourished to join in the struggle for peace and justice. With someone who calls us by name, we are ready to speak the truth in our world!

Belonging to Christ makes us different! We who hear the shepherd's voice also hear the voices of pain in our world. And we hear the shepherd's voice leading us into struggles to change our world.

Belonging to Christ, we here in our own congregation will engage the thieves and bandits of our world. We will actively stand against all the prejudice and hate expressed toward God's creation right here in our community. We will work to give shelter and support to the homeless in our county. We will befriend the lonely and the lost of our society. We will share our wealth with the many who do not have enough even to buy food to eat. We will build up and empower each person we meet. We will do so, not because of our own goodness. Not at all! We will do so because Christ has made us his sheep. Christ has given us a home!

Yes, Melanie, life is worthwhile! In Christ God has claimed you and made you a sheep in the divine flock. God has given you life—abundant life even! With it you will not find a safe, secure womb sheltered away from the world. But with it you will find the power to live in this world. Empowered to struggle against all that is death and destruction in our world.

〜

Faith and Salvation

If unbelief is the basic sin in the Gospel of John, what then is belief or faith? Of course, there is no admonition to have faith in general. It is always faith in a particular object (God or Christ). The verb translated "to believe" *(pis-teuō)* is used ninety-eight times in this Gospel, which suggests its importance. It means a personal trust in the sense that the believer trusts her or his life to Christ and to God, which means entrusting oneself to the revelation of God in Christ. That trust in God's revelation is what enables us to pass from the realm of the below and of the world to that which is not of this world and is above. It is the means of transition from phony self-understanding to authentic life—or what the Gospel calls "eternal life." Salvation in the fourth Gospel means above all allowing God's revelation in Christ to determine our self-understanding. It is salvation from life lived in misunderstanding and to proper understanding of God, Christ, other people, and ourselves.

Faith in What?

Today we hear a lot about faith, which often means thinking in a positive way and not becoming discouraged. Too often, I fear, the popular use of the word fails to indicate the object of faith. Faith in what or whom?

The fourth Gospel uses the verb "believe" in three different ways. In the first two cases, it is followed by one of two prepositions—*en* or *eis*, both of which are translated "in" (for examples of each, see 3:15 and 3:36, respectively). English translations do not always make a distinction between these two.[9] While many believe there is no significant difference between the two, others argue that *eis* has a more personal quality about it. The third use of the verb "believe" is followed by the word "that" *(hoti,* 11:27).

This word suggests that there is specifically something we should believe—that is, some cognitive content as well as some person. This use may be a movement toward a doctrinal understanding of faith, that is, proper faith has a certain content.

In all three of these uses of "believe" we discern what it is that John wants us to believe, if we are to receive and embrace God's revelation in Christ. The passages using one of the two prepositions suggest that faith should believe in God (for example, 14:1), the One who sent Jesus (6:29; 12:44), Christ (7:39), Jesus (12:11), the Son (3:36), the Son of Man (9:35), and the light (12:36). The objects of "believing that" include "I am" (8:24), Christ, the Son of God, the one coming into the world (11:27), Jesus, the Christ the Son of God (20:31), God sent Christ (11:42; 17:8, 21), Christ is in the Father and the Father in him (14:10), and Jesus came forth from God (16:30; 17:8).

Faith is clearly centered on Christ, his identity and his origin. Even belief in God is usually connected with believing in Christ. In the fourth Gospel, therefore, faith has to do with the way we are related to Christ and suggests that relationship is one of confident trust in him. Out of this relationship, we might say, arises the content of faith. The relationship of trust with Christ enables us to affirm who he is—Christ, the one God sent, and so on. This means that for John our Christology is rooted in our faith relationship and grows out of that relationship. We might also say that the content of faith is part of the trusting side of believing, or that the doctrinal view of Christ comprises one aspect of a total trust. In order to trust, we must know who it is we trust and why.

The fourth evangelist also suggests that this kind of faith yields certain results. Believers have eternal life (for example, 3:15—see the next section below), life (11:25), light (12:46), freedom from death (11:26), freedom from thirst (4:13), the Spirit (7:39), persecution (12:42), and the capability of works greater than Jesus' (14:12). The first of these—eternal life, life, light, freedom from death and thirst—are all synonyms for what John means by a saving relationship with God in Christ. These are various ways of saying that by faith in Christ we come to participate in an authentic life or life as God always intended it.

Who Determines Faith?

Now we are up against one of those Johannine paradoxes. The tension is between human decision and divine sovereignty. If we ask who is responsible for our believing, we get a double-sided answer. Obviously, there are passages that suggest that humans exercise their free will in coming to believe. As I said earlier, preaching John can easily be preaching for decision.

A couple of examples of passages where human decision seems to be demanded will suffice. Perhaps the most dramatic of these comes at the end of chapter 6 in verses 60-71. Having heard Jesus make such outrageous claims for who he is, many who had been his followers left him, although this does not surprise Jesus for he knows from the beginning whose faith is genuine. But then he turns to the Twelve (one of only two passages in John where they are mentioned; see also 20:24) and asks, "Do you also wish to go away?" The implication is that they can still decide to leave him, even as they had decided to follow him.

Another example of passages in which free will seems to be part of believing is another question, this time to Martha. After having claimed to be "the resurrection and the life," Jesus asks, "Do you believe this?" The call of the first disciples is a simple invitation, "Come and see" (1:39). Presumably they are free to reject the invitation. The Samaritan woman's witness and Jesus' own words cause the villagers to believe (4:39-42). A number of other passages could also be cited as evidence that John assumed belief was a result of a decision humans make in response to Jesus.

The matter is not so simple however—not for John. There is an equal number of passages that imply only those who have been chosen and acted on by God can believe. Faith is God's doing, not ours. Again, we do not need all the evidence, just enough to exemplify this theme in the Gospel. The most radical of these statements is found in 12:39-40, which is a quotation from Isaiah: Some cannot believe because God "has blinded their eyes and hardened their heart. . . ." Jesus also refers to a mysterious divine force that leads people to him and to believe in him. That force is sometimes stated in terms of those whom God has given to Christ (for example, 6:37, 39; 10:29; 17:2, 6, 9, 24; 18:9) and sometimes in terms of a "drawing." "No one can come to me unless drawn *(helkō)* by the Father who sent me . . ." (6:44; see also 6:65). In 10:26 Jesus suggests that his opponents do not believe because they are not one of Jesus' sheep.

This sense that our origin determines whether or not we can believe is an example of one of the reasons the early Gnostics were attracted to John. Even the famous expression "you must be born from above" may imply an origin with God that enables one to believe. Some are "from God" (or "out of God," *ek tou theou*) and some are not (8:47). Your origin or affiliation seems to determine whether or not you believe. There is something more than human will in the act of believing.

The paradox of willing faith and being given faith is a prize example of Johannine paradox and probably our response to it. Many are inclined to say that one side or the other is what John really meant and then interpret the other side according to that. We might say, for instance, John sought to evoke a willful response of faith in us, and those passages that sound as if

God determines faith simply allude to God's initiative in seeking our response. Indeed, just this might be the best sense we can make of the double-sided language about faith. I invite you, however, to think about the possibility that there is an intractable paradox here. There is a sense in which we must willfully accept God's love in Christ, but our response is really only a reflection of God's gift of faith to us. Such a paradoxical view finds its experiential basis in the simple fact that some of us feel *both* that we choose to believe, but that there are moments when we believe in spite of ourselves! Yes, faith is decision for Christ, but it is also a gift, given by God. Both are true in our lives today: We know we have to embrace the gift of grace, yet there are times when we seem to believe without willing it, without being able within ourselves to believe.[10]

Salvation from What?

The fourth Gospel does not make a great deal of the category of salvation, although the word "save" *(sōzō)* occurs four times in the sense of God's rescue of humanity (3:17; 5:34; 10:9; 12:47) and once Jesus is called "the Savior *(sōtēr)* of the world" (4:42). The real question is from and to what are we saved, according to John?

The fourth Gospel speaks sparingly of any kind of condemnation of unbelievers, but see 12:48 (and below, under "Christian Hope"). The most vivid of the language used for those who are condemned is found in the word-picture of the vine and the branches. Those who do not "abide in me" are "thrown away like a branch and withers; such branches are gathered, thrown into the fire, and burned" (15:6). Many of us doubt that the evangelist intended to picture some sort of eternal fire of damnation, and the language is simply part of the metaphor. However, those who are not related in faith to Christ do experience condemnation. Even though Christ did not come with the purpose of condemning the world, his presence causes a judgment, and some are condemned while believers are not (3:17-21). What is striking about 3:17-21 is that the condemnation is a result of our response to Christ, and the unbeliever is "condemned already" (3:18). In other words, the judgment occurs in this life and in our reaction to God's offer to us in Christ. Actually, the word translated "condemn" is *krinō* and means "to judge." We pass judgment on ourselves by our response to Christ, and Christ's presence always causes a division *(krisis)*, as several passages demonstrate (7:43; 9:16; 10:19).

Perhaps the condemnation to which the Johannine Jesus refers is the fate of living in a world separated from its creation and with a misunderstanding of oneself. In Christ God saves us to Life, that is, to a relationship with God that results in authentic life here in this world and in the world to come. Hence, God saves us from a kind of death, which is inauthentic life or an existence that lacks the meaning our Creator intended for us. What we must discuss later is the fact that the gifts of salvation are given to believers in the present and not reserved only for the future.

Homiletical Implications

Some forms of contemporary Christianity choose to emphasize our eternal destiny and both the promise and the threat that entails. Such a perspective is so widespread that sometimes Christians feel that they have no option but to take the question of eternal destiny as the central issue in the faith. If they are to be Christian, they must concentrate on going to heaven and avoiding hell. The Gospel of John never denies such an eternal destiny but chooses rather to go to its roots in what life means for us. You might say that the eternal is now as well as after death, but more on that in a moment.

The Gospel's perspective is what we might call "existential," in that it focuses on how way we understand our existence and what kind of existence that understanding yields. I believe that many of our parishioners struggle with this question on a daily basis. It still crops up, I think, most often in the question of "what does my life mean?"[11] Preachers can address that gut-wrenching question directly through preaching John. What does John mean by "life" or "abundant life" (10:10)? If we accept the perspective John is offering, what meaning does existence take on? A sermon on the "I am" saying in 11:25 might dig into the matter of what "life" means there. It refers no doubt to a life that is not bounded by death, but surely it means more than that. The meaning of life is that we are God's children (1:12) and belong to our heavenly Parent.

The other thing that stands out in this discussion is the nature of faith. Again, I can only offer an impression for what it is worth. We may have tended to quantify faith and have sometimes become preoccupied with "having faith." Or, as one parishioner once said to me, "If only I had *enough faith*." Certainly there is a truth in this perspective, but we might want to qualify it with the promise that God enables our faith. We are not left on our own to believe; God grants us faith when we need it. Perhaps if we balanced the poles of faith—my believing and God's giving—we would be better able to live faithfully.

A Sermon Example

One way of getting at these issues is dealing with the troublesome portions of the end of the Bread of Life discourse in John 6. The following sermon explores 6:35, 41-51 and is entitled, "Is Faith Possible?" It was prepared for Proper 14 (the Twelfth Sunday after Pentecost, B).

∾

Swimmers learn the dangers of the undercurrent—that powerful force that can suck you down in seconds. It threatens the power and confidence of even the best swimmers. It comes from underneath and is unseen on the surface of water. Without warning, the undercurrent strikes. The swimmer's strength makes no difference. The power of that undercurrent neutralizes all human energy.

As I read the Gospel lesson for today, I felt as if I had been a victim of an undercurrent. It was hardly detectable on the surface of the reading. It came up from underneath to threaten my power and confidence.

Listen to the pull of the undercurrent: *"No one can come to me unless drawn by the Father who sent me."*

"Drawn by the Father?" What puzzling words! I feel myself drowning in uncertainty and puzzlement. What does that mean? How is it that God draws us?

Many of us think of faith as a decision we make in response to the Gospel. One of my seminary professors years ago made an important distinction. He suggested that Christian belief may be divided into two kinds: "Monkey-hold" and "Cat-hold."

A mother monkey sees her little one in distress. She dashes to the baby, turns her back, and the baby leaps on. Holding tightly to the mother, the two race to safety.

A mother cat sees her little one in distress. She dashes to the baby and grasps it by the nape of the neck. The infant dangles helplessly from its mother's mouth. And the mother carries it off to safety.

The baby monkey must cooperate in the rescue mission. Leaping onto mother's back. Holding tight. But the baby cat does nothing. The rescue is all up to the mother. And the baby is totally dependent on the power of its mother.

Many of us like to think in terms of monkey rescue. We like to stress our role in God's saving act. Believing seems to be our act. Surely, an act invited by God's presence in the Good News. We take the leap of faith, cling to our Savior, and we are rescued! We often hear that it is necessary for us to make a decision for Christ. Only by such a decision do we claim Christ's life, death, and resurrection for ourselves.

So, what does Jesus mean here? No one is able to come to him without first being drawn by God? What sense does it make? It sounds like the picture of the mother cat. And we are the helpless kitten, hanging from the mouth of our rescuer.

But maybe we should look at the larger story. The lesson for today is only a small part of the larger discussion. Jesus has marvelously fed the crowd at the beginning of chapter 6. Then they find him. And the discussion begins.

A number of different groups of people engage Jesus in discussion. First comes the crowd. They follow Jesus after the feeding and talk with him. Then in the passage read this morning, the group changes. They are called the "Jews," the religious authorities of the times. They are offended by Jesus' words. They grumble among themselves about the claims he makes for himself. The discussion later continues with the disciples. They too are displeased and cannot tolerate Jesus' words. So displeased are they that some abandon Jesus. Finally, the whole of the discussion ends with Jesus asking the inner circle of the twelve disciples if they too will leave him.

Throughout this whole discussion Jesus subtly challenges his discussion partners. He says that those who come to him are those given to him by God. He says that faith is a "work of God." (Does that mean faith is the work that God does in us?) He says that to believe one must be taught by God. We are baby kittens, dangling from our rescuer's mouth.

All of this feels like a dreaded undercurrent. It pulls me under. Makes me ask, *is faith possible?* At least, is it possible for us humans to decide we are going to believe?

The concluding segment of the discussion is with the Twelve—that intimate circle of followers. The other disciples have left him. So, Jesus addresses the Twelve. Do they, too, want to leave? Are they going to abandon him because of his words? He seems to imply that they have a choice in the matter. Then Peter makes that grand confession, so dear to us Lutherans: "Lord, to whom shall we go? You have the words of eternal life."

Peter encourages me. He makes me feel stronger. Here is a clear decision to continue to follow Jesus. His faith here appears to be a willful act. Peter has considered the options. He decides to remain faithful. He takes that leap of faith. And now clings relentlessly to the one who has the words of eternal life. At least it appears that way on the surface.

But wait! Jesus' response is none too reassuring. To Peter and the others he says, *"Did I not choose you?"* They did not choose to be his disciples. The only reason they are there is that *he chose them!* Their belief is the result of Jesus' choosing them, not they him.

And then comes the most frightening part of this whole discussion. Jesus has chosen the twelve faithful believers. But among them is still a demon. Even if we are chosen to believe, we may be a demon—a Judas! Phoney believers among even the chosen!

The tow of the undercurrent is mighty. Do you feel it? *"No one can come to me unless drawn by the Father who sent me."* God gives believers to Jesus. The disciples' faith is weak, and they fall away. The closest followers believe. But not because they choose Jesus. They believe only because he chose them. And even among the faithful few there may be some who are demons.

Is faith possible? Is it possible for us to decide to believe? There is a troubling undercurrent in the stream of this discussion. That undercurrent forces some of us, at least, to ask what faith really is. This whole discussion brings to the surface that difficult question. What does it mean to believe?

Of course, to have faith is a complicated issue. Belief is not a simple matter. We might put it this way: Faith is total dependence on God. Faith entails renouncing all claims to our own powers and our own merit. We renounce all in order to rely exclusively on God's grace and mercy toward us. Absolute faith is total dependence only on God and not self. That's why faith is sometimes spoken of as a self-emptying. Emptying ourselves of all power and merit. In that empty space then comes absolute dependence on God's acceptance of us. Grace is the powerful undercurrent that saps us of all our strength. Leaves us totally helpless.

I wonder if this understanding of faith helps us see what Jesus is saying here. Perhaps here is the clue to why he speaks the way he does. His choosing. And God's drawing. Here Jesus seems to be dismantling the last bits of our self-reliance. His words remove our last props. The braces that hold up our self-dependence. The very last of those props may be a reliance on our decision. It may be our presumption that we believe as a result of our own *decision to believe.*

"No one can come to me unless drawn by the Father." And down comes my last wall of self-reliance. Now I must depend on God for my faith in Christ. Not on my own powers of decision. And I dangle helplessly from the saving arms of Christ. The arms that have swooped us up and carried us to safety.

Is faith possible? Is it possible for me to believe? No, it is not. God alone makes even my faith in God possible.

But how does God do that? How does God construct a house of faith in the place of our houses of self-reliance? How does God draw us to Christ and to the divine self?

The answer may be found in another passage in the Gospel of John. It is in his last public statement before his passion. Jesus says, *"When I am lifted up, I will draw all people to me."* In his crucifixion, Jesus claims, he draws us to himself. The cross is the divine drawing mentioned in our text for today. That supreme expression of divine love is what pulls faith out of us. Like a mighty suction power, Jesus' death drags us to the foot of the cross and to faith.

Is faith possible? Like a mighty undercurrent the cross answers our question. No, faith is not possible—at least not out of our own power. But our faith is possible by means of the divine love. In that agonizing death God chooses us. In that terrible execution God takes us and gives us to Christ. In that revelation of God's boundless love God's power pulls us down into the depths. Into utter helplessness. And we are made to believe—to believe even in spite of ourselves.

∽

Christian Hope

We find the most widely recognized Johannine paradoxical tension in the view of eschatology—that is, belief about the last things. The classic way of expressing this paradox is in terms of realized and futuristic eschatology (for example, see 5:24 and 5:28-29). John seems to take many of the hopes Christians have for the future and claim that they are present realities. While the Gospel claims that these future events are present, the future dimension is not eliminated entirely. For example, while some passages seem to hint that resurrection is a present reality, there are others that promise a resurrection in the future.

There are some who argue that the Gospel of John has entirely collapsed the future hope into the present. I think, however, that if you read the text carefully you will notice that there are still bits and pieces of promise for the end times. So, it is not the case that the fourth Gospel represents an absolute transformation of Christian eschatology. What it does do, however, is to stress the present along with the future in a new and balanced way. In a sense, I think that you can find the same present-future tension in some of Paul's letters. Compare, for instance, Romans 5:9, where Paul says "we have been justified"; and Romans 13:11, where he speaks of salvation as drawing near. G. B. Caird suggests that the entire New Testament tends to represent salvation in three tenses—past, present, and future.[12] What we find in the fourth Gospel is that the second and third tenses—present and future—are pulled tightly together and articulated side-by-side with one another. Here are some examples showing how the present and future eschatologies are partners.

Resurrection, Eternal Life, and Judgment

One of the most frequently misunderstood phrases in the Gospel of John is "eternal life" *(aiōnios zōē)*. Many understand eternal life as the life that awaits the Christian after death, beyond the grave. As a matter of fact, John makes it quite clear that this future gift is already given to believers in Christ, so that they have eternal life in the present. The Johannine Jesus consistently speaks of believers as having eternal life now (see 3:16, 36; 5:24, 39; 6:47, 54; 10:28; 17:2-3)—not just the promise of such a life in the future but now.

This transformation of eternal life into the believers' present means that the Gospel of John defines this life quite differently than we may think of it. Rather than thinking of eternal life in terms of quantity—endless life— the fourth Gospel suggests that it is a "quality" of life. Eternal life describes the life we live when we understand ourselves to be God's children and when we live in relationship with God in Christ. That kind of life is "eternal" in the sense that it feeds off of the Eternal One and is harmonious with what the Eternal God wants for humanity.

In one sense, the Gospel of John does the same thing with resurrection, except here the tension between the future and the present is sharper, even if the contrast is more subtle. Jesus frequently refers to the promise of resurrection in the "last days." The most obvious of these references are found in the Bread of Life discourse in 6:22-59 (see chapter 6). On four different occasions, while speaking of those who believe in him, Jesus says of them, "I will raise it [or them] up at the last day" (vv. 39, 40, 44, 54). Actually, the Gospel of John rarely refers to the apocalyptic concept of the end time, such as is represent in this verses in the phrase "the last days."

Notice first of all that these promises of a future resurrection of believers are scattered throughout the discourse in chapter 6 along with the promise that believers already have "eternal life." In verses 40 and 54 that statement is even found in the same sentence with the promise "I will raise them up at the last day." But the declaration that believers already have "eternal life" is also found in verse 47. Other expressions of the present eschatology are found in verse 35 ("whoever comes to me will never be hungry, and whoever believes in me will never be thirsty") and in the expression in verse 51 that believers "will live forever" (which is a linguistic variation of eternal life—*zēsei eis ton aiōna* and *hē aiōnios zōē*).

The promise of resurrection in the last day is woven into the fabric of the assertion that believers already enjoy eternal life. With this discourse fresh in your mind, read 11:17-44, the raising of Lazarus. There Jesus declares to Martha that he is "the resurrection and the life" (v. 25) and then goes on to demonstrate this truth by bringing Lazarus back from the dead. (He is really dead, not just comatose, since he has been in the tomb for four days.) One of the points of this story seems to be that in Jesus "the last day" is present. Where Christ is, there is resurrection. If this reading of chapters 6 and 11 in relation with one another is legitimate, the resurrection is promised for the last day, but Christ brings the "last day." Perhaps 5:25 and 5:28-29 summarize this present and future tension. In 5:21 Jesus declares that God has given him the authority to give "life to whom he will," even as God "raises the dead and gives them life." In 5:25 Jesus further claims, "Very truly, I say to you, the hour is coming, and now is here, when the dead will hear the voice of the Son of God, and those who hear will live." The resurrection is a future event brought back into the present, but apparently the future still holds a resurrection. Paradox!

We have already discussed the topic of judgment in the section on faith and salvation above, but Jesus' words in 5:24 need attention. There Jesus claims believers already have eternal life, and then says that they do not "come under judgment, but [have] passed from death to life." To believe is to come to life without judgment. The standard apocalyptic scheme is resurrection, judgment, life (see for example, 2 Thess. 1:7-10); but John bypasses judgment for believers. John 3:18 makes it sound as if judgment occurs in our response to Jesus, and 9:39 seems to make a comparable point. In 12:48, however, Jesus speaks as if there is still a final judgment for those who reject him. They have a "judge," his "word." "On the last day" what Christ has spoken will judge them. It appears that judgment occurs in our initial response to Christ, but those who respond with rejection face some sort of future judgment.

The Gospel of John seeks to nurture a faith in the presence of God's final gifts in the here and now. I think it does so without entirely eliminating our hope for the future. What probably startles us the most is that those events that we usually associate with the future are transformed into present experience thanks to God's revelation in Christ. We can't be sure why the evangelist chose to do this, or the Johannine community held this view, but we can see how it works in our consciousness to honor the present life in this world.

Homiletical Implications

Christianity is constantly under attack for its otherworldliness. We Christians are charged with being preoccupied with what happens to us after death and being unconcerned with life in the here and now. We are totally a waiting people, whose only hope, some claim, is in the future. Moreover, groups within the broader church appear consumed by anticipation of the "last days"—who will be "taken" and who "left behind." Again, critics respond to these groups with the charge that all the attention on the future deprives us of genuine interest in the present. While all such charges are guilty of oversimplifying the Christian faith, we need to take them seriously.

Preaching is one occasion, among others, for nurturing a stronger sense of our being a people straddling the present and future and being equally concerned with both. To live in the interim, as it were, is not at all reason for disregarding the future. We believe that the future transforms the present. However, John would have us preach another message, namely, that *Christ transforms both our future and our present*. Preaching John may provide us opportunity to invite our congregations to find the last days in today, to appreciate the quality of life Christ gives us now while still clinging to hope for the future.

My suggestion then is that we try to preach John's paradoxical eschatology—without ever calling it that. Preachers could lift up and identify Christian experiences in the present that alter our perspective on the present. I do not in any way suggest that we minimize the future. I for one think that a future transformation of society and nature is one of the precious hopes the Gospel provides, but, I think, that we sometimes lack a fuller awareness of God's gifts to us in this present time.

A Sermon Example

Let us see how this might work out in a sermon. Again, this is only a sermon sketch or fragment, but I hope it is enough to suggest a way to sensitize a congregation to the quality of its present life. This example arises from John 17:1-11, the Gospel lesson for the Seventh Sunday of Easter, A. (See chapter 6.) One might simply entitle it "What's Eternal about Life?"

∽

This Gospel lesson for today reminds me of a friendship I had some years ago. It was a somewhat unusual friendship. One of my very best friends was an atheist. Jim is one of the finest people I have ever known. Certainly he was deeply committed to improving our society. Making our society more just and fair. Our friendship was based in part on that kind of commitment. But we also shared some similar life experiences. Jim and I agreed to disagree on some matters, especially religion. He respected my views and I his. And our friendship flourished.

One of Jim's criticisms of Christianity was this: We Christians, he thought, spent too much time thinking about the future and too little time attending to the present. He thought most Christians believed what they did only for the reward they thought they would get in heaven. In the meantime, Jim argued, Christians ignore the problems of this world. He wanted a belief that would make the here and now different. Not one that promised pie in the sky by-and-by.

Jim made me ask some tough questions. One of these questions was something like this: Would I be a Christian if Christianity did not promise a life after death? Am I a Christian only because I want to live beyond the grave?

It's a tough question. What about you? Would you be a Christian even if Christianity did not believe in life beyond death? Suppose that heaven beyond death was not part of our faith. Would you still believe?

How that all comes to mind is the fact that Jesus speaks of "eternal life" in our Gospel lesson. This is Jesus' final prayer before he was arrested, tried, and executed. Here he sums up his life and ministry. In particular, he speaks of what he has accomplished. He prays, "You have given [me] authority over all people, to give eternal life to all whom you have given [me]." And then he gives us a definition of eternal life. The only such definition we have in the Gospel of John. "And this is eternal life, that they know you, the only true God, and Jesus Christ whom you have sent." Eternal life is comprised of knowing God and Christ.

Several questions arise. One is what Jesus means by "knowing." But a prior question is, what does Jesus mean by eternal life? What is eternal about life? we might ask.

The Gospel of John pictures eternal life in a rather strange way. Many of us would say that eternal life is something we are given *after* death. It is life beyond the grave—life with God in heaven. John seems to think differently. Again and again in the Gospel of John, Jesus says that those who believe in him *have eternal life*. He does not say that we have the *promise* of eternal life after death. We *have* eternal life here and now.

So, what is eternal about our lives as Christians now? Obviously, Jesus does not refer to how *long* life is. So, eternal life is not life that lasts forever without end. No, it seems that Jesus has in mind a certain *quality of life*, not a quantity. Eternal life is *how* we live, not *how long* we live. We have grown accustomed to speaking of "quality time." We say that a relationship with our children, our spouse, our friends needs quality time, not quantity time. Jesus suggests the same importance of quality.

So, we have narrowed the question. But the question still remains, what is eternal about this life we Christians live? What sort of quality does Jesus have in mind? Quality time has to do with how meaningful time is for us. We may go on a trip with a friend but never engage in significant conversation. We talk about the weather. We talk about our work. We talk about how our favorite baseball team is doing. But we never approach really meaningful topics. Topics like our loves and our hurts, our hopes and our fears, our feelings about ourselves and about others.

Eternal life for Jesus is a quality time that has meaning and purpose. Meaningful time is part of the theme of the award-winning movie, *Saving Private Ryan*. The army squad is sent behind the enemy's front lines to find and bring back Private Ryan. Some of the squad become increasingly unsure that the risk is worth it. Two of their colleagues are killed in combat with the Germans. And some ask if their mission is worthwhile. It seems meaningless—nonsensical—to risk ten lives to save one life. However, gradually their captain convinces them otherwise. What finally persuades them is his commitment to the mission—his own willingness to risk his life for the life of Private Ryan. Because of his commitment, the others give the mission meaning and purpose. Their time was made quality time by virtue of the meaning they found in it. Quality time is meaningful time.

Eternal life is meaningful time. It is living here and now with a purpose, with a love, with a mission, and with a commitment. The life Christ gives us changes this time—now and here. It is life filled with significance. It is a life that goes on beyond the grave and beyond death. But it is also a life enriched by having a goal and a job to do.

What is eternal about this life? What makes this life meaningful and rich now is our relationship with God, with Christ, and with one another. That's what Christ means by saying that eternal life is knowing him and God. Knowing, in this case, means being in an intimate relationship with another. One of the things that made the mission to save Private Ryan meaningful was the relationship among the members of that squad. As they came to

know one another and care for one another, they became committed to their mission. As we come to know God and Christ—
the divine love poured out on us—our lives become eternal!

Life is made eternal when we love one another. Our life
together as a congregation becomes eternal when we serve the
poor and needy in our neighborhood. One congregation I know
was threatened with losing the eternal quality of its life. They had
become preoccupied with themselves and their social life together. They became a group of like-minded people, enjoying each
other. Then they were confronted with the opportunity to reach
out to the Hispanic population of their community. Because they
knew God's love and care, they knew how to love and care for
others. So, they invited a Hispanic pastor to provide services
of worship in Spanish. They invited the Hispanic congregation
into their social life together. And their life as a congregation
became eternal. That is what is eternal about our lives together.
Knowing God and Christ. Loving one another and others beyond
our congregation! . . .

~

Conclusion

Preaching John is full of possibilities in part because of the richness of
Johannine theology. Of course, preaching the theology of the Gospel of
John does not mean overpowering your congregation with doctrinal language. It does mean, however, identifying connections between Johannine
thought and the life of your congregation. It means stretching our own
views and those of our parishioners with the expansive thought of one of
the most provocative theological writers in the New Testament.

Theological preaching becomes effective, I believe, only when we can
show our listeners the relevance of a theological theme for their lives. We
do this most often by identifying common daily experiences (say a friendship) that both express a particular theological theme (such as grace) and
take on new meaning when viewed from a theological perspective (grace
embodied in daily friendships). Helping a congregation find the eternal
quality of their life together, for instance, makes the theological idea of
eternal life a lived experience and not simply an abstract idea. So to preach
Johannine theology necessitates that we ourselves explore the connection
between it and our own life experiences.[13]

Preaching the theology of John means work for us on two fronts. First,
we need to know Johannine thought as thoroughly as possible. We will

have to read and reread John many times, looking for hints of theological themes, and we will need to read what others have said about the theology of John. The brief discussion in this chapter is far from adequate. Second, if we are to preach Johannine theology effectively in our congregation, we will have to know that congregation. We can hardly relate theological themes to the life experiences of the congregation if we don't know the people. It has become common to speak of preachers doing two kinds of exegesis in preparation for preaching. On the one hand, we exegete the biblical text with all the care we can. On the other hand, and with equal care, we exegete our congregation.[14] Know what they are saying, what they believe, how they live, and what their hopes and fears and joys are. Above all, we need to care for our congregation, insofar as possible, as God cares for us.

The theology of John is closely related, as we have seen, to the language of this Gospel. The fourth evangelist tends to express broad ideas in a few carefully chosen words. Indeed, the theology of the Gospel leads us to ask about its language. How does the evangelist express the Word in words?

3

The Word and Words:
Johannine Language

THE PECULIAR CHARACTER OF JOHANNINE LANGUAGE puzzles interpreters
and teases preachers. It is often strange language, long stories (see, for
example, chaps. 4, 9, and 11), and equally long discourses (chaps. 14, 15,
and 16). Peculiar expressions are often repeated almost incessantly ("abide
in" or "dwell in," for example). Part of the difficulty in the discourses in
particular is the style, which we will examine in the next chapter. The language of John, in and of itself without regard to the general style, is dense
and often perplexing. Invite a lay study group, for instance, to read chapter
17 and offer their understandings of these words. With only a small portion of honesty, we have to admit that the fourth Gospel's language is a
serious impediment to understanding.

We have already noted several of the characteristics of Johannine language: The polemic quality of much of the Gospel's language, the evangelist's fondness for words and expressions that have several different
meanings, and the social character and effect of the language. The goal of
this chapter is, first, to examine what might be proposed as a kind of theology of language implicit in the text of the fourth Gospel. Second, the discussion will focus more intently on the symbolic or metaphorical
character of Johannine language.

John's Language and Preaching

The puzzling character of the language of this Gospel leads us to ask what
understanding of language in general lies embedded in the text. I do not
pretend to be able to unearth the author's understanding of language. To
do so, we would have to enter the author's mind and discern her or his
intentions, which is a historical enterprise fraught with significant dangers.
Instead, I would like to focus attention on what the language of the text

seems to imply about the function and nature of language in general. This discussion arises from a hunch that the text of the Gospel implies a peculiarly profound conception of expression and one that is particularly relevant to preachers.

A Johannine Understanding of Language

The thesis of this chapter is that there is an implicit view of words rooted in what the Gospel's prologue says about "the Word." We begin then by probing that fascinating attribution of word or *logos* to God, which confronts readers at the very onset of the document. The very first verse suggests that Word and words will figure prominently in the narrative that is to follow and that readers are well-advised to reflect on *word* before entering the story of Jesus. For centuries interpreters have been fascinated with the question of the historical, philosophical, and religious context out of which the author drew the term *logos,* and it has been argued that, in order to understand what the text is saying at this point, we must understand the milieu for the *logos* concept.

There is little agreement as to what that specific milieu was. In order to summarize the theories proposed for the conceptual context of *logos,* we will speak only of the three most popular proposals. The first is that the Hebraic concept of *dābār* (and other words, such as *ʾēmer*) provides an adequate and correct understanding of the intellectual context for *logos,* especially since the phrase "in the beginning" with which the prologue begins evokes Genesis 1:1. The second theory takes the Hebraic concept further and proposes that speculation about Wisdom (Greek—*sophia,* Hebrew—*ḥokmā*) provides a more precise context, especially since so much (and some say everything) of what is said about the *logos* has parallels in what is said about Wisdom.[1] For example, like the Word, Wisdom was thought to be an agent for creation in Wisdom of Solomon 9:9. Jewish speculation on Torah and the use of *Memra* provide other options. *Memra* was not only the Aramaic translation of *dābār* but sometimes serves as a circumlocution for God's name.

A Hellenistic background is equally possible, however. In Heraclitus *logos* is the governing eternal and rational principle of the universe, and the Stoics spoke of *logos* as the mind of God. Philo of Alexandria (ca. 20 B.C.E.–50 C.E.) combines Jewish and Greek thought on many topics including *logos.* For him *logos* was God's thought that created order, form, and rationality in the world.

I think we do not need an answer to the thorny question of the source of the Johannine concept of *logos,* since the history of interpretation has demonstrated that it cannot be definitively solved. If one must speak of a context out of which the poem's author drew the *logos* concept, it would be safer to postulate an eclectic milieu, influenced by Hebraic, Jewish, and Hellenistic thought (not unlike the eclecticism of Philo).

Whatever background best illumines the prologue, the first verse states several intriguing things about *logos*. To begin with, "the Word" *(ho logos)* was "in the beginning" *(en archē)*. The *logos* has existed even since the origin of reality. Second comes that confusing claim "the Word was with God and the Word was God" *(ho logos ēn pros ton theon kai theos ēn ho logos)*. The Word is clearly to be understood as either God's own self or as God's divine companion. The preposition "with" *(pros)* suggests a relationship between two entities, while the second "was" *(ēn)* implies identity—*logos* and *theos* are the same. Some have proposed that the absence of the definite article ("the"—*ho*) before the second use of the word God *(theos)* necessitates translating it "was divine." Regardless of the value of that suggestion, the expression *theos ēn ho logos* ("the Word was God") furthers the intrigue of the verse. The following verse goes on to describe the role of the Word in creation itself, still further mystifying the beginning of the hymn. D. Moody Smith summarizes the point of the prologue this way: "the Word's participation in God as the extension of God's creativity and revelation into the universe."[2]

Theologically, the best we can do is find a metaphor that might capture something of what these verses mean. One such metaphor is that of human self-expression. To apply it to what is said about *logos,* we might conclude that the relationship between God and the Word is like the relationship between a person and her or his self-expression. Self-expression occurs when speakers desire to give voice to their own unique selves. For instance, when someone says, "I am depressed today," those words are likely a genuine self-expression. Word is then something like God's self-expression, in which case the expression of self reveals the self—brings it into public view. The christological meaning of John 1:1 is widely discussed and common knowledge. Christ was God's expression of the divine self, and through Christ one sees the true nature of God, as 1:18 says so very provocatively. *Logos* is God's act of giving the divine self-articulation in the form of Word, which in this case and in the light of 1:14 means person.

What does it say about language to attribute word to God and to equate God's word with God's own self? At the very least, it suggests that word—language—is basic reality. Word existed from the beginning; word is identical with the Ultimate Reality. If this is the case, language is given a fundamental role in all existence, not least of all human existence. Humans are noted for their use and development of language, whether or not other creatures communicate through sound in some comparable way. To take the argument one step further, language provides humans access to reality—to the truth—since language is akin to the very basic reality, namely, God. By language, however, I mean more than human speech. Self-expression is accomplished in many ways. Indeed, the more we learn about animals, the more obvious it becomes that they express self and communicate with others. Hence, I intend "language" to mean the broad phenomenon of self-expression.

If something like this emerges from the implications of John 1:1, what does it have to do with the story of Jesus? As we have already said, first of all, it means that Jesus' own self is word; that is, it is linguistic insofar as that basic reality comes to expression in his words and his life. The declaration that "the word became flesh" *(ho logos sarx egeneto)* claims that God's self-expression took the form of a human being. Divine Word is not mere abstraction, nor is it sound or marks on a paper. It is, in this case, the whole of a person, Jesus of Nazareth. Consequently, God not only expresses the divine self in Word but gives that Word bodily physical form in this world. This leads us then to ask the question, What is the relationship between Christ, the Word, and the words of Christ?

Often scholars have noted that the concept of *logos* as a christological category is not found in the rest of the fourth Gospel. However, the word *logos* itself appears thirty-six times in the Gospel, and its synonym, *hrēma*, another twelve times (for example, 3:34). Moreover, these two words are often used in very important statements. For instance, to believe Jesus' words is the equivalent of believing in Jesus himself (see 2:22; 4:50), and his words evoke faith (4:41) and "cleanse" (15:3). Keeping or "continuing in" Jesus' word is the chief characteristic of the believer (5:38; 8:31; 14:23; 15:7; 17:6). Perhaps more important is the power or significance Jesus or others assign to his words. They are "spirit and life" (6:63) and the source of "eternal life" (6:68). Those who "keep" Jesus' words "will never see death" (8:51), and his words are none other than God's words (14:24 and 17:8).

Let's put together what we have found in John 1:1 about *logos* with its use (along with that of *hrēma*) in the rest of the Gospel. The fundamental role of the word in relationship with God is enacted in Jesus' words, so that through his words one has access to the Word, which is access to God. *The Word is incarnated in words.* The revelation of God in Christ is a linguistic revelation insofar as Christ is God's own Word and Christ's words are part of the revelation of the Word. It is clear in this case, however, that the category of "word" is expanded to include act and even person. The Word that is Jesus comes to public view in what he does and who he is as well as in what he says.

Recent theories of "Speech-Act" or "Performance Speech" stress that speaking is itself an act with some desired purpose or goal. Such a view of the relationship between speech and action captures a dimension of the Hebraic concept of word. In Hebrew scripture, the utterance of speech was thought to be an act that brought into being something that did not formerly exist. Hence, the utterance of the words (such as a blessing or curse) caused what is said to be. In the first story of creation, in order to bring into being something that does not exist, God simply speaks (Genesis 1:1—2:4a). God continues to be related to the divine word when it is spoken, so that what is uttered is brought to reality by God's doing.[3]

What then does all this tell us about the language of the Gospel of John? I suggest that, within the Gospel's text, language is assumed to be the medium of revelation. The language of the Gospel re-presents the words of the one who is the Word. The Gospel's words are God's self-expression. It is not the words alone attributed to Jesus that are revelatory but the whole of the Gospel itself. So, the Gospel of John's first conclusion in 20:30-31 includes these words (see also 21:24-25): "these [signs] are written so that you may come to believe that Jesus is the Messiah, the Son of God, and that through believing you may have life in his name." The words of the Gospel are the revelation that evokes faith and bestows life.[4] In other words, the Gospel text asserts that its own language is the means by which God is revealed to readers. Language is not simply one medium among many; it is not just one way of understanding who God is. Rather, language is the chief medium of revelation by virtue of the fact that Christ is the Word of God.

Implications for Preaching

What possible difference could all this make for preachers? It may seem that this rather lengthy and heavy argument is unnecessary; however, if the argument is sound, several things follow logically for preaching John and for preaching in general.

First and obviously, if language is so important in the Gospel, our interpretative process of preparation to preach begins with this principle: *Attention to the specific language of a text is necessary in order to grasp a passage's meaning.* We cannot, for instance, say that this or that collection of words in a Johannine passage is one way by which some abstract content might be expressed. The fact is the selection of words and their order are deliberate and essential to discern meaning and in this case revelation. The relationship between the Word and the words is such that every word— regardless of how small (see the preposition "with"—*pros*—in John 1:1)— is crucial. This attention to linguistic specificity presupposes a view of language that the text of the fourth Gospel advocates and assumes. Specific language is the medium of revelation.

One temptation we preachers face is to skim a biblical text, grab a topic of some sort out of the text, and then run with it—develop a sermon on that *topic*. I have done that very thing when I was in a hurry to get a sermon ready. Such a topic selection method is hardly true biblical preaching. As a matter of fact, one could argue that it is simply topical preaching that seeks a text that provides an excuse for discussing the topic. The alternative, of course, is to take the specific language (among other things) of the text seriously and to probe the details of the language for what they might tell us about the possible meaning.

For instance, the famous "realized" or "present" eschatology of the Gospel is often found in the details of passages. In 5:24, Jesus is credited with saying, "anyone who hears my word and believes him who sent me has eternal life, and does not come under judgment, but has passed from death to life." The startling thing about this statement is the use of the verb "has" *(echō)*. It is not that believers "*will* have" (future verb) but already "has" (present form of the verb). The same is true of verse 25 of the same chapter, where Jesus says, "the hour *(hōra)* . . . is now here *(nyn estin)* . . . when the dead will hear the voice of the Son of God, and those who hear will live." The time of resurrection is present—"the hour is *now here*." It is no longer a distant future hope but a here-and-now reality. Meaning may be tucked away in the details of language, which is naturally the case if language is as important to the writer as we have proposed.

Second, this proposed view of the relationship between the Word and the words suggests something about the preaching task in general. If the Gospel supposes that words give one access to the Word, which is God's self-revelation, then the words of the sermon take on new and inestimable importance. The language of the sermon—and not just its cognitive content—can be revelatory. To say it even more radically, in the sermon the Word once again becomes incarnated in a human and in human speech in particular.

Such a view of preaching has precedent not only in the fourth Gospel's high view of language but also in the Hebraic concept of classical prophetic speech. The "word of the Lord" comes to a prophet, and then the prophet speaks that word in words and does so in the first person, speaking for God. For instance, the title of the Book of Micah reads, "The word of the LORD that came to Micah of Moresheth . . ." (Micah 1:1). Then the prophet Micah declares, "Thus says the LORD . . ." (e.g., 3:5) and proceeds to speak God's words: "O my people, what have I done to you? In what have I wearied you? . . . For I brought you up from the land of Egypt . . ." (6:3-4). The fourth Gospel seems to employ just such a prophetic understanding of the word of the Lord and its translation into human words.

Within this understanding of language and of the Word of God resides the basis for a theology of preaching. For now, all we can do is sketch some of the implications of John's understanding of language for preaching. If language is revelatory, as both the Gospel's prologue and its first conclusion (20:30-31) seem to say, that means the language of the sermon, too, can be—or should be—revelatory. The text becomes incarnated in new words for a new day and brings God's Word into the present. This is, of course, a ridiculously high understanding of preaching—that God's self-revelation is incarnated again in the sermon—but it is one that merits consideration, even if it unbearably increases the weight of responsibility on preachers.

If this understanding of preaching has any truth in it, it means several things for our preaching. Obviously, it means that we take our preaching seriously. This sounds like a truism, and I hope in one sense that it is. Many pastors, however, grow weary from the task of preaching, and many are discouraged about the importance of preaching. If you preach year after year for a congregation and see very little, if any, results from your preaching, it is natural that discouragement sets in. A reminder of the potential of preaching—that it can be the incarnation of God's self-revelation—provides incentive to continue our preaching ministries with new commitment.

The second implication of the Gospel's view of language is more mundane and less lofty. If language is this important in the Gospel of John, then we ought to be very careful in the selection of words and phrases for the sermon. The role of language in God's revelation calls into question the old idea that it doesn't matter *how* you say it as long as it *gets said* (whatever "it" means). The way it is said (or written) seems vitally important in the Gospel of John, and so it should be in our sermons. Given that fact, we are called to scrutinize each and every word, phrase, and sentence of our sermon.

There is, however, a contemporary trend among pastors that works against exercising such a care in the language we use. Many of us are attracted to the practice of coming out of the pulpit for the sermon. We want to be close and intimate with our congregation and less formal and distant. So, as we preach, we move about the chancel or the area immediately in front of the chancel. This is all well and good, although I fear that the popularity of the practice is due to the influence of television preachers who are in many cases not good models for preaching. It is also due to the nature of television itself. When speakers appear on television (such as a news anchor), they seem to be looking right at us and are as close as the tv scene. That immediacy of the speaker leads us to want to be closer to our congregation, and some of them expect that immediacy of us.

The danger in preaching outside the pulpit with only notes, if anything, is that the language of the sermon may become careless. We are liable to use whatever language occurs to us while preaching the sermon. We do not want to break eye contact with our listeners long enough to read our notes—as skimpy as they may be. Yet this is not necessarily so, for we can work diligently enough on the sermon's language that we can duplicate it in the sermon event even outside the pulpit. Notice, the key phrase here is "diligently enough." I suggest that if we take the sermon's language seriously enough and if we are willing to devote enough time to be able to carry our language with us out of the pulpit, powerful use of words and phrases can be used while preaching without notes or with few notes outside the pulpit. In the end, like anything that is worth doing, this requires a great deal of preparation.

A Sermon Example

Since this section does not lend itself directly to an example, I want to propose that we can help our congregations understand this view of language through carefully constructed stories and analogies. What follows is but a fragment of a sermon on John 2:13-22 (the "cleansing of the Temple"), which is the assigned Gospel for the Third Sunday of Lent, Year B. The sermon moves toward the conclusion of the story in verse 22, where the narrator tells us, "After he was raised from the dead, his disciples remembered that he had said this; and they believed the scripture and *the word that Jesus had spoken*" (italics added). This is a way in which we might preach the importance of believing Jesus' words. Admittedly this is perhaps a topic sermon but one that in this case may be justified in some situations.

~

Words, of course, can be very important. They are important for communication. We want to say exactly what we mean. And we want those who hear us to understand correctly what we want to say.

On one occasion, I prepared a pastoral report for the church council. In the course of the report I included an item about the use of the church's nave. But instead of writing nave, I accidentally wrote *navel*. Needless to say, the council got a good laugh out of my error. But it was an error of *only one letter*. Words are very important for communication.

Words are important for another reason. Sometimes words come out of our inner selves. They say who we are, what we are like, how we think, and how we feel. In those cases, words are important in communicating ourselves to others. So, those words are very personal. They are like little bits of ourselves offered to other people.

Two adult men were on a fishing trip in Canada. We'll call them Jim and George. They were sleeping each night in a tiny little cabin—little more than a shed with some beds and a stove. One night, after a successful day of fishing, a storm arose. Gradually the lightning and thunder grew in intensity. Finally the lightning seemed for an instance to illumine the whole inside of the cabin. And then quickly the darkness returned. The thunder rattled the old, fragile windows until they seemed about to fall apart. Then the rain came. Pounding down on the building like stones.

At first the men joked about the storm. "With that lightning, who needs electricity?" Then Jim grew strangely quiet. George continued to offer light-hearted remarks, but there was no response from Jim. Finally, with the storm still raging, George asked simply, "Jim, are you okay?" Silence. George became concerned. "Jim, are you okay?"

Finally, Jim spoke in a soft, thin voice very different from his normal one. "George, I . . . uh . . . I guess I may as well tell you." "Tell me what?" George asked. "Well, I'm . . . scared. There's no other way to put it—scared." George was at first at a loss for words. This was not the kind of thing the two of them talked about on their fishing trips. But now, gradually, they began to talk about fear, about their pasts, and about experiences of fright. Soon, Jim told of his experience as a child in a storm, something like this one. Lightning had hit their home and started a fire. A fire that nearly took the lives of his parents and siblings.

Jim communicated something about himself in that simple admission of fear. His words in this case were a revelation. He revealed something about himself George had never known. A strong, athletic, confident man shared his fear of the storm. As a result, George came to know and—actually—appreciate Jim all the more.

Words reveal something about the speaker. So, believing Jesus' words is believing in Jesus himself. Jesus reveals who he is in words, and those words become the basis of belief. George came to know Jim better as a result of Jim's confession of fear. We come to know Jesus better as a result of his words.

Knowing Jesus through knowing his words, however, is still more important. Jesus is the incarnation of God's Word. He is

God's expression of God's self in human form. So, Jesus' words reveal himself to us. But they also reveal God to us.

"They believed . . . the word that Jesus had spoken." When we believe the word that Jesus has spoken, we believe in the God who sent Jesus. Believing the word—trusting the word—holding the word as the center of our lives. That's what our faith is all about.

~

The understanding of language we find packed into and between the lines of the Gospel of John challenges us preachers with regard to our study of the text for preaching as well as to our understanding of the task of preaching itself. However, our investigation proceeds further by asking how the language of the Gospel of John stretches the limits of words.

The Metaphorical/Symbolic Language of John

In the discussion of the language of the fourth Gospel, special attention is often given to the metaphorical (or symbolic) character of this language and especially to the use of ambiguous words, such as those we have discussed in the previous chapter (for example, "spirit" or "wind"—*pneuma*—and "born again" or "from above"—*anōthen*). Other words and phrases are often thought to have symbolic meaning, for example "water" (4:1-42). This discussion sometimes treats John's language as if it were some sort of code, and, if one could just find the key to the code, one could then understand the Gospel's symbolism. As a result of the newer literary approach, however, we can find discussions of and proposals for how such language works in the reader's consciousness.

The Interpretation of Johannine Symbolism

To say that a word or phrase is symbolic is to say that it has another referent, either instead of or in addition to its obvious one. So, if we say that the word "water" is a symbol, we mean that instead of or in addition to referring to the substance we usually call water, the word points us to something else. The philosophical and linguistic discussion of symbolism is extensive and complicated, particularly in terms of the distinction between symbolism and other literary forms such as metaphor.[5] For our purposes, we need not concern ourselves with that discussion. In his book on symbolism in John, Craig R. Koester writes,

A symbol, in the most general sense, is something that stands for something else. Here, however, we will focus the definition more narrowly: A
symbol is an image, an action, or a person that is understood to have
transcendent significance. In Johannine terms, symbols span the chasm
between what is "from above" and what is "from below" without collaps-
ing the distinction.[6]

Obviously the language of the Gospel of John frequently invites symbolic
interpretation, sometimes subtly and sometimes conspicuously. There is
no question that symbolic language plays an important role in the fourth
Gospel. Several questions, however, emerge as debatable and significant for
our discussion.

First, how do we discern when a word or phrase is to be interpreted as
having "transcendent significance" or pointing us to something else and
when it does not? Some readings of the Gospel of John play heavily on the
possible symbolic meanings of passages. For instance, some have argued
that the episode of the wedding at Cana is properly interpreted as symbolic
and directs us to other realities. Thomas L. Brodie speaks of the story as "an
idealized summary of God's gift to the world and of life in the church," so
that baptism, Eucharist, and marriage should "be understood against the
background of union with the divine."[7] Others claim it to be the institution
of marriage as a sacrament or as having to do with the Eucharistic wine.[8]

When shall we take a word, phrase, or action as symbolic, that is, as referring to something more (and greater) than its obvious referent? Because
the fourth evangelist makes ample use of symbolic meaning, we are
inclined to look for it everywhere. Still another example of the quandary of
identifying symbolic language is the "blood and water" that flows from
Jesus' side after the spear thrust (19:34). The obvious meaning is that
Jesus is indeed dead. Yet should we take these two fluids as representative
of other realities? Do they refer to the Eucharist and baptism? Does water
here mean the Spirit, as it sometimes does elsewhere in John (see, for example, 7:37-39)?[9]

The danger is that we will make up symbolic meaning in a text when it
is not necessary to do so, or when it simply is not indicated in the text
(although that is difficult to discern). The best protection against violating
the text by reading in symbolic references is simply to check it out elsewhere in the Gospel. Is water used symbolically elsewhere? To what does it
refer there? How about "blood?" Is there any evidence elsewhere that the
evangelist assigns it a symbolic significance? To try to be consistent with
the evangelist's style as a whole may prevent our misuse of the text.

Now this is no foolproof method of discerning symbolism. What, for
instance, of the single occurrence of a particular symbol? We cannot find
evidence of its being used symbolically elsewhere, but might it be the case

that this one occurrence is the single time a certain word or phrase is used to point us beyond the literal meaning of the word? A case in point is surely the language of 6:51-58. While there is no other instance in which eating Jesus' flesh and drinking his blood are meant symbolically, surely we are not to take these words in their purely literal sense.

Still, symbolic meanings should be consistent with the general theological thrust of the Gospel, if not its actual use of language. So, the question becomes, does the thought of the Gospel justify reading "blood and water" in 19:34 as symbolic? Does the theological perspective of the whole Gospel allow for a symbolic reading of the wedding at Cana? In a sense, the whole of the Gospel invites us to think how it has "transcendent significance." So, in effect, the distinction between the symbolic and the nonsymbolic language is a matter of definition of symbolism more than anything else, and the distinction seems to fade.

The other question about Johannine symbols we need to face is this: How should we handle symbolic language? I have already suggested that one common method of interpreting language that seems to point us beyond an immediate and obvious reference is to understand symbolism as code. In code, one sign is used as a substitute for another. If you know the code, you know that the sender of the message does not mean the first sign—the apparent meaning—but another one. "The eagle has landed" does not really mean an eagle (bird) has come to rest some place; it is code for the arrival of troops at their destination. Hence, we may decide that "water" in the fourth Gospel always stands for the Spirit (as it seems to in 7:37-39), and we then substitute "Spirit" wherever the word "water" appears. The treatment of Johannine symbolic language as a code to be deciphered dangerously limits the meaning of the language, however. It creates a kind of wooden system of interpreting language. For instance, when Jesus asks the Samaritan woman for a drink of water, it misses the point to interpret water to mean something other than the substance we commonly call water. There is something more going on in John's use of symbolism than coding.

The fact is that Johannine symbolism seems consistently ambiguous, so that it is difficult to pin down exactly what reference beyond the obvious is to be gleaned. My proposal is that, if preachers treat the language of John as frequently *metaphorical,* we can better deal with its so-called symbolic meaning. A metaphor occurs when we use usual words in unusual ways, when we stretch the dictionary meaning of a word beyond its limits so that it says something else.[10] I might say, "She is a gem." Clearly this statement is not to be taken literally, otherwise we have to imagine a woman who appears to be a sort of rock! Rather, the language uses the value of a gem to mean something entirely different.

Metaphors surprise us. They connect two realities that we usually do not connect, and hence they violate dictionary meanings of both. Fresh and new metaphors shock us by asking us to think in entirely new ways. When a metaphor becomes common, it loses its real metaphorical meaning. For instance, speaking of the "head of the bed" doesn't even seem to be metaphorical, even though it is. Perhaps it shocked people the first time someone designated the portions of the bed where people should place their heads and their feet should be the "head" and "foot" of a bed. Now, however, the metaphor has become defused of its unexpected association of two or more realities. Sometimes religious metaphors, too, become so common-place that they lose their shock. That is surely the case with Jesus' words, "I am the good shepherd" (John 10:11). Originally, this association was probably shocking, since shepherds had a bad reputation in first-century Palestine. Shepherds were migrant people who were noted for stealing from villages and then silently moving their flocks away by night to some unknown location. For John to suggest that Jesus is a shepherd surprised his listeners.[11] The difference between metaphor and simile is only that the latter cues listeners that a comparison is coming by using words such as "like" or "as." Otherwise, similes can function the same as metaphors.

Metaphors surprise us and therefore always puzzle us and make us think. Just what does it mean when Shakespeare has Macbeth say, "Life's but a walking shadow . . ." (*Macbeth,* act 5, scene 5)? If the association A=B is strange and unexpected, we cannot easily determine what is meant by the association. So, metaphors keep puzzling us and evoking new possibilities of meaning. One way of putting this is to say that the meaning of a metaphor is always "open," and one cannot simply "close" its meaning by saying with certainty, "this is what it means." Paul Ricoeur writes, "*true metaphors are untranslatable . . .* [This] does not mean that they cannot be paraphrased, but the paraphrase is infinite and does not exhaust the inno-vation in meaning."[12] This feature of metaphor makes some of us uncom-fortable. We want to nail down the meaning of words and phrases and are frustrated when the text does not allow us to do so.

What does all this mean for the interpretation of Johannine symbolic meaning? What happens when we treat John's symbolic language as metaphor? The unique contribution a metaphorical reading of symbols makes is that it prevents our pinning down the meaning of the words and insists that we continue to struggle with their meaning. Symbols are then not simply translated into that to which they point us. Rather, symbols go to work on our imaginations to produce first this meaning, then that meaning.

Take, for example, Jesus' controversial words in 6:56: "Those who eat my flesh and drink my blood abide in me, and I in them." First, looking at this statement as a metaphor allows us to admit the shock it causes. This sort of interpretation understands that surprise, disequilibrium, and confusion are exactly what the language should provoke in us. In other words, it allows us to savor the shock of the words. Furthermore, rather than capturing the meaning of this verse in another sentence or phrase, the words refuse to be shut up in a linguistic cage. We then permit them to work in our imaginations, stirring different meanings and forever bringing new possibilities to the surface. Moreover, if we take Johannine symbolism to be metaphorical, we open our minds to the suggestions of others as to the meaning of the text. There is finally no one true meaning, only a multitude of possibilities. We are to ingest Jesus as we ingest food. We fill our hunger through him and his revelation. We take in the benefits of Christ's death and resurrection in the bread and the wine of the Eucharist.

If the symbolic language of John's Gospel works in a metaphorical way, it means (1) we accept surprise and ambiguity as a natural feature of the Gospel; (2) we never assume that we have nailed down its meaning; (3) we let the language continue to evoke new meaning in our imaginations; and (4) we attend closely to the context in which the language appears. Metaphors are always contextual. They "fit" in a relationship with other language, just as John 6:56 fits so tightly into the whole of the bread of life discourse, 6:27-58 (see chapter 6).

Preaching Johannine Symbolism

How does one go about preaching John's symbolic language? The possibilities are almost infinite (even as the meaning of metaphorical symbol is infinite); however, here are some concrete suggestions for taking advantage of this kind of language for homiletical purposes.

First, our sermons on Johannine symbols we find in the fourth Gospel may try to stir our listeners' thinking rather than give them answers. If the metaphorical quality of Johannine symbolic language tickles the imagination and resists being translated exactly into other expressions, then our sermons ought to function in a similar way. Of course, congregations today are eager to hear answers and are already up to their ears in questions, and hence they do not always welcome a "make-your-congregation-think sermon." Still, we cannot in all honesty claim to know exactly what some of the symbolic language means, and we dare not take on faith the claims of some commentators to know what it means. If the evangelist sought to provoke thought through symbolic language for the sake of the maturation of Christian faith, and if the church at one time seemed to think such a provocative document as this should be included in our canon, then we preachers are in no position to defuse the Gospel's language of its ambiguity.

What exactly does this mean? A sermon on one of the concluding portions of the bread of life discourse (that is, John 6:51-58, the assigned Gospel lesson for Proper 15, B) might explore some of the possible meanings of eating Christ's flesh and drinking his blood, without ever claiming that one or another of these meanings is true and the others false. A sermon on John 10:1-10 (Easter 4, A) might hold up the fascinating "good shepherd" metaphors and turn them around, viewing first one side, then another. It might ask the congregation to take this multitude of interpretations home and reflect on them for the week. A sermon on John 14:6 (part of the lesson for Easter 5, A), for example, might attempt to explore some of the possible meanings of Jesus' identity as "the way, and the truth, and the life," without ever advocating one as more valuable than the others.

While this kind of provocative preaching is, as I have suggested, not always as palatable for a congregation as the more authoritarian assertion of answers to life's deepest questions, it fits what I have come to think may be the best sort of preaching in the twenty-first century. Among others, Lucy Rose sketched a kind of preaching in which the sermon was sharing one interpretation of a text with a congregation simply as a way of furthering the community's discussion.[13] One of the results of her book is that we begin to rethink the authority of the preacher and to value a more dialogical or conversational posture in preaching. My proposal is that preaching the metaphorical symbols of the fourth Gospel in the way I have described contributes to this vision of the future of preaching (see also the conclusion).

Second, we do justice to John's symbolic and metaphorical language by adapting it to our day. If the language of the Gospel works, it most often spawns new metaphors, symbols, and word-pictures. One of the results of metaphorical language is that it pulls other metaphors out of us while we are trying to explore the original one. That is why when we try to understand many good metaphors, we end up using another metaphor to explain the first. Just think of all the metaphors that have been conceived as a result of the image of Christians as "children of God": the family of God, brothers and sisters in Christ, Christ our brother, God as Father or Parent, and so on. It is natural that one rich metaphor provokes another and another. The metaphorical language of the fourth Gospel will excite our imaginations to create other and contemporary metaphors or images. For example, the metaphor of 8:12, "I am the light of the world," invites us to think about how light functions in our world today. (This passage is not included in the RCL but see Lent 4, A.) Like the lights along the landing strip, Christ leads us safely to our destination. Like a night-light glowing softly in a child's bedroom all night long assures the child that darkness is not all there is, so too does God's gift to us in Christ. Like street lights guard us against attackers, Christ's light guards our relationship with God.

The process of birthing new metaphors to say something of what the original suggests is what might be called "relanguaging John for contemporary listeners."[14] "Relanguaging" the sense of a text is part of the process of appropriating it for our own lives. For instance, we might ask a confirmation class to state the first article of the Apostles' Creed in their own words. We are inviting them to relanguage the creed in their own language and in the process take ownership of it.

In the process of interpreting the fourth Gospel for preaching, we allow its language to excite our imaginations, and we "play" with the language to see what happens. How can we express the Johannine word "glorify" in language that allows our congregation to claim the prayer of Jesus in chapter 17 as their own? (See the Gospel lesson for Easter 7, A, John 17:1-11.) As soon as we begin considering this question, we probably find ourselves thinking of contemporary metaphors for God's glorification of Christ. I think of awarding the Noble Prize for Peace, and—probably more interesting—publicizing an otherwise unknown person for her or his rescue of a child from a burning building. Remember, no contemporary metaphor exhausts the meaning of the biblical image. It only points in one possible direction the language might take us.

In chapter 2 we considered the ambiguity of *pneuma* ("spirit") in John 3. Verse 8 is really a condensed little metaphor using wind to enlighten the meaning of spirit. The spirit and the wind are equated, which provokes our consideration of similarities between the wind and spirit. As is the case with the spirit, you can see the evidence of the wind's presence but not the wind itself. The freedom of the wind, its strength, its changing directions all help us articulate the church's experience of the Holy Spirit. All this might inspire preachers to weave their own analogies using wind and spirit. Imagine a child flying a kite and learning the power and mystery of the wind. The language's metaphorical quality invites us to create metaphors for our day out of John's metaphors.

Playing with biblical language is a bold practice. Who are we to try to "improve" on John? Indeed, the creation of contemporary metaphors that work today like John's images might have worked in another day is risky business. We need confidence to undertake the practice for the sake of communicating the gospel message. We need to remember that our metaphors for today can be weak, inadequate, and even corny, but that's okay. There is no single collection of words that absolutely captures the fullest sense of the Johannine language, so we are not trying to equal the power of the text. What we try to do is simply help make the provocativeness of the Johannine symbol accessible for Christians in this day.

Finally, my suggestion for preaching the metaphorical symbols of John's Gospel is that we craft sermons around a single word. While all these words may not be symbolic or metaphorical, many of them are rich with meaning. Like metaphors, it is impossible to capture the entirety of the word's meaning in our own language. So, we can explore the various possibilities of a single word and their relevance for today. Such sermons are in one way simpler than those on one of the more elaborate symbols because they focus on a single word. On the other hand, like treatments of the more elaborate metaphors, they can and should explore a variety of possible meanings for a word.

For example, the evangelist is fond of the word "abide" (the verb *menō*), which is rich with possibilities for preaching.[15] Through the centuries of interpretation, this word has contributed to the argument that the Gospel encourages a Christian mysticism. In this case, the mutual indwelling of the believer in Christ or God, as well as God or Christ in the believer, is taken to mean the personal distinctions among the parties in the indwelling are blurred, and the two or three become one. That is not the way I interpret the Gospel of John in general and the word "abide" in particular; however, it is an understanding of John that has a considerable history.

For me, the word "abide" in John suggests relationship. The Father abides in the Son (14:10), and the believers abide in the Son (15:4). Relationship is the key to knowing God, and how we are related matters in terms of what we know. Relationships constitute the heart of our faith, and in them we discover the deeper dimensions of life, particularly life together. The relationship spoken of with this verb, abide, is an intimate association, what the Gospel itself characterizes as a "friendship" (see also 15:15). The complex of relationships among the Father, the Son, and believers suggests a community in which love and care are paramount.

The powerful concept of abiding can be translated into contemporary understandings of personal relationships. Relatedness is important in our lives and even defines who we are. So, God's effort to bring us into relationship with our Creator can be viewed as comparable to the way in which a new relationship transforms our lives. A marriage, a friendship, a parent-child relationship—all of these are ways in which relatedness forms our personalities.

Another example is the word "world" *(kosmos)*. In this case, the metaphorical dimension of the word is perhaps weaker than what we find in "abide." Still, there is a sense in which the word is sometimes used in a way that suggests symbolic meaning. The fourth evangelist often uses it in a negative sense to speak of the realm of evil and unbelief. The world hates Christ and the believers (15:18). So, the Gospel sometimes employs *kosmos* as part of its conception of a universal polarity (or dualism). In these cases, world represents the negative pole of which the positive is implicitly the divine realm.[16]

On the other hand, God "so loved *the world*" that God sends the Son (3:16) for the redemption of the world (italics added). Moreover, believers are sent into the world, as God sent Christ into the world (17:18; 20:21). By examining this single word in its various contexts in the fourth Gospel, we discover the essential ingredients of a theology of mission. The Christian community lives within the context of evil and broken relationship with God and hence is distinct from the world. Yet the church is in mission to the world. Driven by God's love for the creation, we are invited to engage the world with the gospel message.[17]

A Sermon Example

The following bit of a sermon explores John 14:1-14, the assigned lesson for the Fifth Sunday of Easter, A (see also chapter 6). This passage is also popular for funerals, although I prepared it for the congregation during the Easter season. The sermon attempts to explore the meaning of "rooms" in Jesus' statements. I offer it as an example of a sermon focused on a single word and more precisely on one of the frequent words in the Gospel of John. This sermon is also an example of how preachers can introduce their congregations to the original language of the text without blowing them away with paternalistic superiority. My experience is that laity are always intrigued by explanations of the original language when they are clear, simple, and to the point.

~

These are familiar words. The Gospel lesson for today is a passage we often hear read at funerals. In that setting, the passage offers comfort and assurance that a deceased loved one is safe with God. In another sense, these words of Jesus are puzzling.

Listen again to the first three verses:

Do not let your hearts be troubled. Believe in God, believe also in me. In my Father's house there are many dwelling places. If it were not so, would I have told you that I go to prepare a place for you? And if I go and prepare a place for you, I will come again and will take you to myself, so that where I am, there you may be also.

What a strange promise this is! We most often think that Jesus is promising us a place somewhere beyond this world. It sounds as if God has a gigantic apartment house in the heavenly realm, and we have a reserved room awaiting us. Jesus says that God has a "house" with many rooms. And he speaks of preparing a "place" for us." Those of us who have been trying to think of heaven as something other than a place don't get much help from this passage. If anything, it is just the opposite. This passage seems to affirm that child-like image we had of heaven. A place, up there, out there. A dwelling place much like we have in this world in this life. God's house. A room within the house.

What makes this passage all the more puzzling is the word John uses here for "rooms." It is a particular form of one of the most prominent words in the Gospel of John. The word translated "rooms" is *monai*. John is the only New Testament author to use this word, and it appears twice in the Gospel of John.

In the second place, however, the word appears in John, it is translated differently. English translators have chosen to render it "home" instead of room. Listen to that passage that comes later in John 14. Jesus answers a disciple's question and says, "Those who love me will keep my word, and my Father will love them, and we will come to them and make our *home* with them." That doesn't help us much. A home is a dwelling place. It can be a room. So now we have Jesus promising us a room in heaven that will be our home. Again, very comforting words. But still words that suggest a rather physical idea of heaven and our place there.

There is yet another thing about this word, whether you translate it "room" or "home." The word is related to a verb that is most often translated "abide" or "dwell" *(menō)*. Sometimes in John it means to abide physically somewhere. To live somewhere. For instance, the word is used when Jesus "dwells" (abides) for a time in the Samaritan village after meeting the woman at the well.

Jesus uses it again and again, however, to speak of our relationship with God and with Christ. God abides in Christ, and Christ abides in God. Christ abides in our lives, and we abide in Christ. We are to abide in Christ's word and Christ's love. Finally, Jesus promises that the Holy Spirit will abide in us. To abide often means to be related to another. To be in relationship with another. The word sometimes has nothing to do with physical place and everything to do with personal relationship.

Many of us know what it means to have God abide with us and in us. I once visited a shut-in whose life had been one tragedy after another. Her children had all died while she was still alive. Her husband suffered a stroke and died years ago. She was doomed to poverty with only a pittance from social security to support her. I asked her, "How can you survive on so little?" She replied simply, "I'm never alone! God is always with me!"

This woman knew the meaning of abiding with God. She knew the relationship the word suggests. So, the rooms Jesus speaks of may not necessarily be a place but a relationship. The word translated "place" can also mean possibility or opportunity. "I go to prepare a place for you" may mean "I go to prepare an opportunity for you."

This passage seems to live in two worlds. On the one hand, it tells us about the lives of our loved ones who have died in Christ. On the other hand, it tells us something about our lives here, now, in this world. Christ went to prepare an opportunity for us to live now in an intimate relationship with our God. Our "dwelling place" is in God's presence—both now and beyond the grave. Could it be that the passage means both things—life now and life after death?

But, remember, the word translated here as "rooms" is elsewhere translated "home." So, the Greek word can mean both room and home. Christ promises us a home—a relationship in which we can live comfortably and at peace. What does the word "home" make you think of? A safe place? A comfortable place? A place of rest and relaxation? Maybe all those meanings are caught up in what Christ means by "home."

My wife, Myrna, and I enjoy our home very much. For us, it provides a space for rest and leisure. We also enjoy traveling. Yet it bothers us to be on the road without the assurance that we have a place to stay at the end of a day of travel. We like to have a room reserved just for us. It makes us more comfortable. It makes the journey easier. It's like having a temporary home awaiting us. Without a reservation, we imagine running from motel to motel looking for a place to stay.

Christ promises us a reservation for the conclusion of our journey in life. That reservation is also a part of the journey itself. God and Christ are our traveling companions now in this life. But our relationship with God defies time and place. This is Christ's promise. Thanks be to God!

∼

4

Words and Stories:
Johannine Discourses and Narratives

FROM THE DISCUSSION OF THE SYMBOLISM in John in the previous chapter, it is evident that both narratives and speech can be symbolic. The Johannine account of the "cleansing of the Temple" (2:13-22), for instance, is explicitly symbolic by virtue of Jesus' words about raising up the Temple (v. 19) and the narrator's explanation (v. 21). Johannine narrative and discourse materials share in the possibility of symbolism. There are, however, still other important connections between these two literary forms in the Gospel.

For our purposes, the distinction between narrative and discourse is simply in the prominence of the voice. In narrative, of course, the narrator's voice telling the story is predominant, even though a narrative may include Jesus' words and those of other characters (for example, 2:13-22). In what we call discourse sections, Jesus' voice is dominant, even though the narrator and other characters in the story may speak. For instance, in the long Bread of Life discourse in chapter 6, the preponderance of the words are attributed to Jesus, even though other characters contribute (see vv. 28, 41b-42, 52b), and the narrator makes comments along the way (for example, vv. 41a, 52a, 66). Narrative and discourse are sometimes woven together so that calling some passages discourse or narrative may be misleading (see 9:1-7).

This chapter will lead us through three concerns. First, we will discuss Johannine discourses and how to interpret them, including some special attention to the "farewell discourses" of chapters 14–17. Second, the chapter explores the features of the narrative materials. In both the sections on narrative and discourse we begin by briefly summarizing the problems each of these two literary forms pose for preaching. In the chapter's conclusion, our attention will turn to the complicated but fascinating relationship between discourse and narrative in the Gospel. As usual, we will try to isolate the relevance of these matters for the preacher and provide three sermonic examples.

Johannine Discourse

Many preachers would say that preaching on the narratives of the Gospel of John is easier in most cases than preaching on the speeches or discussions included in the Gospel, and I would heartily agree with that judgment. The narratives are, in a sense, relatively straightforward. In many cases, they are transparent, except when they seem to be symbolic. However, the discourses are more obscure. Simply put, the narrative material usually flows with a natural sequential logic, while the discourses seem to have been put together with little regard for logic.

The Problem of the Discourses

Read the following passage out loud:

> Then Jesus cried aloud: "Whoever believes in me believes not in me but in him who sent me. And whoever sees me sees him who sent me. I have come as light into the world, so that everyone who believes in me should not remain in the darkness. I do not judge anyone who hears my words and does not keep them, for I came not to judge the world, but to save the world. The one who rejects me and does not receive my word has a judge; on the last day the word that I have spoken will serve as judge, for I have not spoken on my own, but the Father who sent me has himself given me a commandment about what to say and what to speak. And I know that his commandment is eternal life. What I speak, therefore, I speak just as the Father has told me." (John 12:44-50)

What dense and allusive language! A reader needs to be well acquainted with the major Johannine concepts in order to understand what Jesus is saying, and even then the sense is not entirely clear. When I teach John, I often assign the interpretation of this passage for an examination, and ask students to isolate and discuss the major themes exemplified here. But note the flow of the speech! One is hard-pressed to identify anything like a logical movement in the speech. Maybe there is a reason that you will not find this passage in the RCL, even though it is a pivotal speech in the design of the whole Gospel!

This is but a single example of the character of Jesus' discourses in the fourth Gospel, and many others could be offered to illustrate with what the interpreter has to deal. The discourses in John are remarkably different from those in the Synoptic Gospels, as we noted in the introduction. Not only do the speeches of the Johannine Jesus tend to be longer, they also tend to be far more complex and even obtuse. Instances of the misunderstanding motif of which we have spoken do not surprise us, since, like the Gospel's characters, we readers often find it hard to understand the Johannine Jesus and are liable to misunderstand him just as characters in the narrative do. What can we make of these long and complex speeches?

The Style of Johannine Discourse

The structure of the discourses is one of the classic problems in Johannine studies and one that is not easily explained. Usually, when we read a discourse, we look for and discern a kind of structure that most often is logical. Let's say we are reading a good sermon. Chances are that with some care we can identify a clear structure or line of development. Sometimes the development hinges more on tone or emotion than logic, but the movement through the constituent parts of the sermon makes some kind of sense to us. We expect the same of a speech we hear or watch on television.

It is precisely this discernible structure or movement that puzzles us about much of the discourse material in the Gospel of John. The passage quoted at the beginning of this chapter (John 12:44-50) is a good example. We search mostly in vain to find connections between the separate parts of the speech. Why does Jesus say one thing after having said another?

To cite but a few stumbling blocks in this particular passage, why is the imagery of "light" introduced at verse 46? What connection does it have with belief in Jesus? Is "darkness" what evokes the words of judgment in this speech (vv. 47-48)? What is the logic that leads Jesus to "a commandment" from the Father in verse 49? How are the words Jesus speaks "a commandment," and how is that commandment "eternal life?" If we were forced to construct a structure out of the sequence of these sayings, it would be very difficult to claim that we have not read our own structure into the passage. This example of Johannine discourse also suggests how the use of individual words and phrases complicates the discernment of a pattern in a speech. "Judgment" is one such example here.

A number of ways of understanding the movement of discourse passages have been suggested. Of course, we need to consider, first of all, the possibility that there simply is no structure or pattern to these speeches. The evangelist brought together fragments of traditional words of Jesus, expanded them, and connected them without regard to anything like what we would call logic. This view supposes that logical argumentation was not a high priority for this author, so we are foolish to try to impose it on Johannine passages. If that is the case, is there another way by which the discourses proceed?

It is not uncommon to find New Testament passages that move on the basis of *word association*. One word sparks the consideration of another.

Word association is sometimes employed on the basis of the content or meaning of two or more words. That might be the case in the relationship of light and darkness to judgment in the passage from chapter 12. The connection among words may also arise from the sound or spelling of the words. One possible example is found in the bread of life discourse. The word "descended" or "came down" *(katabainō)* appears repeatedly in 6:33-58, when suddenly in verse 62 Jesus speaks of the Son of Man "ascending" (a form of the verb, *anabainō*). Notice the concluding sound of the two words—*bainō*. This creates a unity in this portion of the discourse and also a dramatic reversal.

Other times a single word may allow us to patch a longer speech together (as "came down" does in 6:33-58). That is clearly the case in 16:1-15, where the discourse is held together by the words "these things" *(tauta* and *ta)*, "many things" *(polla)*, and "all things" *(panta)*, which occur in verses 1, 3, 4 (twice), 6, 12, 13, and 15. The unity is purely linguistic since the "things" have different references. For example, in verse 1 "these things" refers to what Jesus is saying to the disciples, and in verse 3 it refers to the acts of others toward the disciples. Notice, too, how the single Greek word *mikron* ("a little while" or "time") saturates 16:16-19, holding the verses together, and then abruptly ends with the "truly, truly" declaration in verse 20. (See also the connection forged by "work" and "works" in 14:10-12.)

These are but a few simple suggestions for how word association creates structure in some Johannine discourses, and how noting word association may be a way we can discern that structure. Still another way of doing this is to view these discourses as *spirals* rather than straight-line argumentation. In fact, this proposal is a relatively old one and is still sometimes embraced. Essentially, this proposal appeals to the repetition of words and phrases in a passage to demonstrate a circular form of statement. This is relatively easy to do, as you know from your reading of John. But, then, with that circularity established, the greater difficulty is to find a progression of thought from one occurrence of a word or phrase to a later occurrence.

Let us use the speech in 5:19-30 as an example. First, we establish the repetitions within these verses: Father-Son (vv. 19, 20, 21, 22, 23, 26); the relationship between these two proceeds from see-show (vv. 19-20) to gives (vv. 21-27), to honor (vv. 23-24), and finally to hear (vv. 24-28). Then with these in mind we note the progress that takes place in the speech. The Father-Son theme concludes with "him who sent me" in verse 30. Giving life leads to resurrection in verse 28, and judgment (v. 24) to Christ's judgment (v. 30).

A second example demonstrates a combination of word association and spiraling. In 17:6-19, verses 6-14 seem held together by the word "given," but the word "world" begins to appear with it (vv. 9, 11, 13, and 14). Then in verses 15-19 the sentences are linked with the word "world." In this case, a kind of spiraling effect is evident, but there is clearer evidence of another way of spotting the progression of a discourse. In such passages, movement is occasioned more by connections between words than by ordinary logic. Perhaps we should not look for logic but for association of ideas and concepts, whether in spiral succession or not.

Chiasm is another literary form sometimes used to isolate structure in Johannine speeches. The name of this form arises from the claim that a speech or narrative fashions something similar to the Greek letter *chi*. Peter F. Ellis suggests that 5:19-30 forms a chiastic parallelism, which he summarizes this way:

(a) The Son *can do nothing* of his own accord (5:19-23).

  (b) *The hour is coming when the dead will hear the voice* of the Son of God (5:24-25).

    (c) The Father gives the Son the power to judge (5:26-27).

  (b[1]) *The hour is coming when all who are in the tombs will hear his voice* (5:28-29).

(a[1]) *I can do nothing* on my own authority (5:30).[1]

According to this analysis, the discourse moves through two steps (a and b) to its turning point and most important point (c). Then it retraces its movement through the first two steps (b[1] and a[1]).

Raymond Brown proposes a chiastic pattern in 15:7-17. To summarize this structure, Brown sees a parallel between the statements in verses 7-10 and 12-17. For instance, the whole passage begins with "If my words remain in you" (v. 7) and concludes with "This I *command* you"(v. 17, italics added), and Brown sees "words" and "command" as parallels. Other parallels are found in verses 7 and 16 ("ask"), 8 and 16 ("bear fruit"), 9 and 15 ("Father" and "loved-beloved"), and 10 and 12-14 ("commandment" and "commandments"). The central point of the chiasism, in Brown's analysis, is verse 11: "I have said this to you that my joy may be yours" (Brown's translation).[2]

All such proposals for dealing with the style of a discourse passage are fraught with dangers. In each case, it seems to me, we are liable to find what we want to find in the passage's pattern. Nonetheless, there is value in each of the proposals we have discussed—an absence of structure, word association, spiral structure, and chiasm. It may well be that there are different discourses in which one of each of these is present. In addition, it may also be our need for structure that compels us to find one of these structures in a passage. Might it be that the fourth evangelist did not care much about structure, and that the discourses are patchwork collections of sayings attributed to Jesus and the church's interpretation of them? My warning to preachers is simply be careful that our own necessity for structure does not take precedence over the text itself.

In light of this warning, let us consider a modest proposal that lacks the sophistication of the analyses described above, but one that perhaps is better because of its simplicity. I call this approach "stream of consciousness," which, in literature, refers to the free flow of thoughts and feelings tumbling along in no particular direction. You don't analyze a stream of consciousness. Rather, you try to enter it and allow it to carry you along. You go with the flow. Should you care to try treating a speech as a stream of consciousness, I suggest you read it aloud (in the Greek, if possible). Simply allow words to hand you on to the next words. By bracketing our critical capacities—suspending them, as best we can, for a moment—we may find sense in a speech that would otherwise evade us. This suggestion is not very scholarly, but it may allow the passage to speak for itself without the imposition of this or that structure on it.

What we call the "stream of consciousness" character of the discourse has been identified by some as the poetic quality of the passages. Many have argued that in the discourses John writes in a style that is more poetic than prosaic. The poetic quality is most evident in the use of parallelism, the classic feature of Hebraic poetry.[3] Examples of such parallelism are found in 3:11, 16, and 20-21. Some have even argued that a Semitic source was employed in the Johannine discourses; however, that is probably stretching the evidence too far. I prefer to say more simply that the discourses are in many ways more like reading poetry than reading prose.

The Farewell Discourses

Before addressing the homiletical implications of the style of the discourses, we need to take some time to consider that special section of discourse materials found in chapters 14–17, if for no other reason than their prominence in the RCL. Chapter 6 deals with the lectionary passages from this section, so our primary attention now is the nature of the discourse materials in these chapters. These chapters have traditionally been called the "farewell discourses" because of Jesus' special concern in these teachings to prepare his disciples (whoever they may be in this case) for his death and resurrection. So, the theme of Jesus' "departure" (13:1) or his "going away"(14:28; 16:7) pervades the chapters as well as concern for the disciples' faithfulness amid persecution (see, for example, 16:1-4).

C. H. Dodd offers this analysis of the structure of the farewell discourses: (1) An "opening dramatic scene" (13:1-30); (2) "Dialogue on Christ's departure and return" (13:31—14:31); (3) "Discourse on Christ and His Church" (15:1—16:33); (4) "The Prayer of Christ" (17:1-26).[4]

Many have suggested that the genre of these discourses was a standard form found in other literature in which a leader gives his or her disciples final instructions.[5] Chapter 13 is sometimes included in the farewell discourses and sometimes thought to be an introduction to them. Either way, it is clear that chapter 13 is integral to Jesus' final instructions to his disciples.

These chapters have often been thought to be a compilation of at least three separate collections of Jesus' words and their interpretation.[6] For instance, 14:1-31 focuses on "loss and restoration"; 15:1—16:4a on "intimacy with Christ and hostility with the world"; and 16:4b-33 on "tribulation and assurance."[7] Most important is that we should note that there are numerous repetitions in the discourses. For example, the power of asking God is found as many as five times (14:13-14; 15:7, 16b; and 16:23-24, 26), and Jesus speaks of the disciples' joy at least three times (14:28; 15:11; and 16:20-24).[8] Preachers ought to take each passage in its immediate context but also investigate and compare similar passages elsewhere in the farewell discourses.

From the perspective of the evangelist, these passages address the church in its postresurrection life. As such, then, they address us and the church in our own day. The themes of the discourses are easily related to the contemporary church. For instance, the theme of antagonism with the world, which is so prominent in these passages (for example, 15:18—16:4a), is important for us as we find ourselves more and more at odds with popular culture. In my opinion, the farewell discourses are a paramount resource for rescuing the contemporary church from excessive accommodation to culture.

Chapter 17 requires special mention, since it is very different from what we find in chapters 13–16. The prayer flows in a way typical of what we have called "stream of consciousness" and is filled with Jesus' emotion and love. John sometimes portrays Jesus as rather cold and aloof, but here Jesus' words about love become incarnated in his final prayer, even as they will be enfleshed in his suffering and death.

This is not the place for a protracted discussion of the Paraclete (John 14:16, 26; 15:26; 16:7; and 1 John 2:1—see chapter 6).[9] What interests us at this point is how the passages repeat certain themes while also extending the interpretation of the Spirit. Several examples will have to do. First, note that in 14:26 Jesus promises that the Paraclete will "teach you all things *(panta)* and bring to your remembrance all *(panta)* that I have said to you" (RSV). Then in 16:13 he declares that "the Spirit of all truth . . . will guide you into all truth *(alētheia pasē)*" (again RSV). There is clearly a relationship between these two sayings, but the second seems to carry the promise further, while at the same time defining Jesus' revelation as "truth."

Second, a careful reading of the sayings reveals that the one who sends the Paraclete varies. In 14:16 the Father sends the Paraclete as a result of Jesus' request, and 14:25 affirms that the Father sends the Paraclete in Jesus' "name." Then in both 15:26 and 16:7 Jesus says that *he* will send the Paraclete. (The saying in 16:13-14 does not mention the one who sends the Spirit.) Rather than claiming this evidence for a redactor's hand in the Gospel, consider what is accomplished in these discourses with their contradiction. Christ and God are at once both separate agents and the same Agent. In other words, a Christology emerges from an apparently simple contradiction.

Suffice it to say, the Paraclete is the means by which the revelation of God in Christ is continued after Christ's "departure." The Spirit, according to these passages, continues to make that revelation accessible and continues to guide and teach the church. So, the fourth Gospel suggests that the Paraclete is the extension of Jesus' ministry. Jesus speaks of the Paraclete as "another Advocate" (14:15), suggesting that the Spirit replicates Jesus' ministry. Consequently, the Paraclete has been labeled "Jesus' alter ego." In John, the risen Christ bestows the Holy Spirit on the disciples (20:22); however, the distinction between the Spirit and the presence of the risen Christ is blurred. This is due, in part, to the fact that John never narrates a conclusion to the appearances of the resurrected Christ, as if to suggest that he continues confronting the church and leading it (see chapter 5). The later church drew the line of distinction between the presence of Christ and the presence of the Spirit more clearly than does the fourth Gospel.

Homiletical Implications

The representation of Jesus' final private ministry with his disciples is filled with the typical Johannine discourse material we have discussed above. There are perhaps two things to keep in mind as we study passages from these chapters for preaching. The first is to recognize *their setting*, at least as the Gospel presents them. Immediately after chapter 17, Jesus is arrested, and the remainder of the Gospel's story describes his passion and resurrection. John has arranged this material for dramatic effect—putting it in the context of Jesus' impending passion. Therefore, preachers have an opportunity to emphasize the personal quality of Jesus' teachings: Jesus' concern for the disciples who are faced with their loss of his presence, and Jesus' preparation of the disciples for his departure and the crisis they will experience as a result of his execution. As such, the discourses are appropriately interpreted in the context of contemporary crises in the lives of Christian individuals and the congregation.

Second, preachers should not hesitate to take passages as they are in themselves without trying to relate them exactly to what comes before and what comes after. By saying this, I am not encouraging interpretation out of context, but recognizing the simple fact that these discourses seem to be segments loosely joined together under the broader context we have just mentioned. For instance, 15:18-25 is sandwiched between 15:12-17 (the love commandment) and 15:26-27 (one of the Paraclete sayings). The words of Jesus regarding the disciples' relationship to the world in verses 18-25 are certainly not entirely unrelated to what comes before and what follows them. Preachers are free, I think, to preach on those passages themselves without feeling the necessity of discerning and understanding their place in the immediate discourse.

Third, preaching the discourse materials in nearly every case requires that we offer explanations of words and phrases that so often puzzle us and our congregations. We cannot, of course, once and for all determine entirely what Jesus means by some of the large theological categories (such as "Truth"), but, if we are to lead listeners into these texts, it is incumbent on us to offer clear and basic understandings of the key words in them. For example, in several passages we need to make clear just what Jesus seems to mean by "world" (see 15:18-27). Or, in our sample discourse passage (12:27-36), what does "judgment," "lifted up," or "draw" mean? Preaching John taxes our capacity for explaining complicated terms and phrases in understandable ways without distorting or oversimplifying them.

As an example of what I mean, suppose the sermon is on John 17:6-19 (assigned for Easter 7, Year C). In verse 17, Jesus asks God on behalf of the disciples, "Sanctify them in the truth; your word is truth." How shall we clarify the word "sanctify?" (see chapter 6). Rather than burdening our listeners with a complicated doctrine of sanctification (which is probably not Johannine), we might resort to the basic meaning of the Greek verb *hagiazō*, "to set apart." Jesus is asking that God confer on the disciples a distinctiveness from the world and from their surrounding culture. If we can say simply that "truth" refers basically to God's revelation, then by understanding who God truly is, Christians become distinct from our society in terms of whom we worship and from whom we derive our values. Much as we set apart certain days in our calendar as special (such as the Fourth of July or Martin Luther King Day), so God sets apart those claimed by the divine love. The danger of this practice, of course, is that for the sake of simplicity we oversimplify and even in some cases trivialize. From my experience in preaching it is clear to me that our listeners (who are perhaps increasingly unsophisticated in their theological acumen) are eager to be assisted in their efforts to grasp biblical ideas and themes. Preaching Johannine discourse can never be made easy, because the interpretation of

John is seldom easy. Still, probing the depths of Jesus' words in John promises to lead us to riches beyond our expectations.

A Sermon Example

This sermon, entitled "Peculiar Peace," on John 14:23-29 (Sixth Sunday of Easter, C) is a revised form of one I preached some years ago. I offer it here as an example of one way we might deal with a Johannine discourse passage. The sermon was first prepared for a rather affluent congregation—one in which there was a good deal of evidence of upward mobility while at the same time a great deal of dissatisfaction and emotional misery. You will notice, too, that this is a rather personal sermon in which my wife, Myrna, and I are mentioned. This is part of what I regard the value of the personal story, if it is not overdone (see if I overdid it!).

~

At a retreat with lay persons not long ago, I asked the group to imagine what God most wanted for humans. The thing that was mentioned first and most often was peace: Universal Peace. Peace and Beauty. Peace and Serenity. One person told me afterward that what he wanted to say was "[sigh] . . . Peace."

I suppose that he expressed the desire lots of us may have. The older I get the more I want just one thing: [sigh]. . . *Peace.* Take away all of the hassles, the troubles, the worries. Spare me the conflicts with other people and with machines. I can do without the storms. Just give me calm seas. Don't rock the boat!

I used to think that I yearned most for success and wealth and all those things that we think we would like to have in life. Now I would trade them all for simple peace in life. And it appears that I am not the only one who would like peace above all. There is a huge market for medications for "peaceful sleep." We still put on grave stones, "Rest in Peace." The best-selling books still include the most recent proposals for "peace of mind." And there is a widespread attitude among us that goes something like this: "Just leave me alone; I don't want to be bothered." I felt like that once this week when weariness overcame me.

Peace is the most precious of the treasures we seek.

And so you would think that the words of the Johannine Jesus in today's Gospel lesson would be very relevant. In his last conversation with his disciples, Jesus bids them farewell with these words: "Peace I leave with you; my peace I give to you. I do not give to you as the world gives."

But it is a peculiar peace Jesus gives. "I do not give to you as the world gives." The peace Jesus gives is not the same as worldly peace.

Try an experiment with me: Close your eyes. Try to visualize yourself in absolute peace. Picture what the situation would look like. What do you see in a fully peaceful setting? Open your eyes now. Let me guess that the scene you just pictured was most characteristically a setting in which certain things were absent. The peace of the world—the peace you and I most commonly seek—is best described as the *absence* of certain things. The absence of war, the absence of crime and strife and violence, the absence of pain, conflict, struggles, unfulfilled desires. It almost sounds as if the peace we seek is something like a vacuum.

A friend of mine once said that the peace most of us seek can never be attained short of the grave. What we strive for is the absence of all struggle, which sounds like the absence of life itself.

But Jesus gives a peculiar peace. A peace characterized not by an absence but by a *presence*. What Jesus gives his disciples is the assurance of the presence of God in the Holy Spirit: "[T]he Advocate, the Holy Spirit, whom the Father will send in my name, will teach you everything, and remind you of all that I have said to you. Peace I leave with you. . . ."

The peace Jesus gives is a result of the presence of God in the Spirit, not the absence of other things. It is a peculiar peace. Jesus' peace is not the absence of the struggles of life. His peace is a divine presence that does not annihilate the unpleasantness of life but empowers one to live with the unpleasantness. His peace does not insure a hassle-free life but an abiding presence that makes the hassles of life bearable. This peculiar peace does not allow us to be left alone, to be not bothered. Just the opposite! This peace comes as a result of a presence—a presence that sensitizes us to the pain of others. We feel their pain along with our own—a presence that makes us concerned for the life conditions of others, so that we cannot rest easy while others are oppressed.

Far from a contentment, this peculiar peace may make us discontent. It is a presence that makes us dissatisfied so long as our brothers and sisters anywhere in the world have no freedom and know no justice. It is a presence that makes us discontent so long as there is segregation of the races in our nation or anywhere in the world.

This Jesus peace is a peculiar peace. I am not sure it is the kind of peace for which I yearn. Because the peace I seek is the peace of the world.

But this is a peculiar peace, too, because it is *given to me*. The peace most of us seek is a goal out there in the future after which we strive. We seem to think that peace is hiding somewhere for us to find. Life is a game of hide-and-seek. Peace hides from us, and we try to find it. Or peace is a commodity to be acquired, a goal to be achieved. Peace is something we earn!

So, Jesus does not make much sense to our way of thinking when he insists that he *gives* peace. It's a gift! It's not found. It's not achieved. It's not earned. It's given to us. Jesus' peace is not the result of something we do but something that is done for us. The gift of peace comes as a result of God's abiding presence in our lives. All that we must do is accept and be sensitive to that gift of divine presence.

A counselor once gave me some advice by which I wish I could more consistently live. He said that the things we most desire in life are never found when they are sought after. Peace and happiness come to us, not because we seek them, but as gifts when we seek other goals. The precious gifts of peace and happiness are always by-products of our efforts to seek other goals.

The Kysars are devoted to the effort to have fun. Our precious day off comes, and we set out to *have* fun. We seek fun—try to "have fun." As if fun is something we can take possession of! And in the course of the day we are liable to ask ourselves—as the saying goes—"Are we having fun yet?" But strangely the most enjoyable moments for us occur when we have not tried to plan them. They just happen! They are not programmed, designed, or plotted. They come at unexpected moments, usually when we are concentrating on something else rather than having fun. A committee meeting proves to be fun. A council meeting is fun! Going to the grocery store—believe it or not—proves to be fun!

This peculiar peace Jesus offers us comes unexpectedly as a gift and not as a goal of our striving. It comes as we give of ourselves in service of others. It comes as we care about other people and Christ's ministry. It comes as we work for justice in our world and dignity for all people.

By the standards of our world this Jesus peace is peculiar. "Peace I leave with you; my peace I give to you. I do not give to you as the world gives."

Maybe this peculiar peace is not what I seek after all. It is not that peace of calmness and contentment I want. Or, is it?

I guess we learn in the course of life that what we think we want is not always what we really want. I think I want a steady diet of candy, ice cream, and popcorn. Yet I want even more to live a long and healthy life. I think I want no hassles and no troubles in life. Yet I want even more to serve my Lord. Do I really want the kind of peace I think I want?

Sometimes in teaching, a student will ask a question to which the teacher cannot give an answer, because it is simply a wrong question. "Which of the snake's legs are the stronger—the hind legs or the front legs?"

Perhaps our search for peace is a wrong search. It cannot be fulfilled because it seeks the wrong thing. A lottery prize of over one hundred million dollars. Now that will bring me peace! Or maybe I can get on the "Who Wants to Be a Millionaire?" program and win it all. Even if this would not bring me peace, I would sure like to try it anyway! Apparently thousands of people think so. The lines at the state lottery windows seem to grow longer and longer, especially as the jackpot increases.

And who of us does not at least secretly wish that we might win that kind of money? Instant millionaires! It is tempting, isn't it? Would one hundred million dollars bring us the peace we really want? Would any amount of money? Can you buy the peace that comes from knowing the presence of your Creator in your life?

It is a peculiar peace Jesus offers us. But perhaps it is the peace we really want.

~

Johannine Narrative

The whole of the narrative in the fourth Gospel is generally clear and relatively smooth. One has little problem following the story. The two major problems in reading John's narrative are, first, their symbolic nature and, second, the peculiar difficulties we encounter at some points. Having discussed the symbolic possibilities of narrative as well as Jesus' words, we will consider briefly the so-called "aporias" in John's narrative. Aporia is defined simply as "a difficulty, as in a philosophical or literary text, caused by an indeterminacy of meaning for which no resolution seems possible" (*Webster's New World Dictionary*). In this case, the difficulty is in narrative flow, which of course intrudes on meaning. The fourth Gospel is notorious for its narrative rough spots or "potholes."

The Problem of Narratives

The most conspicuous of the narrative difficulties is found in 14:31. Here Jesus sounds as if the farewell speeches (see above) are ended, and he and the disciples should make their way to the "garden" (18:1). However, the discourse goes on for another two chapters, and in a third chapter Jesus prays! Scholars have spent considerable time in trying to decipher this strange break between chapters 14 and 15.

Another such break or rough spot in the narrative is the order of chapters 6 and 7. In this case, the problem lies in geography. In 5:1 the narrator tells us that Jesus went to Jerusalem, and no geographical movement is mentioned in the remainder of the chapter. Yet 6:1 reports that Jesus went to the other side of the Sea of Galilee, even though there is no mention of his return to Galilee. These difficulties in the flow of the narrative result in theories of displacement and rearrangement.[10] Displacement proposes that papyrus sheets of the Gospel were accidentally "disordered" and then incorrectly reassembled. It is that mistaken reassembly that comes down to us as the structure of the Gospel. The efforts at rearrangement seek to reestablish the original order of the Gospel. The most famous of these theories is that of Rudolf Bultmann.[11]

Theories of disorder and rearrangement have fallen into disapproval and, for the most part, have been replaced with literary claims that we need to take the order of the Gospel as it is. Culpepper made the astute observation that the fourth Gospel as a whole "is magnificent but flawed. Magnificent in its complexity, subtlety, and profundity, but oddly flawed in some of its transitions, sequences, and movements." He goes on to claim that the Gospel is "more unified and coherent than has often been thought" because it consistently develops its major themes.[12]

We preachers can for the most part disregard these problems of the narrative flow for two reasons. First, contemporary literary criticism of John demonstrates the present order of the Gospel makes sense, and we benefit from assuming and looking for that unity. Second, while preachers need to build their interpretations on context, we seldom need to depend on the text's perfect narrative order to structure our messages.

The Features of Johannine Narrative

Readers of the Gospel of John will note that there are two kinds of narratives in this Gospel. The first group includes narratives that seem to be told for the sake of the story itself, the anointing of Jesus (12:1-7), for example. While the story concludes with Jesus' important pronouncement about Mary (vv. 7-8), it is valuable in and of itself. You could, for instance, appreciate the story without Jesus' final saying.

The second kind of narrative we find in John are stories that are told, it seems, simply to frame or provide a context for a speech. One example is the story of Nicodemus coming to Jesus (3:1-9). Once the narrator has brought Nicodemus on stage, and the scene is set and arranged, the character of Nicodemus fades away and Jesus' words dominate the remainder of the passage (see chapter 3). Think of all the speculation about Nicodemus this story has inspired. Because it is so truncated, we wonder, whatever became of Nicodemus? Did he believe what Jesus was saying or not? You will recognize that this sort of narrative—one that simply sets the stage for Jesus' speaking—is much like some passages in the Synoptic Gospels. The so-called pronouncement stories do little more than arrange the stage so that Jesus has occasion to speak[13]. Examples include Mark 2:18-20; 10:13-16 and 17-22. Note, too, that brief narrative settings provide the context for a good many of Jesus' parables in the Synoptics. For example, Luke 15:1-3 introduces no less than four parables—three in chapter 15 and another in 16:1-13.

Readers of the Gospels will also almost immediately realize that the stories told in the fourth Gospel tend to be different from those in the Synoptics. The first three Gospels include an extended narrative relating Jesus' passion, but otherwise, their narratives tend to be rather short. Most typical of the Synoptics are the short narrative bits identified by the form critics years ago as stories transmitted orally before they were written. For instance, Mark 2 contains at least four relatively independent short stories, verses 1-12, 13-17, 18-22, and 23-28. On the other hand, the fourth Gospel relates a number of lengthy stories, including Jesus' encounter with the Samaritan woman (4:1-42), the healing of the man born blind (9:1-41), and the raising of Lazarus and the plot to kill Jesus (11:1-54). These three are assigned Gospel lessons in Lent, A, for the Third, Fourth, and Fifth Sundays, and as such they have caused considerable frustration among preachers simply because of their sheer length.

We need not probe the questions of how the fourth Gospel obtained these stories and how much each of them is rooted in early tradition. As literary units they exemplify the dramatic quality of Johannine narratives in general. These longer stories suggest the way in which the fourth Gospel's narratives nurture suspense, dynamic interchange, tensive action, multiple layers of reference, and symbolic reference (see chapter 1.)

The raising of Lazarus literally exudes *suspense*. It begins with Jesus' delay in going to the aid of the Bethany family (Mary, Martha, and Lazarus, vv. 5-6). The disciples's remark in verse 8, followed by Thomas's exclamation "Let us also go, that we may die with him" (v. 16), heightens readers' sense of suspense by reminding us of the dangers that await Jesus in Judea. Then his progress to the tomb itself is delayed by his conversations with first Martha (vv. 20-27) and then Mary (vv. 28-32). Jesus' unusual weeping and his strong emotional response (vv. 35 and 38) lead us to wonder what exactly he will do, if anything. Maybe that suspense is tightened even more by Jesus' request that the tomb be opened (v. 39). Then suddenly all the tension is relieved and the suspense lifted when Lazarus comes out of his tomb at Jesus' command. Here the text uses intense suspense to keep readers on the edge of their seats.

For another prize example of suspense, read again the story of Jesus' trial before Pilate, focusing on the question of what Pilate will finally decide to do. Our familiarity with these stories tends to numb us to the narrative suspense in them. We know how the story of Jesus and Lazarus will turn out and are quite familiar with Pilate's decision. Familiarity with the stories sometimes keeps us from recognizing what is going on in them. Perhaps on occasion we should pretend we don't know this story and that we have no way of knowing where the story is going to lead. When we can do this simulation of ignorance successfully, we begin to see a lot in the stories we did not previously know was there.

Another feature of Johannine narrative is *dynamic interchange,* by which I mean Jesus' give-and-take with other characters in a narrative. These interchanges are rich and move the stories along at a rapid speed. However puzzling the dialogue between Jesus and his mother may be in 2:1-11, clearly the development of the problem and Jesus' mother's request that her son do something about it (v. 3) pushes the narrative along. Jesus first seems unwilling to act, but yet his mother's request apparently influences him. His orders to the steward at the wedding creates the setup for the wonder, and then the steward's remark about the quality of the wine heightens the wonder. Again and again in narratives, Jesus' encounter with other characters serves as a kind of motor in the narration. Another similar example of dynamic interchange is the story of the healing of the royal official son in 4:46-54. Again Jesus speaks as if he is going to refuse the official's request (v. 48). Then the words of the desperate father move Jesus (or so it seems) to heal the official's son. The official's simple statement of faith ("Sir, come down before my little boy dies," v. 49) triggers Jesus' act of healing. Clearly the dynamic interchange between Jesus and his mother at the wedding and between Jesus and the royal official also contribute to the suspense of both stories.

A third feature of John's narrative is what we might call *tensive action.* In this case, "tensive" means simply that which causes tension. I also have in mind the tension that arises from a lack of clarity. Language is tensive when it is ambiguous or can mean several things at the same time without our being able clearly to resolve the tension among possible meanings (see the previous chapter). Narrative action is tensive when we frankly don't know what to make of it. What does this story mean? Does it mean this or that? The fourth evangelist is not content to keep us off guard by using words and phrases with multiple meanings but bolsters that practice with stories that evoke a number of possible interpretations regarding their meaning.

In 7:1-13 there is a rather curious story of Jesus' decision to go to Jerusalem for the "Feast of Tabernacles." It is first stated, "He did not wish to go about in Judea because the Jews were looking for an opportunity to kill him" (v. 1). Then the mysterious characters of "his brothers"—whom we are soon told did not believe in Jesus (v. 5)—suddenly appear and try to persuade him to go, so that his "disciples also may see the works you are doing" (vv. 3-4). Jesus first refuses (vv. 6-9), but then inexplicably he goes secretly (v. 10). The little story concludes by stating how the people were divided over what to think of Jesus (vv. 11-13).

This story may be more than simply a difficult one to understand in the context of the Gospel's narrative. The fact is that it evokes numerous questions which float around in our imaginations as we try to assign some meaning to the tale. First, who are these "brothers" who are mentioned nowhere else in the Gospel? Then, why does Jesus first refuse to go and then does go? Is this another case in which the evangelist demonstrates Jesus' freedom from human manipulation, like his responses to his mother's request in 2:1-11 and to the royal official's plea in 4:46-54? And what's this about Jesus' publicly doing his "works" so that his disciples will believe in him? Is that not exactly what he has done on several occasions earlier in the narrative (e.g., 2:11; 4:1-42, 54; 5:1-9; 6:1-14 and 16-21)? What are the "brothers" asking of Jesus that he has not already done? Because of their unbelief, does the story suggest that they themselves have evil intentions?

We cannot pretend to know what the author intended by this story, and certainly we cannot say that the evangelist intentionally wrote such ambiguity into the story. All we know is that the present story evokes a lot of questions. My suggestion is that the text encourages us to ponder the tensive quality of the narratives and never claim finally to have nailed down exactly what they mean. This practice is not popular, because we are trained by our culture to want to settle firmly on the meaning of a passage. Yet if we declare unequivocally that we know what a story means, we cheat ourselves of the pleasure of continuing to imagine different possible meanings.

Related to what I have called tensive action in narratives is another feature of Johannine story-telling, namely, *multiple layers of reference*. As we note in chapter 1, the proposal that the Gospel was written out of and for a community that had recently suffered separation from the synagogue is based on the possibility that its narratives sometimes refer both to the historical time of Jesus and to the contemporary situation in which the church found itself when the Gospel was written.[14] Without necessarily endorsing the whole of this theory for the Gospel's origin, we are safe in believing that the fourth evangelist interpreted the Jesus story for the church's contemporary situation. In this sense, it is an example of good preaching, insofar as the author addressed current issues in the church by means of the Christian tradition.[15] Of course, this double reference— to Jesus' time and the church's time—is not peculiar to the Gospel of John. At least most scholarly interpretations of each of the Synoptic Gospels attempt to read them as expressions of the Christian message for a very specific and concrete situation in the church.

In chapter 1 we discussed the most obvious of the occurrences of such a double reference is in John 9. This story may indeed reflect an antagonism between the synagogue and the Johannine church, but more importantly for our purposes it indicates the evangelist's effort to empower readers of her or his own time.

John's story of Jesus' entry into Jerusalem (12:12-19) departs from the Synoptic versions of this event in several interesting points. (The story takes this traditional name fashioned for the Synoptic accounts, even though in John it is never actually said that Jesus entered Jerusalem.) The quotation of Hebrew scripture in verse 15 is a blending of Zechariah 9:9 ("Look, your king is coming, sitting on a donkey's colt") and Zephaniah 3:16 ("Do not be afraid, daughter of Zion"). (Compare Mark 11:1-10; Matt. 21:1-9; and Luke 19:28-38.) In Zephaniah the king is Yahweh and is not a reference to a nationalistic ruler. The fourth evangelist seems to tone down the nationalistic implications of the story. "Jesus' entering Jerusalem on a donkey is a prophetic action designed to counteract that nationalism."[16] This is so even though the Johannine narrative has the crowd explicitly call Jesus "king" (v. 13). Jesus will be a universal king when he is lifted up on the cross.

Some of us suspect that the narrative of the entry into Jerusalem in John refers both to the Jesus story of the past and his story in the church contemporaneous with the writing of the Gospel. The hints this story provides, plus the obvious fact that the fourth Gospel emphasizes and redefines Christ's kingship (see chapter 5), invite us to wonder what was going on in the community that is addressed by this understanding of kingship. Speculation will get us nowhere, but the evangelist gives the story of Jesus' entry into Jerusalem two levels in order to stress an understanding of kingship that is devoid of nationalism. It is fair, then, to conclude that John, the preacher, was addressing a specific issue in the Johannine congregation. Note that this concept of double-layered reference entails a historical interpretation of the Gospel and not simply a literary one; however, it is entirely compatible with literary criticism (see chapter 1).

The double-layered narrative brings us finally to the *symbolic* feature of some of the stories the Gospel's narrator tells. Symbolic meaning is closely related to both tensive and double-layered narratives. What is peculiar about symbolic narrative is that it is an enactment of another theme—one that has "transcendent significance."[17] As we noted in the previous chapter, symbolic narrative functions the same way as symbolic speech, except that the pointing beyond itself occurs not in single words or phrases but in actions and events. Like linguistic symbolism in general, when we think we are reading a narrative that stands for and points toward something else, we confront the same interpretative problems, most especially that of determining when a narrative is symbolic and when it should be read only for what it seems on the surface to say. An example of one narrative that seems to function symbolically is all that we need·to supplement what has already been said about symbolism or metaphor in John. Moreover, when we ask the question of whether or not a narrative is symbolic, we are looking for some of the same features of Johannine narrative we have already mentioned in this section, such as tensive narrative.

John's account of the feeding of the multitude in 6:1-14 provides us a good specimen to put under our microscope. Chapter 6 deals with the passage in greater detail, but here we want to examine it as a possible symbolic narrative. Some of the features of the Johannine version of this story that are unique and not found in the Synoptic versions include the following: First, the narrator provides a setting that is distinctive. The crowd follows Jesus to this place because "they saw the signs he was doing" (6:2). The place is a "mountain" (v. 3), a feature missing from the Synoptic versions. Moreover, the narrator also tells us the Passover was "near" (v. 4). Second, the transition into the feeding is entirely different in John. Jesus' self-determination is emphasized in verse 6. The role of the "boy" with the "five barley loaves and two fish" is a Johannine detail missing in the Synoptic stories of this event. Strangely, the narrator makes a point of telling us "there was a great deal of grass in the place," a puzzlingly distinctive feature. Third, Jesus' actions with the bread and fish are different in two ways. He first gives "thanks" (the verb *eucharisteō*),[18] and then he himself "distributed" the food to the crowd (v. 11). In the Synoptic versions, the disciples distributed the bread and fish (Matt. 14:19; Mark 6:41; and Luke 9:16). Fourth, when the crowd has been fed, Jesus commands the disciples, "Gather up the fragments left over, so that nothing may be lost" (v. 12). Unlike the Synoptic Gospels, the Johannine narrator never mentions the number of the crowd that has been fed but describes their reaction, saying that they "saw the sign that he had done," called him "the prophet who is to come into the world," and tried to "take him by force to make him king," requiring Jesus to flee (vv. 14-15).

Is this story a symbolic representation of the Lord's Supper? Some of the peculiarly Johannine features could be set aside as typical of the Gospel's language or theology, for example, the Passover setting in verse 4 (which might also account for the "great deal of grass" in v. 10), the mention of signs in verses 2 and 14, and the crowd's eagerness to make Jesus king (v. 15). Other details may be present just for the sake of good story-telling (such as the boy and his loaves and fishes, v. 9). What spurs the possibility of symbolic and eucharistic reference are (1) the Passover setting, (2) Jesus' thanksgiving, (3) Jesus' distribution of the food, and (4) gathering the leftovers that they not be lost. The context furthers the possibility. In 6:51-58 we find the most explicitly Eucharistic language in the Gospel. If the discourse in verses 22-71 is an interpretation of the feeding story (see the next section below), then verses 51-58 augment the possibility of a Eucharistic meaning in 6:1-15.

One of the easiest ways of determining whether a passage is symbolic is to look for support for the theme elsewhere in the Gospel. In this case, when we look elsewhere for confirmation of a symbolic reading of the feeding of the crowd, we come up empty-handed. The absence of an account of the institution of the Lord's Supper, however, may make us wonder if this story some how stands in its place. Many commentators read the feeding of the crowd as an enactment of the Eucharist, some saying that this is John's account of the institution of the Lord's Supper.[19] There is a good case, then, for believing that with this story the fourth evangelist subtly points beyond it to the Eucharist. Note, however, that the story is not an artificial construct to stand in place of the institution of the Lord's Supper. Rather, the Gospel repeats the traditional story that was also known by the Synoptic evangelists but adds another dimension to it. Therefore, the story represents another of Jesus' marvelous signs as well as stimulates us to think of the Eucharist.

Unfortunately, we have just wandered into a swamp! The question of the sacraments in the fourth Gospel is muddy and treacherous terrain. Suffice it to say that interpreters are all over the map with their answers to this question.[20] That does not prevent our making some observations about this matter. The first is that, in the case of the symbolic interpretation of John 6:1-15, we encounter tensive narrative, and, like symbolism as a whole in John, we are left with a stimulating narrative that should not finally be closed in its meaning. Instead, this narrative provokes us to thought and puzzlement over its symbolic reference. Let's just remember, we do not have to nor can we finally settle the question, because the nature of the story is that its meaning remains open.

Second, I believe preachers have a certain license at points such as this. For centuries the church has interpreted the feeding of the multitude as Eucharistic, and for that reason we are free to read it the same way. Perhaps we should openly acknowledge to our congregation that its Eucharistic meaning may seem evident to us today (as it did to our predecessors in the church), but that may not be what the text actually conveys.

Homiletical Implications

The homiletical implications of this discussion are, I hope, already evident. However, I want to shape several suggestions for preaching Johannine narratives to make them as explicit as possible.

First, this is a good place to offer one suggestion having to do with preaching on all the Gospels: Emphasize the unique features of a particular Gospel's telling of a story. Suppose we are going to preach on a passage that has parallels in other Gospels, and one of those other versions is assigned in the lectionary for reading at another time. I suggest that we find what is unique about the story as it is told in the particular lesson for that day.

For instance, the lectionary includes both the Matthean (14:13-21, Proper 13, A) and the Johannine (6:1-21, Proper 12, B) accounts of the feeding of a multitude. In order to deal with as much of the New Testament thought on the feeding as we can, it might be wise to isolate the unique features of each of these two accounts and emphasize them in our sermons. When we preach on the Johannine story, we use its unique qualities we have mentioned above in fashioning our sermon. When we come then to Year A and find the Matthean account, we ask what is different about this account from John's. For instance, like Mark (6:34) Matthew says Jesus was motivated by his compassion for the crowd (14:14), something conspicuously absent from John's account. The role of the boy who has five loaves and two fish in the Johannine account (6:9) is played by the disciples in Matthew (14:17). The disciples offer their lunches in order to feed the hungry, just as the church today is asked to offer what it has for the sake of the hungry of our world.

If we make a practice of stressing what is peculiar to one Gospel's telling of a common story, we accomplish two things. First, we are more likely to put our finger on the reason the evangelist tells this story and therefore are truer to the assigned lesson. Second, we don't exhaust all we can say on one version of the story and then have nothing left to say when another version appears in the lectionary. Another good example is Peter's confession at Caesarea Philippi that appears in the Matthean form (16:13-20) for Proper 16, A, and in the Markan form (8:22-38) for Proper 19, B.

A second suggestion is to pay attention to discourse or narrative depending on the function of the narrative. Above, we suggested that some narratives in John do little more than provide a setting for Jesus to speak. In those case, the text invites us to attend more closely to the speech than the narrative. In those cases in which the narrative stands on its own without necessarily needing a discourse, let the narrative be the center of our attention. (For more on this see the next section of this chapter.) Clearly, this simple suggestion does not do justice to the particular text before us. This is not to say that we should ever ignore Jesus' words but only that we should keep the narrative in mind as we interpret Jesus' words.

By way of example, the Johannine account of the "cleansing of the Temple" (2:13-22—Lent 3, B) has a saying attached (2:19)—and an important one that interprets Jesus' treatment of those who are profaning the Temple. Still, the saying makes little sense without the narrative, so it must be carefully set within the narrative when we preach on the saying. The Nicodemus episode (3:1-16, Trinity Sunday, B, and alternate reading for Lent 2, A) ought not seduce us into a sermon on the character of Nicodemus at the expense of Jesus' speech. In this case, Nicodemus is a good example, however, of a character whose encounter with Jesus moves the story along.

Third, when the text highlights suspense, we should imitate that narrative suspense in our sermons. Now, it is easy to spot elements of suspense in a narrative, but it is a good deal more difficult to build suspense into our sermons. The main feature of a suspenseful sermon is that it does not give away its essential message before leading listeners through a couple of turns that make them wonder where is the pastor going with this?[21] When some of us try to write sermons that employ suspense, we end up wandering around and losing our listeners entirely. I know this from personal experience! When it is done well, however, it captures listeners' attention and keeps them wondering how this sermon will end. Several good examples of structuring suspense into sermons are found in Eugene L. Lowry's book, *How to Preach a Parable: Designs for Narrative Sermons*. I recommend in particular Lowry's own sermon, "Who Could Ask for Anything More?"[22]

As an example, preaching the story of the raising of Lazarus in John 11 invites us to re-present the suspense the narrator builds into the biblical story. We can do that by our retelling of the story itself, or by telling a contemporary story that has the same kind of suspense in it (such as a story of waiting for the doctor to arrive while she is delayed again and again). This leads me to express one of my pet peeves: preachers who give away the whole point of the sermon in the first three minutes! That practice is widespread, because it roots in the old slogan, "Tell them what you're going to tell them. Tell them. And then tell them what you've told them." Why would I want to listen to the whole sermon when the preacher gives me a summary of it to begin with?

A fourth suggestion is to try to use dynamic exchange to preach a narrative that incorporates dynamic exchange. Suppose, for instance, that we are preaching the account of Jesus and the Samaritan woman (4:1-42, assigned for Lent 3, A). Here is a passage in which narratives and discourses are creatively interwoven. What moves the story along, however, are the woman's comments and questions. Notice, for instance, that the woman introduces the question of who Jesus is in verse 12 and the topic of worship in verse 20. Such a passage invites preachers to employ dialogue in the sermon. Sure, it might involve actual dialogue with the congregation, but it could also be the presentation of dialogue between another party in the pulpit with the preacher or simply the preacher's playing both roles in the dialogical exchange.

The form of such a sermon comprises structuring the sermon's movement from beginning to end by means of exchange between two people or two perspectives. (See my sermon on Jesus and Pilate in the next chapter.) Sometimes this is accomplished by the preacher imagining an inquirer who is asking questions, or imagining an opponent who is challenging the preacher at every point.[23] I invite you to experiment with any of these forms, using exchange—dialogue, discussion—as a way of preaching a narrative in which such exchange moves the story.

Fifth, when a narrative exhibits a tensive quality, try employing *tensive narrative in the sermon*. In this case, there are several possibilities. One would be to take a narrative whose meaning seems suspended between several different possible interpretations and explore each of those meanings in tandem in the sermon—without ever resolving the unresolved character of the story itself. For instance, suppose on the Fifth Sunday of Lent, B (or the Tuesday of Holy Week, A, B, and C) that you preach on John 12:20-33 (or 20-36)—a passage that begins with a narrative (vv. 20-22) and concludes with Jesus' speech (vv. 23-33). The story of the "Greeks" coming to see Jesus is wonderfully tensive.[24] What in the world does it mean? They approach Philip and say, "Sir, we wish to see Jesus." Philip reports this to Andrew, and then the two of them tell Jesus about the Greeks' request. Jesus proceeds to ignore entirely their request and launches into a speech. Why?

A sermon on this passage might explore the puzzle of its narrative portion. One structure for this exploration would be to consider several possibilities, giving equal credence to all of them, without showing favor for one or the other.

(1) The Greeks represent the church's mission to the Gentiles
after the resurrection and the universal nature of God's revelation

in Christ. "The whole world has gone after him," as the Pharisees say (v. 19). In this case, the passage asserts the inclusiveness of God's revelation and calls into question our tendency to restrict access to God through Christ.

(2) The eagerness of the Greeks to see Jesus contrasts with the Pharisees, whose negative concern has just been expressed in verse 19. The Pharisees represent the religious establishment and are a paradigm for how institutionalized religion always protects the status quo and resists change, even change initiated by God. The Greeks, on the other hand, offer a paradigm of openness.

(3) The Greeks fear they may not be accepted by Jesus, which Philip seems to think is a possibility since he first goes to Andrew. What makes Philip think that Jesus might not welcome this group? Has Philip failed to grasp the inclusiveness of Christ's ministry? Have we?

No matter how you might organize these options, there is a resolution available in the text. Leaving the precise role of the Greeks to one side, the passage implies that their advent occasions Jesus' declaration in verse 23: "The hour has come for the Son of Man to be glorified." In one way or another, the narrator claims the widespread interest in Jesus has brought about circumstances that involve Jesus' death and resurrection. The Greeks are the key to God's preparation for Christ's glorification. (See chapter 5).

Sixth, use the multiple layers of meaning in a narrative to *connect the message of a story with our own day*. Here preachers may want to offer brief summaries of historical ideas about the way the evangelist addressed the church in her or his own day through stories about Jesus. As I have said before, the story in chapter 9 offers the easiest glimpse into what might have been the struggle going on between the church and the synagogue when the Gospel was written. My suggestion is that preachers point out this second layer of meaning and then ask how a story's deeper layers might address us today. (For examples, see the discussions above.)

Finally, of course, preachers should *employ the symbolic meanings of narratives* whenever it is possible to do so. That is to say, there may be some passages in which symbolic references are so uncertain or unclear that they are better treated only in terms of their obvious meaning. For instance, the baptismal symbolism in the wedding at Cana (2:1-11) is so tenuous that it may be better to avoid such interpretations for homiletical reasons. (Of course, this is only my own view of the passage.) When the symbolic meaning of a narrative is comprehensible and relatively clear, preachers have a marvelous bridge to sermonic interpretation.

A case in point is foot washing (13:1-20 or 13:1-17, 31b-35, the lesson for Holy Thursdays all three years). Many interpreters believe that there are two meanings of Jesus' servant act. One is suggested in the exchange between Jesus and Peter in verses 6-11 and the other in Jesus' words in verses 12-20. The latter is called the *moral meaning*—that is, interpreting the foot washing as an example (v. 15) of how the disciples are to treat one another. The previous meaning is the "cleansing" of which Jesus speaks. Of course, these two are not necessarily mutually exclusive. The symbolic interpretation, however, invites us to understand Jesus' death as his servant act by which God cleanses us of the dirt of our alienation from our Creator. On Maundy Thursday we can offer a figure—an image—for what God is about to do through Christ on Good Friday.

A Sermon Example

The Johannine account of the call of the disciples is in 1:35-51; however, the lectionary divides this single narrative into two parts. The first part is verses 29-42, which links John the Baptist's witness (vv. 29-34) with the call of the disciples in verses 35-42. This reading is assigned for the Second Sunday after Epiphany, A. The second part—verses 43-51—is read a year later on the same Sunday, B. This second part continues Jesus' calling of disciples, this time entailing Philip who enlists Nathanael. The Lectionary unfortunately divides 1:35-51, which is a single unit.

What follows is a sermon prepared and first preached by my wife, Myrna, and revised slightly for use in this volume. My thanks to Myrna for allowing me to include it. The occasion is the Second Sunday after Epiphany, A, and the text is John 1:29-41. The sermon builds on the dynamic exchange between Jesus and the first disciples. It also digs out the deeper layer of meaning for the church today. Another feature of the sermon is the way it uses the words of both the disciples and Jesus within the narrative. The original title was "What Are You Looking For?"

～

On one of those rare occasions when I had the time, I went shopping for a new blouse. I entered a woman's clothing store anticipating they would have just what I was looking for. There before me were racks upon racks of blouses. Different styles, different colors. Some designed for leisure, some for formal dress. Some lacy and delicate, some heavy and warm.

I stood there among the racks, looking this way and that, fingering this material, holding up that blouse. "May I help you?" the kind sales woman asked. I told her I needed a blouse. "What kind of blouse are you looking for?" I paused, muttered something, and then declared, "I'll just look around a bit." The sales woman politely invited me to do so and offered her help anytime I might need it.

I looked through a few of what seemed to be thousands of blouses on display. The more I looked the less sure I was of what I wanted. Then despair set in. Men are so lucky—shirts are not so complicated. Finally, I left the store. Maybe I didn't really need a blouse after all. Maybe it was just my restlessness that led me to shop for one. I had one consolation amid my failure: I could always just wear a clerical shirt!

What are you looking for?

That's the question Jesus asked of those first curious disciples who began following him. They had been followers of John the Baptizer. But John declares of Jesus, "Here is the Lamb of God who takes away the sin of the world." And the two disciples hear John say he had seen the Spirit descend on Jesus.

So, that day when Jesus walked by, they followed him. They just up and leave John's side to follow this stranger. When Jesus notices them, he asks them, "What are you looking for?" They sound as dumbfounded as I did in the blouse shop! At a loss for words, they ask Jesus a question in return, "Where are you staying?" That's a strange—dare I say a dumb—way to respond: What's your address? What's your room number at the hotel?

What are you looking for? The question is too profound for those two disciples. Too searching a probe. It reaches deep into their lives—so deep that they cannot respond. They have only a vague sense of what it was they sought in following Jesus. Only a vague, ambiguous sense that there was something they needed. And Jesus might just offer it.

What are you looking for?

Christ goes on asking that question. What are we looking for? What are we seeking in life? What brings us to this place week after week in order to follow Jesus in our lives? And most of us are no better at answering the question than were those first two disciples. *We have no way of knowing what it is we are looking for.*

Imagine this. When you return to your home after this service, you find a huge box in front of your door. Suppose on the box is an announcement: "Contained in this box is what you have been looking for all your life." With that announcement, what would you expect to find in the box when you opened it? Would it be a bundle of cash? Happiness? Peace? Good health? Maybe a magic formula that would keep you forever young?

Freedom from suffering? Immortality? What would the box have to contain to satisfy what you want in life?

Let's face it! My confusion in the blouse shop is nothing compared with the confusion most of us experience regarding this question, *What are you looking for?* Some of us are at least vaguely aware of a need, a hole in our lives, a vacuum. But we may have no idea what it is that will fill that vacancy. We may shop around for some solution to that gnawing gap in our lives. But, if we do, we are then confronted with a bewildering display of options. Rack upon rack of different solutions to what we think is our need. Different styles of answers. Some lacy and fancy. Some plain and simple. Some fashioned for warm and comfortable weather. Some for the cold winters of life.

Which of this vast array of solutions would you find in that imaginary box left on your doorstep? Unfortunately, probably what we would say we would find in that box is not really what we need. Most of what we would like to find are probably only remedies for *symptoms* rather than our real need. That's certainly true of me. What I say I need is probably not what I really need. It is only a consequence of the much more significant and real need.

Many of us do not even know what it is we seek. We may think it is one thing, only to learn that it is another. Like children who think they need soda and candy, when they actually need vegetables.

- Some of us may think—as I am inclined to think—that we need money and security. Yet eventually in life we find those things aren't the real source of our discontentment.

- Sometimes we may think we seek only to be relieved of the pain, when actually it is the removal of the source of the pain that we need. We may think we seek an aspirin, when we actually need surgery.

- We all have our personal wants, desires, hopes, dreams, but is some thing else needed?

And the more we think about it, the more depressing it all becomes. That was the case with Joel, in an episode of the old TV series, *Northern Exposure*. Joel is faced with a crisis. He is the medical doctor forced to live in this isolated Alaskan village of Cecily. He hates it there. Resents having to be there. But he has found that he can at least survive by practicing medicine there. Yet now there is a terrible and unexplained epidemic of health in the village. No one is ill. There are no aches or pains—not even a common cold. Joel is bored silly. Not a single patient in weeks! He can't stand it!

He complains about the situation to his friend, Bernard. Bernard ventures the suggestion that Joel is going through an identity crisis. Without his work, Joel doesn't know who he is. Joel becomes depressed and mopes about. Now he is entirely immobilized by the experience. Bernard, of course, is right. What Joel is looking for is his work. The practice of his skill. He thinks that is what he needs. But Bernard makes him ask, *What are you looking for?* If the world were suddenly made healthy, where would he be?

Joel did not like to be asked that question. And a good many don't like to be asked, *What are you looking for?* That's the pinch! This question won't go away. It continues to haunt us. If we avoid it now, it will just challenge us again later. If we avoid it now, it will leap out at us from the shadows of some crisis in our lives. It will ambush us! When the troubles of life become too much for us to handle. When our lives are disrupted or threatened. Then, the question stares us in the face: *What are you looking for?*

What are you looking for? We face the question as individuals. But we also face it as a congregation. What are we looking for as a congregation of God's people in this place? Some would say we are looking for the return of the "good old days." The days when church attendance was better. The days when we were a small community, and everyone knew everyone else. The days when the church was at the center of people's social lives. But deep within ourselves some of us know that is not the solution.

Jesus asks the two disciples that terrible question: *What are you looking for?* They bumble about and ask, "Where are you staying?" Jesus responds, "Come and see!"

Come and see! Yes, Jesus invites these two befuddled fellows to follow him to the place where he is staying. But, of course, Jesus is saying more. He invites the two of them to trust him. He invites them to follow along with confidence that in doing so there is something important to be discovered.

Christ still asks us, *What are you looking for?* And most of us still haven't the foggiest notion. But Christ also still invites us to "Come and see!" Those words are a promise of sorts. Come, follow me, trust me, put your confidence in me. *Then you will see!* You will understand. You will perceive something more profound than all of your supposed wants and needs.

So, like those first disciples, we follow. We are not sure what we are seeking. We are not sure what we expect will happen. We have no idea what the results will be. But we trust the promise: Come and see.

Do you remember trying to learn to swim? Do you remember your teacher inviting you to "come and see" what the water was like? Your teacher promised you the water would hold you up. You'll float! But you can't believe it! I'll sink like a stone in that water! But you finally trusted the instructor's promise. You accepted the invitation. You entered the water, turned over on your back, extended your arms, took a deep breath, and let your feet leave the security of the bottom. What a surprise! The water did support your body! You didn't sink like a stone! You did float! *The promise was true!*

The promise is true! Come and see! The promise will sustain you. We still do not know what we are looking for. We still do not know where Jesus will lead us. We doubt that we will ever learn the backstroke. But *the promise is true!* Christ does sustain us in the dangerous waters of life.

Yet, there is still one more curious feature to our Gospel lesson for today. One of these two disciples was Andrew. Andrew does not know what precisely he is looking for in Jesus. Yet he trusts the promise and accepts the invitation to come with Jesus to see.

On this slim basis he does something more. Andrew shares the good news of Jesus. Shares it with his own brother—none other than Simon Peter. "We have found the Messiah." You must wonder at Andrew's brazen announcement. Does he have reason to make such a claim—the claim that in Jesus he has found the long-awaited agent of God? He doesn't even know actually what it is he seeks in this Jesus. He doesn't have anything to go on except John's witness and Jesus' promise: He will see. But he makes his announcement nonetheless.

It's interesting! Our Gospel lesson begins with John's witness, "Here is the Lamb of God!" And the lesson concludes with Andrew's witness to Peter, "We have found the Messiah!" Everything else happens within those bookends—bookends of witness.

We who are part of this congregation may not be sure *what we are looking for.* We don't know to what we will be led by following this Jesus. But we trust the promise. The promise that we will see! We will learn! We will grow!

But everything for us happens within the bookends of witness. Our trust in Christ's promise compels us to share the news: *We have found the Messiah!* If challenged, we cannot really substantiate our claim. If our claim is doubted, we cannot subdue doubt with evidence. We can only believe and entrust our lives to Christ. And because we have done so, we cannot be quiet about it. We find our brothers and sisters, wherever they may be. And we share the news: *We have found the Messiah!* Join us and *come and see!*

⁓

Discourse and Narrative

How are the narratives and the discourses related? In provocative ways, the Gospel juxtaposes Jesus' discourses and narratives of his actions. For example, when are we to understand a discourse passage as commentary on a previous narrative? In other words, getting some handles on the discourse passages requires us to have some sense of how the evangelist weaves narrative and discourse together and uses one to comment on the other.

Many scholars have noted and tried to analyze the structural relationship between discourse (or dialogue) and narrative in the Gospel of John. C. H. Dodd, the famous English New Testament scholar, years ago said this about the relationship of narrative and discourse in the first twelve chapters of John:

> The unit of structure is the single episode composed of narrative and discourse, both related to a single dominant theme. The incidents narrated receive an interpretation for their evangelical significance in the discourses; or, to put it otherwise, the truths enunciated in the discourses are given dramatic expression in the actions described. Act and word are one; this unity of act and word is fundamental to the Johannine philosophy. . . .[25]

Dodd helped me realize how often the Gospel interlaces narrative and discourse, so that the former often interpreted the latter. Moreover, he triggered my reflections on what this relationship means by speaking of the "unity of act and word." Recognizing that unity of narrative and discourse has some important implications for preaching. Still, Dodd's statement needs some qualification.

Dodd's view of the relation of narrative and discourse is echoed in the work of Mark W. G. Stibbe, a contemporary narrative critic of the Gospel: "John often has a narrative in the context of discourse material, which deepens the reader's interpretation of the details in the narrative sequences." Stibbe goes on to temper Dodd's broad generalization, however, by saying, "This relationship between the narration and dialogue is a feature of the gospel as a whole, though *the exact nature of the relationship between the two is used with variety.*"[26]

John's Variation of Speech and Action

The Gospel tends to relate its stories about Jesus with speeches, but the pattern is hardly fixed and inflexible. Rather, the text keeps readers off-balance by the way in which this relationship is varied. The chart below (which continues on the next page) may help us grasp the wider picture of the connections between speech and action.

STRUCTURE OF NARRATIVE AND DISCOURSE-DIALOGUE IN THE GOSPEL OF JOHN	
Narrative	**Discourse-Dialogue**
	Prologue (1:1-18), Narrator's Discourse
John's Testimony and Call of Disciples (1:19-51)	
	Wedding at Cana (2:1-11)
Cleansing of the Temple (2:12-23) Nicodemus Comes to Jesus (3:1-10)	
	God and the Son (3:11-21)
John the Baptist and Jesus (3:22-30)	
	The One from Above (3:31-36)
Samaritan Woman (4:1-42) Healing Official's Son (4:43-54) Healing of Man at Pool (5:1-18)	
	The Son and the Father (5:19-47)
Feeding the Multitude (6:1-15) Jesus Walks on Water (6:16-21) Crowd Comes to Jesus (6:22-24)	
	Bread of Life Dialogue (6:25-59)
Response to Jesus' Words (6:60-71) Jesus Goes to the Festival (7:1-13)	
	Festival Speech (7:14-24)
Division over Jesus (7:25-31) Failed Attempt to Arrest Jesus (7:32-36)	

continued on next page

continued from previous page

Conclusion of Festival and Division (7:37-52) [Woman Taken in Adultery (7:53—8:11)]	
	Light of World—Jesus from Above (8:12-30) Jesus and Abraham (8:31-59)
Healing of Man Born Blind (9:1-41)	
	Sheep and Shepherd (10:1-39)
Jesus Crosses Jordan (10:40-42) The Raising of Lazarus (11:1-44) The Plot to Arrest Jesus (11:45-57) Mary's Anointing of Jesus (12:1-8) The Plot to Kill Lazarus (12:9-11) The Entry into Jerusalem and Greeks Come (12:12-22)	
	The Hour Has Come (12:23-36)
The Unbelieving Response to Jesus (12:37-43)	
	Believing in Jesus (12:44-50)
The Foot Washing (13:1-11)	
	Servants, Love, and Betrayal (13:12-38) The Farewell Discourses (14:1—16:33) Jesus' Prayer (17:1-26)
The Passion Story (18:1—19:42) The Resurrection (20:1-29) First Conclusion (20:30-31) Resurrection Appearance at Sea (21:1-14)	
	Discussion with Peter (21:15-23)
Second Conclusion (21:24-25)	

Laying out the divisions between narrative and discourse dialogue helps us see several characteristics of John's use of these two. First, notice that narrative sections are more frequent than speech sections, but by virtue of their length chapters 14–17 adjust the sheer amount of speech as compared with narration. Second, there is no obvious and predictable pattern in the occurrence of the two kinds of material. Although my divisions are not intended to be exact, it is interesting to note how many times there are three narrative bits before a speech. There are three events in 1:19—3:10 before Jesus' first speech in 3:12-21. There are three narrative bits in 4:1—5:18, followed by the speech in 5:19-47. The same pattern is found again in 6:1-59 and 7:32-52. However, speech and act alternate in 3:1-21 and in 12:12—13:1. Furthermore, 10:40—12:22 is one long narrative section.

Stibbe is correct in saying that the relationship between speech and event is varied and entirely unpredictable. Still, we see the point that both Dodd and Stibbe claim with regard to discourse commenting on narrative. At least in the following instances, a preceding narrative segment is enriched by Jesus' words:

- 3:11-21 comments on the narrative of Nicodemus's visit with Jesus.
- 3:31-36 sheds light on the conversation about John the Baptist.
- 6:25-59 deepens the meaning of the feeding story.
- 10:1-39 comments on the religious leaders in the story of the healing of the man born blind.
- 12:23-36 seems somehow related to the Greeks' seeking Jesus.
- 12:44-50 heightens the tragedy of the unbelieving response to Jesus.
- 13:12-38 is no doubt a commentary on the foot washing.

Scattered throughout the stories, though, we find cases in which Jesus seems to anticipate an event that is yet to be narrated. Does the speech in 3:31-36, for instance, point ahead to the story of the Samaritan woman when Jesus speaks of himself as "above all" (see also 4:12)? Are the mentions of "life" and "eternal life" anticipations of the feeding story, as Jesus later interprets it in 6:25-59? If so, the feeding story is encased in two commentaries, one before and one after it.

Indeed, this is quite enough to suggest that the relationship between narrative sections and speech sections in the Gospel is very complicated and rich. Because of that relationship, when discerning readers try to interpret any one section, they need to keep in mind all that has come before it. This requirement has led to a critical analysis of John called "re-reading," meaning only that nearly every section requires us to reread other parts of the Gospel.[27]

What interests us the most is the dynamic unity of word and act, as Dodd correctly puts it. The complexity of the relationship suggests that word interprets act, and act interprets word, without either having priority over the other. Theologically this suggests that act and word are one and the same in their revelatory quality.

GOD'S REVELATION

ACT ◄─────────────────┴─────────────────► WORD

The incarnate Word reveals God both in what God does and says, and characters' responses to both Jesus' words and deeds express the human dilemma. Note, for example, how Jesus' speech sometimes evokes disbelief (for example, 6:60-71) and sometimes his actions evoke the same rejection (9:1-41). Word and deed are different forms of the same revelation, which leads us to the homiletical implications of this discussion.

Homiletical Implications

The first implication is a general one about preaching. The fundamental question is how story enacts words and words characterize actions. How do the two play off one another and enhance each other? We know that only when word and deed are one is Christian life fully integrated and authentic. That simple truism is rooted in God's revelation in which Christ was both word and deed in one single event—that he walked the walk as well as talked the talk. Because God's self-revelation is in the combination of word and deed, so those of us who are embraced by that revelation are called to combine the two in daily life.

Preachers, however, are interested in another implication of this unity of speech and action. Preaching is linked intimately with the preacher's life beyond the pulpit, where we demonstrate whether or not the word is embodied in action in our own lives. That too is a truism founded on the singleness of Christ's revelation of God.

Moreover, the preaching event itself is an expression of the relationship between word and act. The sermon is not just spoken words! All we have to do to realize this obvious truth is to listen to an audio tape recording of a good preacher whom we have seen and heard in the flesh. The disembodied words on the tape lack something vital to the sermon experience. The preacher's body is part of the sermon as much as her words are. How the preacher acts in the pulpit combines with his words to communicate through the whole person to the whole person. If we sometimes think that the words of the sermon are all that count and that gestures, body movement, and posture are only trimmings on the substance of the homiletical meal, we have vastly misunderstood a fundamental feature of preaching, namely, that the Word is proclaimed by one who embodies the word at that moment.

The second implication of the relationship of narrative and discourse has more to do with the interpretation of a Johannine text for preaching. What we have observed about the close relationship between narrative and discourse has some obvious consequences for our study of a Johannine text for preaching. First, clearly we need to pay close attention to the sections surrounding the passage on which we plan to preach, always keeping in mind the details of that chosen passage. This means reading several sections both before and after the passage, and sometimes even rereading the whole of the Gospel. Second, we look for connections between narration and speech. Is there something Jesus says before or after the passage that becomes enacted in narrative form? For instance, preaching on Mary's anointing of Jesus (12:1-8) on the Fifth Sunday of Lent, C, we might note that the "costly perfume made of pure nard" (12:3) looks back at the burial of Mary's brother Lazarus as well as points forward to Jesus' burial (19:38-40). Technically, the passages that point the reader ahead in the text are called *prolepses,* and those pointing back to earlier parts of the text are *analepses.*[28] Mary's act is both, for it stands between God's gracious act through Christ in raising her brother, on the one hand, and, on the other hand, Christ's own and supreme resurrection that makes life available to all who would believe.

A Sermon Example

Mary's anointing of Jesus (12:1-8) provides a good opportunity to explore homiletical possibilities with the interconnections of passages in mind. This is only a fragment of a sermon—the fragment that would set the direction and considerations of the sermon. It focuses on the interpretation of text, but at two places I have inserted a note in brackets about how parts of this fragment might be developed into a full sermon.

~

Do you remember being warned as a child about crossing the street? The standard warning was something like this: "Look both ways before crossing the street!" Oddly enough that parental command has become more useful than we ever imagined it would be. As drivers, we are constantly having to look both ways before pulling out onto a street. Checking the traffic before proceeding. One of my pet frustrations has to do with looking both ways in one of these large parking lots—like those at a mall. It seems you must look every direction at once. It's not easy to look both ways!

But this Gospel lesson asks us to do just that. Look both ways. Mary's anointing Jesus' feet is a beautiful gesture of love and affection. Exactly what does it mean? Especially, what does John mean by placing this story here—at this junction in Jesus' ministry? The whole of chapter 12 of John is like a hinge on a door. The entire Gospel story pivots at this point and turns in another direction. All the preceding chapters deal with Jesus' public ministry. After chapter 12, however, Jesus and his disciples retire into private. And chapters 13 through 17 have to do with Jesus' private ministry with his disciples.

So, what is the meaning of Mary's loving act? The "costly per-fume" Mary uses is like that used in the preparation of a body for burial. The body was covered with perfumes and other anoint-ments. Then it was wrapped in clothes. This was all a way of pre-serving the body and reducing the unpleasantness of its odor. Hence, when Mary uses a whole pound of this perfume, we can-not help but think of the preparation for burial. And that makes us look both ways.

First, we look back. Mary's act of anointing Jesus reminds us of her brother Lazarus. As you know, this Gospel lesson comes imme-diately after Jesus has rescued Lazarus from his tomb. Mary had seen her brother prepared for burial. Perfume, spices, all wrapped in cloth. And now she uses that same perfume to anoint Jesus' feet.

Mary's act of anointing is a profound gesture of gratitude. It is Mary's way of expressing her love and thanks to Jesus. The power of the act is found, then, in what it tells us about Mary. She and her sister Martha are portrayed as faithful disciples of their Lord. Mary's anointing is an act of a disciple's love for her master.

[How is gratitude part of our discipleship and by what acts do we express it?]

Mary's act asks us to look backward to Jesus' restoration of Lazarus. It also asks us to look forward. We know the rest of this story. Jesus is eventually arrested, tried, crucified, and then buried. In this pivotal spot in the story, John hints at what is coming in the future. Just as novel will sometimes gives us a hint in the middle of the story as to how the story will end. Mary is preparing Jesus for his burial. Perhaps unknowingly. Maybe not intentionally. But in the context of the whole of the Jesus story, this anointing antici-pates what's to come. It anticipates Jesus' death and burial.

Mary's act asks us to look both ways. By pointing us forward, it anticipates what Christ will do for us. Her anointing hints at the sacrifice Jesus will make for the sake of his friends—you and me. In that way, the act invites us to remember what God does for us in Christ. The love expressed in Jesus' laying down his life for people like us. The anointing reminds us of the love God has shown us.

That forward glance empowers us to look back. There we see what Jesus does for Mary and hence stirs in us the kind of grati-tude Mary expresses. Mary represents you and me. She does for us what we cannot do directly. She models for us a dimension of discipleship. We cannot anoint Jesus' feet. But we can serve those for whom he gave his life.

[Anointing as an image of loving service in our world today.]

༄

5

The King Is Enthroned:
The Johannine Passion Story

Passages from John's Passion story appear in the RCL on seven occasions: Good Friday (Years A, B, C), the Reign of Christ (Christ the King, B), Palm/Passion Sunday (alternate, B), Holy Saturday (A, B, C, alternate), the Resurrection of our Lord (Easter, A, B, C, alternate), Pentecost (A), Easter 2 (A, B, C), and Easter 3 (C). Four of the assigned passages report appearances of the risen Lord; one is the whole passion story (18:1—19:42), another concerns the trial before Pilate, and one the crucifixion story. Clearly the church uses Johannine passages for some of the high festivals of the church year—the Reign of Christ, Good Friday, Holy Saturday, the Resurrection of our Lord, the Easter season, and Pentecost, as well as others.

Yet the fourth Gospel presents a unique story of Jesus' arrest, trial, crucifixion, and resurrection. The pattern of the Johannine Passion story is the same as those found in the Synoptics, but, as usual, the fourth evangelist gives individual episodes peculiar twists. Most important is the fact that the meaning of Christ's death and resurrection appears to be one that is at least peculiarly emphasized if not entirely unique. For instance, Christ's kingship figures in the Johannine story in a slightly different way, even though we can identify the same theme in the accounts found in both Matthew and Luke.

The precise meaning of Christ's suffering, death, and resurrection in John remains ambiguous, however, which by now should not surprise us. Like those uses of tensive words, phrases, and narratives, the Gospel casts this climatic conclusion to the Jesus story in a puzzling and thought-provoking way. Preachers are not alone in wondering if the Johannine Passion account contains more than meets the eye. Scholarly interpreters have had the same experience in this section of the Gospel.

Our task in this chapter is difficult. We will first move through an overview of the Johannine narrative of Jesus' arrest, trial, and death in chapters 18 and 19. With that overview, it is necessary for preaching John that we come to some comprehension of the unique theological themes expressed within the Passion narratives proper. Then we will also approach the resurrection stories in the same manner, with an overview and then a discussion of themes.[1]

Arrest, Trial, and Crucifixion

The Johannine Passion story is told with drama and suspense. Some episodes seem a bit garbled, as we will see, while others are exquisitely told. The best way to gain an overview is to move through the Passion story, making some general observations about what is unique in John and what is shared with the Synoptic tradition.

An Overview of Chapters 18 and 19

The Arrest in a Garden (18:1-11)

In John, the account of Jesus' arrest emphasizes Jesus' control over his destiny—including two passages that are unique to the fourth Gospel. The first of these is Jesus' self-identification in 18:4-9, which begins with the narrator telling readers (in case it was not already clear) that Jesus knew exactly what was going to happen to him (v. 4). The simple dialogue between Jesus and "some soldiers together with police from the chief priests and the Pharisees" has tremendous results. Jesus asks whom they are seeking, and they reply, "Jesus of Nazareth." Jesus identifies himself as that person with the enigmatic "I am" (*egō eimi*—English translations usually supply the predicate, "he"). As if struck by lightning, the soldiers and police fall to the ground. If there is any doubt that this expression has reference to God in a unique and powerful way, this incident settles the matter. The power of the divine name bowls over the arresting squad. It is also clear to readers that Jesus has great power. Immediately the Passion story begins by stressing that Jesus willingly *allows* these events to transpire. He is by no means a victim of evil forces beyond his control.

The same point is communicated in 18:10-11. The Johannine narrative identifies Peter as the one who draws the sword, and it names the unfortunate slave, Malchus, upon whom Peter unleashes his wrath. Those two details are not as important as the words with which Jesus brings a halt to this silliness. He simply commands Peter to put away his sword, for Jesus has to fulfill God's will for his life. His reference to "the cup" *(to potērion)* reminds us of the words of Jesus in the Garden of Gethsemane (Matt. 26:39; Mark 14:36; Luke 22:42), but the fourth Gospel does not include a story of

Jesus' painful struggle to accept God's will for his life. The Johannine Jesus is so committed to the divine will that he never sways from his determination to fulfill it. Yet there is a striking similarity between the Synotics' accounts of Jesus in Gethsemane and John 12:27-28, in which Jesus is "troubled." But even in that passage Jesus suggests that he needs no confirmation from God, and the heavenly voice is for the crowd's sake, not his own (12:30).

Jesus remains in control throughout the whole arrest scene, knowing what is going to happen to him, committed to God's will, and allowing the events to transpire, although he has the power to prevent them. By giving the arrest story this particular spin, the Gospel alerts us to the role of Jesus throughout the Passion story.

Jesus' Religious Trial and Peter's Denials (18:12-27)

The religious trial in John is a bit confusing, as though something has been lost from the narrative. Some have proposed that the Gospel story has already narrated the religious trial in several parts, making the final hearing before the religious leaders unnecessary (see 5:18; 7:1, 32, 45-52; and 11:45-53). In a sense, the whole of the Gospel's story is told like a legal trial, with Jesus as the defendant and the religious leaders as the plaintiffs.[2]

Unlike the Synoptic accounts of the religious trial, Jesus never appears before the Sanhedrin (see Matt. 26:57-68; Mark 14:53-65; and Luke 22:54-71). Instead, we are told he is taken to Annas, "who was the father-in-law of Caiaphas, the high priest that year" (18:13; compare 11:48-53). The scene immediately shifts to Peter in the courtyard, and, when it returns to Jesus, he is being questioned by "the high priest" (18:19). When the questioning is over, we are told, "Then *Annas* sent him bound to Caiaphas, the high priest" (18:24). Again, the scene shifts back to Peter in 18:25-27, and 18:28 reports the end of the appearance before Caiaphas and Jesus' being taken to Pilate.

A few questions remain: (1) What does John mean by "high priest that year," and (2) Who is the high priest—Annas or Caiaphas—or does John call both of them "high priest?"[3] When "the high priest" mentioned in 18:19 questions Jesus, he responds by saying simply that he has taught openly and has nothing to hide. In verse 23 Jesus invites the chief priest to name the "wrong" he has taught or to explain why he is being punished. His posture toward this religious authority is straightforward and bold. He dares the establishment to find anything in his teachings that is offensive.[4]

John interlaces the religious trial with Peter's denial. Whereas in Mark and Matthew Peter's denials follow the religious trial, Luke reverses the order, telling us first of Peter's denials (Luke 22:54-62) and then his appearance before the Sanhedrin (22:63-71). John, however, has the camera moving back and forth between Jesus and Annas (18:12-14, 19-24, 28) and Peter in the courtyard (18:15-18 and 25-27). The story moves something like this:

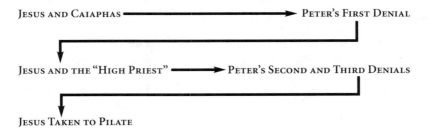

JESUS AND CAIAPHAS ────────────────► PETER'S FIRST DENIAL

JESUS AND THE "HIGH PRIEST" ──────► PETER'S SECOND AND THIRD DENIALS

JESUS TAKEN TO PILATE

Therefore, we see Jesus standing firm against the religious authorities while at the same time Peter is caving in out of cowardice. The "camera" moves back and forth to give us the full effect of the contrast, which gives preachers a marvelous opportunity to recreate the contrast through an interlacing of Jesus and Peter.

Jesus' Trial before Pilate (18:28—19:16)

In contrast to the rather confusing religious trial, this passage is one of the literary masterpieces of the Gospel. Raymond Brown has described the "inside-outside" structure of the passage. He finds seven scenes, which alternate between settings within the praetorium and in an outside court of the building. Moreover, Brown sees a chiastic structure in the seven scenes. Scenes one and seven, two and six, and three and five are parallel with one another, while the fourth scene is pivotal. He identifies the scenes as follows: (1) Outside. The religious authorities demand Jesus' death (18:28-32). (2) Inside. Pilate interrogates Jesus on the theme of kingship (18:33-38a). (3) Outside. Pilate can find no reason to convict Jesus and offers to release either him or Barabbas (18:38b-40). (4) Inside. The soldiers beat Jesus (19:1-3). (5) Outside. Pilate declares Jesus innocent (19:4-8). (6) Inside. Pilate and Jesus discuss power (19:9-11). (7) Outside. The crowd insists that Pilate hand Jesus over to be crucified, and he does so (19:12-16). Brown says of this in-and-out movement: "Pilate's constant passing from one setting to the other gives external expression to the struggle taking place within his soul, for his certainty of Jesus' innocence increases at the same rate as does the political pressure forcing him to condemn Jesus."[5]

As Brown observes, the character of Pilate is fascinating. The story makes perfectly clear that Pilate finds Jesus innocent of the charges against him but senses trouble if he does not do what the religious authorities want done. Discussions of Pilate often find him spineless and weak, while others see him as the politician trying to do the expedient thing for his career. Rudolf Bultmann makes a case for Pilate's representing the responses of governments to the revelation. The state "understands the concept of king only in the political sense." As such Pilate epitomizes the futility of a position of neutrality regarding Jesus.[6]

The contrast between the political leader and the crowd enhances the drama of Pilate's situation. Historically correct or not, John portrays the crowd (and the religious leaders) as vehement in their opposition to Jesus. They will not settle for anything but his execution. They represent out-and-out opposition, while Pilate symbolizes a subtler but no less vile opposition. He lacks the courage of his convictions and allows the situation to produce the opposite of his judgment. He is as aligned with evil as are Jesus' open opponents.

If Pilate is a fascinating character, Jesus is a figure of kingly strength. The heart and soul of this narrative is the question of kingly authority (18:33-37). Is the political system, represented by Pilate, the ultimate authority? Or is Jesus? John quietly reverses the roles of these characters. Before long you understand that Pilate is the one being judged, and Jesus is the judge. Political power stands over against spiritual power. One should not, however, take Jesus' words in 18:36 to mean that his lordship has nothing to do with worldly and political matters. The whole story reveals that the opposite is the case. "Not from this world" translates *ek tou kosmou* and uses that favorite Johannine preposition, *ek*. It often implies the source of one's being—the roots out of which something comes. Jesus is saying that his authority comes from another source outside this world. His confrontation with the state in the form of Pilate, however, suggests that this kingship confronts, judges, and calls into question all political systems (including our own).

Jesus' kingly stature is evident in this narrative, both by his manner of dealing with Pilate and the contrast between the two characters. In order to strengthen the narrative's royalty theme, the evangelist or the Johannine tradition before the evangelist integrated the "flogging" of Jesus (19:1-3) with Pilate's interrogation of him. While the Gospels of Mark and Matthew include this brief episode after Jesus was sentenced but before he is crucified (Mark 15:16-20; Matt. 27:27-31), the fourth Gospel wants readers to see it within the context of the question of "who's the real king?" Through it all, Jesus is again in control of his destiny. He allows Pilate and the religious authorities to have their day, but he holds ultimate power.[7]

The Crucifixion (19:17-37)

John's account of Jesus' execution follows the traditional pattern that arose in early Christian tradition but with an abundance of Johannine peculiarities. The movement of the crucifixion scene goes something like this:

Crucifixion (vv. 17-18)

 Inscription (vv. 19-22)

  Seamless Tunic (vv. 23-24) *(Prophecy fulfillment)*

   Words to Mother and Beloved disciple (vv.25-27)

    Word: "I thirst" (vv. 28-29) *(Prophecy fulfillment)*

     Word: "It is finished" (v. 30a)

      Death and Handing Over Spirit (30b)

       Piercing Jesus' Side (vv. 31-34)

        True Testimony (v. 35)

         Prophecy Fulfillment (vv. 36-37)

The climax of the narrative is Jesus' declaration that he has completed his mission and his handing over "the spirit" (v. 30). The story moves predictably toward that climax, but what follows it is somewhat unusual. The spear thrust seems somehow to interpret the meaning of the death and to support that interpretation as a "true" statement. Prophecy fulfillment is common in the crucifixion scenes in the Gospels. John's footnoting of events with Hebrew scripture citations, however, is unique to this Gospel: Jesus' seamless tunic (vv. 23-24, citing Ps. 22:18), his thirst (v. 28, citing Ps. 69:21), and the truth of the witness that none of Jesus' bones were broken (v. 36, apparently combining Ps. 34:20 and Exod. 12:46 with Num. 9:12) and his side pierced (v. 34, citing Zech. 12:10). Both Psalms 22 and 69 are cited in Mark and the parallels in Matthew (see Mark 15:34 and 36), but the fourth Gospel refers to other parts of these Psalms. The early Christians were convinced that Jesus' death could and should be understood in terms of themes in the Hebrew scriptures. The inclusion of the citations in John 19:36 and 37 is another matter, however. The use of the reference to Zechariah in verse 37 is unique to John, and those suggested in verse 36 have to do with the Passover lamb. The latter reinforce a Johannine theme that we will explore below.

The implication of these citations is that Jesus is fulfilling God's mission for him. Thus, the climatic words of verse 30 are very appropriate: "It is finished" or completed *(tetelestai)*. Most important, however, is Jesus' kingly posture throughout the crucifixion. He carries his own cross to the site of his execution. His tunic is seamless, suggesting royalty and wholeness. He says he is thirsty only to fulfill Scripture and not to fill a human need. There is no indication of his suffering, no words of pain or pleas to God (contrast Mark 15:34). His executioners dare not mock him (contrast, for example, Luke 23:35-37) because of his noble posture. His last act is to care for his mother and establish a new community of followers. He does not die but freely "hands over (the) spirit" *(paredōken to pneuma)*. English translations, unfortunately, substitute "his" for the article *to*, "the." As he told his followers, "No one has greater love than this, to lay down one's life for one's friends. You are my friends. . . ." (15:13-14). He now does this very thing—out of love, Jesus willingly "lays down" his life.

Ironically, the verb "to hand over" *(paradidōmi)* has been used throughout the Passion story to speak of the authorities committing Jesus to the process of trial (18:2, 5, 30, 35, 36; 19:11, 16). Jesus has been the object of the verb in all these references, but now he is the subject of the verb, not the leaders of evil, and the object of the verb is his own (or God's) "spirit." Jesus takes command of his death and gives up life willingly. The reference of the expression, "the spirit" *(to pneuma)*, has been debated. Does it refer to Jesus' life-spirit or to the Holy Spirit. Most argue, of course, that it refers to the former and means simply that Jesus died; others however have tried to maintain that it implies the gift of the Spirit, which will be explicitly given to the disciples in 20:22. It would be perfectly harmonious with the use of language in this Gospel that the word "spirit" evokes both possibilities without resolution. In giving over his life-spirit to God, he gives the Spirit of God over to the world.

The enigmatic story of the piercing of Jesus' side and the blood and water that flowed out is difficult to interpret. (See chapter 3 above.) It clearly stands in a key position, suggesting that it is an interpretation of Jesus' death—an impression enhanced by the narrator's comment in 19:35. In that comment, however, we are not sure what the unnamed witness "sees." Is it the whole crucifixion scene or only the piercing of Jesus' side? Whichever it is, the "blood and water" *(haima kai hydōr)* are surely important. On one level, they mean most certainly that Jesus died, which is important enough in itself. However, if the Gospel was written or revised when the Johannine church struggled with those who denied the physicality of Christ and his death (see also 1 John 2:22; 5:6), it may have been important to put to rest any idea that Jesus only "appeared" to die.

On another level, the blood and water may represent the gifts bestowed as a result of Jesus' revelation and especially his death. What Jesus has just "finished" is God's mission to make love and redemption a reality in this world. The Greek word for blood is used in John 1:13, where it means nothing more than human life. In 6:53-56, however, it takes on special meaning as Jesus' human life by which we are given eternal life. "Water" is more often used as a symbol of the new life God offers in Christ (for example, 3:5-8; 4:10-14). The symbolism may be more complex, but it may be enough to say that the blood and water from Jesus side, while being evidence of the reality of his death, also indicates that his life is the source of new and eternal life. The cross represents the whole of God's self-revelation in Christ by means of which humans are reconnected with their Creator and are given an entirely new kind of existence, which was what God had always intended life should be.

Of course, the whole crucifixion scene takes place under the placard Pilate has placed on the cross, "Jesus of Nazareth, the King of the Jews," written in Hebrew, Latin, and Greek (19:19-22). The story focuses on this sign with a clarity and emphasis not found in Matthew 27:37 and Mark 15:26, where it is the charge against him, or in Luke (23:38), where it is mentioned almost incidentally as part of the mockery. In John, Pilate's placard is ironic. Pilate means it to mock the Jews; he hopes to get back at them for forcing him to have Jesus crucified. Unwittingly, Pilate announces the meaning of the cross to the whole world—in each of the three languages spoken in the Greco-Roman world. Christ is indeed enthroned as King in his death.

The Burial (19:38-42)

This brief episode is marked with several distinctively Johannine features. First, suddenly Joseph of Arimathea, who is a "secret disciple," pops up along with Nicodemus, whom we know from earlier accounts (3:1-9 and 7:50-52). Nicodemus's association with another who has not made his faith public stimulates the possibility that he too was such a disciple. While the Synoptics mention Joseph, there he is called a "disciple" (Matt. 27:57) or one who was "looking for the kingdom" (Mark 15:43; Luke 23:50-51). Does the reference to a "secret disciple" mean that in the evangelist's day there were believers who were afraid to make their confession public? We cannot know for sure, but it is interesting that the Gospel never really condemns such a secret faith. It poses the question of the possibility of "secret discipleship" today.

In the Gospel of John, Joseph and Nicodemus prepare the body for burial, so that such a task is not the motivation for the women coming to the tomb on the first Easter morning as it is in Mark 16:1. The Synoptics each say that Joseph wrapped the body in cloth but not that he anointed it. The anointing reminds readers of Mary's act in 12:1-8. The "new tomb" takes on special meaning, so the narrator specifically refers to "a new tomb in which no one had ever been laid" (19:41). In the Johannine context, the narrator wants us to understand it was a tomb "fit for a king."

Jesus moves through each of the stages of his arrest, trial, and execution with a royal dignity, for by his death he is "lifted up"—enthroned as the supreme one.[8] The image of Jesus in these chapters is such that we might even raise a question about calling it a "passion" narrative. The emphasis is far less on how much Jesus suffered than it is on what he revealed in his glorification. This leads us to consider the major themes in the stories in chapters 18 and 19.

Themes in the Johannine Passion Narrative

Tracing the narrative in chapters 18 and 19 has already stressed what is likely the most important Johannine theme in the Passion story, namely, his *enthronement as king*. There remains little to say about this, except to explicate what might be the meaning of kingship in the Gospel of John. This is necessary, of course, since Christ inverts kingship into servanthood and replaces sovereignty with love. Note, however, that John has almost nothing to say about the "kingdom of God" but a lot to say about the "king." The phrase "kingdom of God / Heaven," which dominates the Synoptic accounts of Jesus' teaching and preaching, is mentioned only in John 3:3 and 5. "Kingdom" *(basileia)* occurs in John only in those two references to the kingdom of God and three times in Jesus' discussion with Pilate (18:36). What does it mean that John has redirected attention away from the kingdom to the king?

Terms of the Passion

At this point we should pause to consider the various expressions of Jesus by which he speaks of his trial and execution, and indeed the fourth evangelist packs the Passion story with just such theological themes. Moreover, the Gospel's narrative anticipates the climax of the story through a number of key expressions. Unlike the Synoptics, Jesus does not make three (or four) predictions of the suffering the Son of Man must endure. Rather, Jesus speaks of his death and resurrection with terms that remain somewhat vague.

The Hour

Probably the most evident of these expressions by which Jesus points us ahead to his arrest, trial, crucifixion, and resurrection is the enigmatic *hōra*. The word is used twenty-five times in the Gospel, of which eight are simply references to the hour of the day—clock time (see 1:39; 4:52; 5:35 [translated "a while" in NRSV]; 11:9; 19:14, 27). The others, however, seem to speak of a crucial and decisive time. In many cases it refers explicitly to the time when Jesus is arrested, crucified, and raised from the dead; however, in some cases, the reference is to the crucial time of others (for example, 16:2, 4, and 32).

The use of the term *hōra* to indicate the decisive time for Jesus' revelation is what interests us. Sometimes Jesus speaks of the eschatological time as the "hour" (4:21, 23; 5:25, 28). Yet on several occasions he says that his "hour has not come," indicating that the occasion of his revelation is in the future. Examples of these include Jesus' reluctance to reveal himself at the wedding in Cana (2:4) and times when his opponents cannot arrest him because the right time has not yet come (7:30; 8:20). Then dramatically for the first time Jesus declares, "The hour has come for the Son of Man to be glorified" (12:23), and from that point on in the narrative the conclusive period of time is spoken of as present or near (see 12:27; 13:1; 16:25, 32; 17:1).[9]

The importance of this expression is at least threefold. First, Jesus' "hour" proves to be that series of events that we call the Passion and resurrection, meaning that in those events God accomplishes the divine purpose through Jesus. While the Gospel's earlier narratives are clearly important, they exist in anticipation of the full revelation of Christ in his death and resurrection. Second, there is an inherent determinism in the use of this term, as if the time is set, the moment fixed, and it cannot be altered. Third, if scholars are correct, this use of the word "hour" may well have its root in the notion of the "day of the Lord" in Hebrew scriptures and especially the prophets (see Isa. 2:2-20; Ezek. 30:3; Joel 1:15; Amos 5:18-20; and Zeph. 1:7-18). If that is the case, then Jesus' day is the moment when God acts decisively in human history to right wrongs and bring justice. It links God's revelation in Christ with the notion of God's crucial acts in Israel's history.

Preachers recognize in this use of "hour" the basic idea of *kairos* as lived time as opposed to chronological time. In that sense it refers to the moment of encounter with God that calls us into question and evokes decision. In Johannine thought Jesus' "hour" is both his own kairotic moment and the decisive moment in time for all humanity.

Glorification

The concept of "glory" *(doxa)* is indispensable in the fourth Gospel and appears at least fifteen times. The verb, "to glorify" *(doxazō)*, is even more frequent, appearing approximately twenty-two times. Most important about these words is the fact that Jesus often speaks of his death and resurrection as his "glorification." The first ten verses of Jesus' prayer in chapter

17 are an excellent example of this use of glorification. (See chapter 6.) Note that Jesus prays that God will "glorify" him and that he will "glorify" God (17:1). Jesus has glorified God already in his work and words (17:4), and now he asks that God glorify him "in your presence with the glory that I had in your presence before the world existed" (17:5). What does glory and glorification mean in John?

To begin with, glory means above all the presence of God and as such is rooted in the Hebraic concept of *kabōd*, meaning glory or honor. God's glory in Hebrew scriptures is synonymous with the divine presence (see Isa. 6:1-3). If this relatively simple understanding of glory is what is present in the Johannine language and thought, it means that "glorification" is simply synonymous with God's presence. The cross and the resurrection, then, glorify God in that they reveal the divine presence in these events, and they glorify Christ insofar as they demonstrate God's presence in Christ.[10]

Social studies of the Palestinian world of the first century c.e. have stressed the importance of "honor and shame." Honor in this sense is simply reputation, and it comes when the public bestows it upon a person; that is, it is ascribed. Honor and shame functioned in the Greco-Roman world as a primary value. Furthermore, family members were responsible for upholding the honor of their family. If we read John's use of glory and glorification in terms of social honor and shame, they become even clearer. As God's Son, Jesus glorifies God and thus ascribes honor to his Father. God glorifies Jesus by attributing honor to him, especially in the cross and resurrection.[11]

We are safe, I think, in holding that both of these views of glory and glorification are contained in the Johannine use of the terms. God and Christ possess the highest of honor in an honor-shame society, and that fact is expressed any time God reveals the divine self. What we need to note with the greatest of care is the fact that God's presence and honor are expressed in the blood of the cross. The most shameful death declares the honor of both God and Christ. Cultural values are turned upside-down.

Lifted Up

We have already explored the meaning of this expression in chapter 3 and noted its dual meaning. We can then summarize the use of this expression in the fourth Gospel in a few words. The Greek verb *hyspoō* occurs five times in John (3:14 [twice]; 8:28; 12:32, and 34). In each case, it carries the ambiguity we have noted above, namely, both an enthronement and a crucifixion. As strange as it is that Jesus and God should be honored by Christ's shameful execution as a common criminal, it is equally strange that a crucifixion should function as the empowerment of a royal figure. This raises the question, What kind of king is this Jesus?

What Kind of King?

This emphasis on Christ's supremacy arises from Johannine theology. Jesus is God's own Word enfleshed, so that God's kingdom is Christ's kingdom. The Revealer is more than a medium of the revelation; he is himself the revelation.[12] His presence is God's presence bringing the divine rule into the world. "Eternal life" is the essence of that divine rule—or "better life." There is some truth to the idea that John substitutes "eternal life" for "kingdom of God." Perhaps this is so because the Johannine tradition wanted to speak less about God's domination (as in kingship) than about God's gift of life as the Creator intended life to be. For that reason, a king enthroned by being lifted up on the cross is a peculiar kind of king. He is a king who rules not by sheer force (as did the Romans) but by suffering love. Unlike worldly kings and rulers, God has no interest in coercing humans, compelling us to obey. Instead, the "kingship" of Christ through crucifixion is supremacy through love.

The meaning of John's passion narrative is therefore above all *divine love*. One is hard-pressed to discern in John's passion narrative a kind of atonement through ritual sacrifice. Unlike Mark, for instance, there is no talk of "ransom" (Mark 10:45). Nor is there mention of "expiation" as in 1 John 2:2 and 4:10, as well as Romans 3:25. The absence of the institution of the Lord's Supper means that Jesus never says his body and blood are given for the salvation of the world (Matt. 26:26-28; Mark 14:22-24; Luke 22:19-20; 1 Cor. 11:23-26). These references all appeal to Jewish sacrificial worship as metaphors for understanding the meaning of Jesus' death, and all are missing from John. If we want to speak in a Johannine sense of Jesus' "sacrifice," we speak of a "personal" sacrifice, not a cultic one. Even so, you have to wonder if sacrifice is an appropriate word. Jesus never speaks of his death on the cross as a sacrifice but always as a "glorification." Jesus does not make a sacrifice when he "lays down" his life for his "friends." It is less a sacrifice than an act of love.[13]

Too often, I fear, the church tends to read the Johannine passion narrative through the lens of Paul and the Synoptics and in doing so misses the radical meaning of the cross in John. The simplest way of speaking of the Johannine theology of the cross is to say that in his glorification Christ reveals the message of 3:16: "God so loved the world. . . ." Therefore, the friendship theme mentioned in the previous chapter and found in John 15:12-15 (see the next chapter) offers the best way of explicating how John represents Jesus' death.[14] In 12:32, Jesus says, "And I, when I am lifted up from the earth, will draw all people to me." That means the power of God's love is unleashed in the world, and it is irresistible in its attraction. Christ's kingship is the preeminence of love, and as such is hardly kingship as understood in John's day or ours.

A New Family and New Passover

This is the place, finally, to consider the unique episode in which Jesus acknowledges his mother and makes her the mother of "the beloved disciple"[15] and that disciple the son of his mother (19:25b-27). There are in this act at least two (and perhaps more) layers of meaning, as is so often the case in Johannine narratives. On the surface, Jesus sees to it that his mother is cared for after his death. If his death leaves his mother without the care of a male in the society of the time, her life would be unbearable. Unfortunately, women had to be linked with a man who could support them. If Jesus had performed that service during his lifetime, he now gives it over to the disciple closest to him, the unnamed and mysterious disciple whom he loved.

Below the surface, however, there is another meaning to this act. Jesus' mother and the beloved disciple represent the elements in a new community. What Jesus does in commending his mother to the beloved disciple and him to her is to form a community of those who stand at the foot of the cross. (See chapter 1.) In other words, this is the Johannine story of the formation of the church. In his final act before his death, Jesus fulfills what is said of him in the prologue to the Gospel: "But to all who received him, who believed in his name, he gave power to become children of God" (1:12). Here he gives the beloved disciple and his mother power or authority *(exousia)* to create a *koinonia* of believers who would continue the revelation he had brought to the world. In the light of our discussion here, the community formed by Christ is one bound together in mutual love, even as he had asked that they "love one another . . . just as I have loved you" (13:34-35). The church is then the community of love that continues God's revelation in Christ. It is the church within which the divine love is concretely enacted and through which that love is brought into the world. (See the discussion of John 17 in the next chapter.)

Another dimension to the Johannine passion narrative that is widely acknowledged is the emphasis on Jesus as the new *Passover lamb.* The evidence for this emphasis is found in several facts, the most important of which is that the Johannine story of Jesus' crucifixion is one day earlier than in the Synoptics. Jesus is crucified at exactly the same time the lambs are being slaughtered for the Passover meal after sundown the same day.[16] The narrator interprets the fact that Jesus' legs are not broken but his side pierced as a suggestion of the prohibition that the bones of the Passover lamb are not to be broken (Exod. 12:46 and Num. 9:12). Hence, it is most likely that John the Baptist's reference to Jesus as the "lamb of God" (John 1:36) has in mind the Passover lamb rather than a sacrificial lamb.[17]

What might the Gospel mean by aligning Christ with Passover and the lamb eaten at the Passover meal? The simplest answer would be that the Gospel presents God's revelation in Christ as a *new Passover.* Much as God liberated the Israelites from slavery by means of the first Passover, now God liberates humans from slavery to alienation and falsehood through Christ. God does battle once again to free humans from oppression, and this liberation is a concrete expression of God's love. Moreover, being embraced by the divine love frees us from the oppression of lovelessness and isolation. This interpretation of the Passover liberation does not diminish the political and social dimensions of such liberation. Indeed, the Johannine community may have read this account of Christ's death within the context of their bondage within a society that ostracized and demeaned them. They knew the reality of oppression and through this story were grasped by God's freeing love.

The enthronement of the king is not really an enthronement of a ruler as we usually think of it. It is rather the glorification of Christ and God and the emergence of the reality of the divine love for all the world and its inhabitants. Since the "world" was in the grips of evil and alienated from God, God's Revealer-Agent, Jesus, is arrested, tried, and put to death. However, his revelation is that the world is in the hands of a Creator who prizes humans and their lives. Hence, through the most vivid expression of the evil of the world—the execution of God's agent—God's radical goodness is made known. Ironically, God reveals the divine self through an act perpetrated by the worst of the forces opposed to God.

Homiletical Implications

How does this help us preachers when a passage from John's Passion story appears in the RCL? The themes explicated above are not to be taken as topics for individual sermons or to be imposed upon the readings. Rather, I hope these themes can enable us to deal with individual passages in chapters 18 and 19 by seeing how the assigned lesson might relate to what seem to be John's primary emphases in the Passion narrative.

Actually, the RCL offers portions of John 18 and 19 on only three occasions. It assigns 18:33-37 as the Gospel lesson for the Reign of Christ, Year B. Since these verses involve the discussion of kingship by Pilate and Jesus, this is a good opportunity to ask what kind of king the Gospel of John portrays. Moreover, it raises the issue of power and authority. Our contemporary culture tends to emphasize physical force as the expression of power and absolute dominance as the character of authority. It is for the most part the very sort of power and authority Pilate assumes to be true. Placing the two side by side, as the text does, sheds light on the nature of our understandings of power and begins to deconstruct them in favor of Christ's power and authority.

Thanks to the RCL, Good Friday is the occasion for dealing with the Passion narrative as a whole (18:1—19:42, A, B, C). Preachers have several possibilities. One is to speak on the drama of the whole narrative, the way it flows from event to event, and the final tragic but penultimate conclusion in Jesus' burial. Another option is in many ways easier, namely to select one of the episodes as the subject of a sermon, for example, the arrest or the religious hearing and Peter's denials. If you have a Holy Saturday service, the assigned alternate lesson for all three years is the Johannine crucifixion story (19:38-42). Again, one can tackle the whole of the story or focus on a single part, such as Jesus' commendation of his mother to the beloved disciple and he to her, or on the dramatic and triumphant words, "It is finished."

Understanding John's Passion narrative reflects light back over the whole of the Gospel. For instance, in the Passion story one finds the clue to what Jesus means by "lifted up," what exactly "glorification" means, and how Jesus' death completes his ministry. Having read the Passion story also helps us to understand what Jesus means in much of his discussion with Nicodemus (3:1-17 on Lent 2, A; Trinity Sunday, B; Holy Cross Sunday, A, B, C; and 3:14-21 on Lent 4, B). Likewise, it enlightens 4:5-42, assigned on Lent 3, A, and the whole of the bread of life discourse on Propers 13, 14, 15, and 16, B, and Thanksgiving, C. Study of the Passion narrative is crucial to the whole task of preaching John, whatever the assigned Johannine text might be.

Sermon Examples

On the Trial

The following is an adaptation of a sermon I preached in chapel at Candler School of Theology, soon after joining the faculty of Emory University. The occasion was the celebration of Christ's Reign. The sermon attempts to replicate the dialogical form of the Jesus-Pilate discussion—the assigned text for Reign of Christ, B (John 18:33-37)—and to give expression to my understanding of Christ's authority and rule. The second assigned reading was Revelation 1:4b-8, and it is cited toward the end of the sermon. The sermon is entitled, "Who's in Charge Here?"

◦﹋◦

In the last few months, since coming to this place, I've been asking a lot of questions.

As a new member of the faculty—one of the new kids on the block—I've had a great deal to learn about this institution and its operation. Who's the right person to see about this? To which office do I go for that? Who's in charge of this matter? Who's responsible for that situation?

I've been seen wandering aimlessly through the halls in search for such-and-such office. I've spent time searching the list of administrators, asking ceaseless questions of colleagues, and especially my friend and secretary, Janet Gary. But this is a friendly place, and I have received gentle and courteous guidance.

Still, with all of my inquiries, I have yet to find out who's in charge of Emory campus parking!

Who's in charge here?

Reading John's story of Jesus' trial before Pilate may raise that question. You may get the feeling that it is not at all clear just who is trying whom. Is Pilate really in charge? And Jesus the accused? Or, is it Jesus who's in charge? And Pilate who's on trial? For me, at least, the lines begin to blur just a little. Then disappear entirely. And Pilate himself even seems to wonder, *Who's in charge here?* He seems to say, let's cut to the core and settle the issue now. (Jesus' responses are in italics.)

Are you a ruler of some kind—Do you aspire to political office?

Do you think I am, or is that someone else's idea?

Ah, come on now—I'm no religious fanatic! It's your own people who brought you here? What in the world have you done?

My dominion is not from this realm. If it were, there would be fighting. But my dominion is not from this realm.

Ah, ah! So you do have a dominion! You are some sort of ruler, huh?

You say so! But I came to witness to the truth. Those who belong to the truth listen to me.

Who's in charge here?

I'm nearly as confused as Pilate. Almost as lost as the Roman. How about a straight answer to a simple question: *Are you a ruler? Are you in charge here?* Pilate's question is reasonable. An important query. He'd make a good theological student. He knows the right questions to ask.

Like Pilate, we too may sometimes ask that question, *Who's in charge here?* We really do need to get this straightened out! It can make a lot of difference. It makes a lot of difference to me now. Trying to find my way around this school. *Who's in charge here?*

Six months ago it was even more important. Myrna and I held that letter in our hands—that final word of the long interview process. Dean LaGree's invitation to me to join this faculty. And we struggled to make that decision.

Who's in charge here? Our own ambitions, our own desires, our own plans for the future? Or, is there something else or someone else in charge here? It makes a lot of difference who's in charge.

And, with me, some of you may wonder each day who's in charge. Especially when we consider the daily news. Are the special interest groups in charge? Or the drug cartels? Or the empowered affluent? Do the lobby groups make our legislation or does Congress? Are the chaotic forces of violence in charge of our cities and our world? Or will the forces for order, justice, and peace have the final word in all of this?

Order and peace seemed in charge that lovely October morning as I rode to work. The sun was bright, the air warm, the foliage brilliant green. I was delighted to be in Atlanta. But then the message of that billboard devastated my serenity and threatened order. A seemingly simple message but a frightfully ambiguous one: *"The Bull is taking charge!"*

"The Bull is taking charge?" What Bull? Which Bull? How's it taking charge? My mind filled with possibilities, none of which I wanted to believe. Then I realized that it was a beer advertisement. But that hardly calmed my anxiety. The words linger on in my mind and the possibility still haunts me: *"The Bull is taking charge!"*

Who's in charge here? Or, is no one in charge? Is the Bull of chaotic nothingness the C.E.O. of this world? Is life utterly without an ultimate rule or final order? Absolute disorder, anarchy, chaos!

Who's in charge here? We want to know—we need to know: Who's in charge, if anyone? Is it any different for us Christians? Is it as problematic for those of us who cling to the Gospel? Don't we already know? Doesn't our faith affirm the sovereignty of God? Don't we claim it is Christ who's in charge? The incarnate Word of God. The one through whom everything was made and without whom nothing was made that was made. The Christ of God.

And Pilate—this puny, arrogant representative of the Roman Empire. The Word of God made flesh and the enfleshment of Caesar in this one place. Don't we know who's in charge? Don't we know that it is Christ who judges Pilate, and not Pilate Christ? Yet, the powers-that-be hand Jesus over to be executed. Pilate actually seems to have thought Jesus was innocent. In the end, however, he caves in. And this one—said to be a pretend ruler—was put to death. Yet in the end, Pilate is not even sure that he is in charge. The best he can muster out of this whole nasty affair is that sign hung from the cross: King of the Jews. *"What I have written, I have written,"* he insisted. His last and only fragment of dignity. His sole act of defiance against the forces that had their way.

So, Who's in charge here? Do we really know? Are we all that certain? The king—our ruler—is crucified. Executed. Lifted up on a cross. If he is king, his throne is a cross. If he is the ruler, his reign is a ghastly affair. If he is in charge, his dominion is the place of the skull. Indeed, his dominion is not of this world! A strange dominion! A strange dominion, indeed!

But Sarah's dominion seemed a strange one, too. She stood there at the bedside of one of her most beloved parishioners. And she watched the cancer win the last decisive battle. He had put up a gallant struggle. And mustered a courageous defense. But now the dreaded cancer would have its way with him. The cancer was in charge here. Its judgment final. Its verdict without appeal.

Sarah saw the excruciating pain, the terrible torment. She heard the last sobs, the last gasp. And there was silence. . . . All she could do was touch—oh, so gently touch—the still trembling arm. Somewhere among the tubes and needles, her fingertips touched his flesh. All she could do was mutter a half-audible prayer—maybe more for her own sake than for his.

All she could do was to be there—to be a presence—a presence of the congregation, a presence of Christ's care. All she could do was to be present to share a little of the suffering, to be vulnerable to another's pain, to love.

Who's in charge here?

Christ—in charge through simple presence? Christ—in charge through helplessness? Christ—in charge through broken love? Through vulnerability? Through suffering care? Who's in charge here? The One who is, who was, and is to come? The one who loves us and has freed us to make a dominion of lovers and liberators?

Is that any way to be in charge? Maybe if there were powerful visions. Perhaps a show of force. Surely a revelation of strength.

If only there were a torrent of fire to purge the evil.
    But instead there's only a splash of water.
If only there were powerful armies to right the wrong.
    But instead there are only crumbs of bread.
If only there were potent rulers to reign in his name.
    But instead there are only sips of wine.

Because . . . because his dominion is from another realm. Another realm. Another rule. ⁓

On the Crucifixion

The following is only a sermon sketch, developed for a Good Friday service in which the whole of the Johannine Passion story (18:1—19:42) has
been read. It focuses on 19:26-27, Jesus' words to his mother and the
Beloved disciple. The form of the sermon might be called "a ladder" in the
sense that it moves through a number of succeeding steps in exploring the
meaning of these words and comes finally to the meaning with which the
preacher wants to leave the congregation. This fragment was inspired by a
sermon I heard my friend, colleague, and co-author, Robert G. Hughes,
preach for a chapel service at the Lutheran Theological Seminary in
Philadelphia several years ago. You may not blame Hughes for my weaknesses in trying to develop the sermon as he did his.

～

"*Woman, here is your son.*" "*Here is your mother.*" With these
words Jesus commends his mother to the care of the unnamed
disciple. And he commends the disciple to his mother. We don't
know the identity of this disciple. In several places in the Gospel
of John, he is called simply, "the disciple whom Jesus loved." Nor
is his mother named Mary in the Gospel of John as she is in
Matthew and Luke. She is always referred to only as his mother.

What do you suppose Jesus had in mind when he uttered these
words from the cross? Here he is, suspended on the cross, suffering the torture of crucifixion. Here he is humiliated by being
made a public spectacle. Sweat pouring off his body in the intense
heat of the day. Flies swarming around his head. Blood dripping
down from his head. And increasingly finding it harder and
harder to speak. His posture on the cross put pressure on his
lungs so that breathing was more and more difficult.

And yet he turns his gaze toward his mother and speaks to her
and then to the disciple who would become her son. What do you
suppose he meant?

Perhaps Jesus is simply concerned for his mother's welfare
after his death. In the culture of the time, widows depended on
their sons for support. A woman without a male in her life
became vulnerable to poverty and isolation. In all likelihood,
Jesus' mother was a widow. Jesus wanted his mother to be cared
for, looked after, and loved.

Jesus' words may, in the simplest sense, be like our own concern for our parents. Who's going to look after mom and dad in
their later years, if the children are all dead? How can we insure
that they will always be cared for? So, we buy insurance, connect

our parents with a retirement home where they can live their lives out, or ask a friend to look after them. It is the kind of concern any child would have for her or his parents.

Now, of all times, is when Jesus says these words! Amid his suffering, he thinks not of himself but of his mother. His care and compassion embraces his mother even in the final moments of his life. That's the kind of person he is. One who always cares for us. Wants the best for us. Is concerned about the poor and the needy, the lonely and the hurting. His care for his mother in these last moments is an expression of God's love expressed in his life.

There are sometimes moments in life when our love of others is tested. Perhaps you know those moments. It may be a crisis in which we are challenged to ask for whom we care the most. There's a woman who faced one of those moments. Her life was endangered by an abusive husband. On this occasion, he was in a drunken rage and turned on their six-year-old daughter. The mother was already on the floor, bleeding from the blows she had received. But when she saw her husband lift his hand to strike their daughter, she struggled to her feet and threw herself between him and their daughter. As a result, she was beaten until unconscious. Then, however, the husband staggered to the bedroom and collapsed on the bed in a drunken stupor. The story has a brighter ending. This incident finally convinced the woman she must take her child and seek shelter elsewhere.

In the moment of crisis—when her daughter's life was in danger—the depth of the woman's love for her child motivated her to risk her own life. Her love came to expression in that moment. In much the same way, Christ offers his life as a means of expressing the divine love for us. He throws his body between the forces of evil and us. And that love—that measureless compassion—is expressed in these simple words spoken to his mother and his disciple.

"Woman, here is your son." "Here is your mother."

Clearly, these words arose from a heart of divine love. This act of uniting his mother and disciple in a new family. Is it possible that Jesus is creating a new human family?

At the beginning of the Gospel of John we find some intriguing words. The writer says that Jesus is God's Word who comes into this world. But he is rejected by his own people. The author says, *"to all who received him, who believed in his name, he gave power to become children of God. . . ."* Power to become children of God. Christ would create a new family within humanity. The family of God. United in the love Christ revealed, believers would become like brothers and sisters. And all would find parental love and care in their relationship with God.

We hear a lot these days about family and about "family values." The traditional form of the family as we have known it is changing. Single parents with children. Couples who choose not to have children or to adopt children. Even people of the same sex uniting and raising children. The traditional family is changing.

Amid this change, we have had to think again about family. What constitutes a family? What is essential in the environment in which children are raised? As a result of rethinking the family, we have rediscovered what it is we treasure in the family. It is an association of people who care deeply for one another. A relationship of love among adults and children. A caring, nurturing environment in which children can be raised to live healthy lives. We have also become acutely aware that families can be destructive as well as nurturing. We have learned how devastating a dysfunctional family can be in our lives.

When I was in seminary, years and years ago, I had a part-time job. I worked at a home for emotionally disturbed children. These were children who were so injured by their backgrounds that they were not suitable for adoption. In this home, they learned to live together and share their lives while they worked with counselors. Along with a number of others, my job was simply to be in a hall with about ten of these children. To help them get along with one another, to play together, to do chores. In general, we were trying to be adults whom these children could trust.

For nearly every one of these children, parents and family were ugly words and concepts. Many of them had abusive parents, and, if they had any family at all, it was more destructive than helpful. I came to realize that we were trying to be "family" to these children. They had been cut adrift in life without love and nurture. And we were attempting to provide an environment in which they knew they were loved and in which they could mature.

Isn't that what we all need? Even if our families are healthy and strong, we need a family that stretches out beyond blood relationships. We need a family that does not exclude some in favor of others. We need a family of trust and security, no matter what kind of blood relatives we have.

It is that kind of family Jesus creates from the cross. Gathered at the foot of the cross sharing Jesus' agony were the components of a new family. *"Woman, here is your son." "Here is your mother."*

And the family of faith is born. A family in which you and I can thrive and grow. Amid all the social change in the family, God's family becomes all the more important. In our baptisms God welcomes us into the divine family. We are given new parents, new siblings—a new family.

Yes, with these words Jesus was providing for his mother. Out of his love and care for her, he was assuring that she would live a secure life. But he was also making us a family. Creating God's family in this world. Both of these meanings have one thing in common. Jesus expresses God's love—love of parents and love among believers. And so he commends us to one another. Look around you. See your brothers and your sisters. All of us united in faith and love.

"Woman, here is your son." "Here is your mother."

∽

The Resurrection Appearances

In John, Christ's crucifixion and his resurrection are indivisible—they are a single event. So, the enthronement we looked for in the crucifixion is found in the stories of the Risen Christ as well, and the glorification of which Jesus speaks is as much his execution as his resurrection. Rudolf Bultmann argued that Christ's resurrection is not really necessary in John, since "Jesus' death on the cross is already his exaltation and glorification." He went on to say that Christ's resurrection is simply another of the "signs."[18] I think, however, it is better to regard the two episodes—crucifixion and resurrection—as a single event. The Gospel seems to transcend temporal categories so that time is collapsed in on itself in the events that have transcendent value. In this way, the fourth evangelist's work is very different from the Gospel of Luke and Acts of the Apostles in which temporal sequence is of utmost importance.

In this section we look first individually at the stories in chapters 20 and 21 and then discuss general themes in John's account of the resurrection. Finally, we will consider homiletical reflections on preaching the Easter stories and an example of one such effort.

An Overview of Chapters 20 and 21

John has four stories of the appearance of the risen Christ to disciples. Three of those are found in chapter 20 and one in chapter 21.

The Discovery of the Empty Tomb
and Christ's Appearance to Mary (20:1-18)

The first story combines the discovery of the empty tomb by Mary Magdalene (20:1-10) and the risen Christ's appearance to her (20:11-18). While
these two stories may have been separate in early Christian tradition, here
they constitute a literary whole. (See also Matt. 28:1-10.) One of the few
things on which the four Gospels agree in their accounts of resurrection
appearances is that a woman or a group of women were first to find the
tomb empty. The precise names and number of the women vary, but in
each case the evangelists report their discovery.

It is rather remarkable that women play this crucial role in the resurrection story. (See Luke 24:11 for evidence that the testimonies of women
were not trusted in that day.) To be sure, in the culture of the time, they
were probably expected to mourn and take care of the grave. In this case,
they are given a pivotal place in the story, which suggests that women were
not necessarily confined to preconceived roles in the early church. That is
surely the case with Mary Magdalene, as we will see. The Gospels agree that
a woman or group of women went to the tomb early on the first day after
the Sabbath. While Mark (16:1) and Luke (24:1) say that the women went
to the tomb with the intent to embalm the body, Matthew agrees with John
in not mentioning a motive. John's account assumes the earlier mentions
of the preparation of the body for burial (19:39-40). Matthew too seems to
take for granted such an earlier preparation, although there is no explicit
reference to it in the first Gospel.[19]

In John's case, we may safely assume that Mary goes to the tomb first
thing in the morning because of her love for Jesus and her desire to be near
him. In modern popular imagination, Mary Magdalene has been seen as a
prostitute who was converted into a follower of Jesus. The New Testament
gives us no clear evidence that this is the case, and the "rumor" that has
become commonplace in Christian circles must be laid at the doorstep of
male interpreters who have so often been inclined to find immoral women
in the Bible. The fact is that we know little about her, except that her home
was Magdala, that Jesus had cured her of demon possession, and that she
was among a group of women who followed Jesus (Luke 8:1-3). She is not
necessarily to be identified with the "sinful" woman who anoints Jesus in
Luke 7:36-50 (and we are not told that the woman's sin was sexual!). In
John, Mary Magdalene first appears as one of the disciples gathered at the
foot of the cross (19:25) and is now featured in this remarkable story.[20] I
believe preachers have a moral responsibility to correct the scandalous
image of Mary, if for no other reason than the sake of biblical faithfulness.

Some commentators have interpreted the reference to "dark" in verse 1 as symbolic of John's dualistic separation of light and darkness (for example, 1:4-5). See also 3:1-2 where Nicodemus comes to Jesus from the darkness of night. The mention of the darkness in 20:1 is a good example of the difficulty of deciding when the Gospel's language is symbolic (see chapter 3). It is not too much, however, to think of Mary's gloom and grief at this moment. When she finds the tomb empty, she quickly informs Peter and the beloved disciple, and they dash to the site to see for themselves. The relationship between Peter and the beloved disciple in the Gospel of John is a complex one, and this story only deepens the mystery of that relationship. In every case, when these two appear in the same story, Peter is in some way or another put in a inferior place to the beloved disciple (see 13:23). In this story, the beloved disciple not only enters the tomb first but also is the first to "believe"—"he saw and believed"—whatever it is that he believes (20:8). Given this Gospel's emphasis on "seeing" (for example, "come and see," 1:39, 46), we can assume that the beloved disciple exercised faith in perceiving the tomb. In an apparent contrast with Peter, the beloved disciple dares to see through the eyes of faith, which becomes an essential theme in John's stories of the risen Christ.

Mary remains at the tomb, captured by her grief and her fear that someone has stolen the body. She makes the assertion or asks the question about the body being stolen and laid elsewhere no less than three times (20:2, 13, 15). Her love of Jesus leads her to think the worst about the empty tomb, and it is that which prevents her at first from recognizing Jesus. The appearance of angels (20:12-13) does not faze her at all! She is not overcome by awe or filled with fear. She just wants to know what has happened to her master. And she is about to find out.

The angels' question, "Why are you weeping?" (20:13) and Jesus' question, "Why are you weeping? Whom are you looking for?" are loaded with Johannine themes. A basic question for this Gospel is the issue of seeking (see also 1:38). The verb "seek" or "look for" *(zēteō)* often characterizes the human quest for meaning and commitment (see chapter 4). Combine that with the question of our grief—the grief that seems integral to life in this world (why are you weeping?)—and you have a potent pair of basic human questions.

The idea that the risen Christ is not immediately recognized is part of the ancient tradition, or so it seems. Like the two disciples on the road to Emmaus (Luke 24:13-35) and the disciples who hear the report of their two colleagues but have to be convinced they are not seeing a ghost (Luke 24:36), so Mary does not immediately recognize Jesus. I think Mary is preoccupied with her grief, blinded by her tears, and simply not expecting ever to see Jesus alive again. All that blurs her vision. What we are looking for often determines what we see, as the psychologists have taught us. Jesus simply utters her name, designating her as one of the sheep of his flock (10:3, 14), and Mary knows who he is. Names give us identity and even existence, as the ancient Hebrews thought (see also Gen. 1:5), and when Jesus names us we are given new life and new sight.

Mary naturally wants to hold on to Christ now that she has found him alive again. The Greek of verse 17 is unclear, but many think that the sense is "do not keep holding on to me." Mary cannot cling to Jesus for several reasons. Not least of all is the fact that she has a mission to perform; she cannot wallow in her newly found joy but must share it with others. Moreover, Jesus is now not the purely physical Jesus but the risen Lord and cannot be contained by human grasp. What Jesus means by "I am ascending to my Father and your Father. . . ." is also unclear (20:17). Is the ascension a process, and the risen Christ appearing to Mary only one stage of that process? Of course, John does not narrate Jesus' ascension as does Luke (24:50-53), but in the fourth Gospel Jesus' ascension is his crucifixion; that is, it is synonymous with glorification and occurs in both the cross and the resurrection. Raymond E. Brown writes, "'Ascension' is merely the use of a spatial language to describe exaltation and glorification," and claims ascension as glorification should be distinguished from "a levitation symbolizing the terminus of the appearances of the rise Jesus."[21]

Jesus commissions Mary to share the news of the resurrection with his other followers, and she immediately does so with the simplest of words: "I have seen the Lord." Mary becomes the first apostle—one sent to announce Christ's resurrection—and moreover is "the apostle to the apostles," as some have so forcefully puts it.[22] No social station prohibits one from becoming an apostle, only the basic conviction that Christ lives among us.

Jesus' Appearance to Disciples in a Locked Room (20:19-23)

The representation of Mary as a disciple and apostle alerts us to be careful that we do not assume the word "disciple" (mathētēs) means only one of the twelve men, whom we know from the Synoptic Gospels. In John disciple means one who follows Jesus, a learner, a pupil. Actually John mentions the "twelve" only in 6:67 and 20:24 and seems to have little interest in either the history of an intimate circle of disciples or the symbolism of the number twelve. Consequently, we have no idea who these "disciples" were in the room on the evening of the first day of week, which makes considerable difference in how we read this resurrection story.

This group of followers is fearful for their lives, presumably because they might be associated with Jesus of Nazareth and suffer the same fate as he. "For fear of the Jews" must mean fear of the religious authorities, because the disciples were themselves Jews. The New Testament represents Christ's risen embodiment in such a way as to suggest that he was bodily but not limited as human bodily existence is. Hence, in this story, he passes through a locked door. In Luke 24:31, he disappears as mysteriously as he first appears to the two disciples on their way to Emmaus, even though he eats in the presence of his followers in 24:42. Paul speaks of the resurrected body as a unique kind of body appropriate to the situation and calls it a *sōma pneumatikos* ("a spiritual body") to be distinguished from a *sōma psychikos* ("a physical" or "earthly body," 1 Cor. 15:44).[23] Perhaps the clue to the mystery of the body of the risen Christ is to think of it as a transformed body (1 Cor. 15:51) that is not purely spiritual or physical but a unique sort of personal unity.

In John's story in 20:19-23, the resurrected Christ passes through the locked doors but then shows the disciples "his hands and his side" (20:20). The New Testament stories of the appearances of the risen Christ often indicate a special importance to the fact that this is the crucified Jesus (see Luke 24:39) to ward off any kind of suspicion that a different "Christ" appeared. In this way the resurrection is tied closely to the crucifixion and would make little sense without that connection.

The risen Jesus offers four gifts to the disciples gathered in that room. This first is simply "peace," expressed in the common greeting, "Peace be with you" (20:19, 21). As Jesus had promised to give his followers peace (John 14:27), so now as the risen Christ he does so. Christ's peace, however, is not a passive contentment, and he gives the disciples a second gift, a mission. Believers now become apostles *(apostoloi)* because Christ "sends" *(apostellō)* them into the world. God's sending of Christ is the pattern for Christ's sending the disciples, meaning among other things that they are sent out of God's love for the world and for the world's redemption (3:16). Jesus had prayed similar words in 17:18, "As you have sent me into the world, so I have sent them into the world." (See chapter 6.) Moreover, given John's tendency to use the word "world" *(kosmos)* to represent the realm of evil and separation from God, it means that those who follow Jesus go into the midst of the world's suffering, violence, and brokenness. It is an awesome mission in more ways than one. To follow Christ as God's agents in the world is frightening enough, but to be sent in his place for the salvation of the world is nearly paralyzing! It is little wonder that the church has trouble digesting and living such a commission as this.[24]

Christ does not send the disciples into mission without empowerment, so the third gift is the Holy Spirit. He now fulfills his promise to "send you [another Counselor]" (16:7). This is the Johannine Pentecost, but the gift of the Spirit comes at the same time the risen Christ is among Christians. John does not bother to distinguish the period of the risen Christ and that of the Holy Spirit, as does Luke, but collapses them together and thereby suggests their identity. Actually, the Greek reads, "he breathed on them and said to them, 'Receive a Holy Spirit'" (without the definite article); however, the authorization (the fourth gift) that comes with the Spirit leaves no doubt that this is *the* Holy Spirit. Christ's breath is the divine Spirit, and the risen Christ continues breathing on his people, implanting the Spirit in their lives. As it is elsewhere in the New Testament, the Spirit here means guidance and comfort but also empowerment for witness.

The fourth and final gift is authority. With the Spirit, Christ gives the disciples power to forgive sin and to withhold forgiveness. It is important for us to recognize that we cannot attribute this authority to some elite group in the church, such as the clergy, because it is not strictly the twelve to whom this authority is granted but a representative group of all believers. This authority is like those famous words spoken to Peter in Matthew 16:19 and to the church as a whole in Matthew 18:18.[25] The church is empowered and given authority to announce God's forgiveness of sin when it is appropriate and to withhold it when it is inappropriate. A student in a class on John once asked when it would ever be appropriate *not* to offer forgiveness. One of the suggestions made in response has to do with those addicted to spousal abuse. Too often, this woman said, the church is too quick to forgive those guilty of abuse and allow them to continue in their pattern of behavior. Forgiveness is better withheld until the offender is ready to change her or his behavior—a point in the process of therapy for such persons.

With the bestowal of this authority, the appearance scene ends—or is suspended until later. The risen Christ in this scene is active in providing for his followers and empowering and equipping the church. There was a believer, however, who was not present to witness this grand scene.

The Appearance of the Risen Christ to Thomas (20:24-29)

This is the last scene of the Gospel as many think it ended. Assuming that chapter 21 is an appendix added to the Gospel at a later time, 20:30-31 concluded the book, and the scene with Thomas offered its climax. There is much about this story to merit its prime position in what we think might have been the original Gospel, and it is rich with meaning for the church in all centuries.

Verses 24-25 set up the situation for the third appearance of the risen Christ. Thomas is called the twin, and the Greek word for twin, *Didymos*, seems to have been part of his Greek name. He is mentioned by his full name, "Thomas, the Twin," in two other places in the Gospel of John (11:16 and 21:2), and the Thomas referred to in 14:5 is probably the same person. Efforts to discern in these other passages that Thomas was a skeptical and doubting person are more eisegesis than exegesis. His insistence that he share the experience of his colleagues before he is willing to believe is reasonable. In fact, he demands the experience of seeing (v. 25) that is so important in Johannine thought (see above). From his demand, it is clear that Thomas needs to be convinced that this one whom his colleagues saw is indeed the crucified Christ: "Unless I see the *marks of the nails in his hands and put my finger in the mark of the nails and my hand in his side,* I will not believe" (italics added). In other words, he fears his colleagues may have seen a spirit of some sort (see Luke 24:36-43).

Thomas denies the power of the witness of others. In John witness (*matyreō*) is a major theme and is the means by which faith is transmitted to others. The word appears thirty-three times in this Gospel. Jesus himself witnesses (1:7), his works and signs are witnesses (10:25), the Father witnesses to Jesus' identity (5:31-38), the Paraclete witnesses to Jesus (15:26), and the disciples are called to witness (13:35). The special character of witness in the fourth Gospel is that it is almost always a testimony to the person and work of Jesus.[26] In this Gospel, belief is discerning and trusting the unique person of Jesus. The conclusion of the story of Jesus' appearance to Thomas highlights this very point.

Thomas has said that, unless he has a personal and direct experience of the risen Christ, he will not believe, so Christ accommodates him (20:26-29). Jesus invites Thomas to touch him and learn that he is indeed the crucified Christ now risen from the dead. The story does not say that Thomas actually touches Jesus—and that is important. Jesus' words to Thomas alone convince him and bring him to faith. In a clear manner we see in this story the same emphasis on the words of the risen Christ that is found in his appearance to Mary. Seeing and hearing are the keys to the birth of faith. It is indeed, as Paul said, the hearing of the Word (Christ) that occasions faith (Rom. 10:14-17).

Furthermore, Thomas's confession of faith in 20:28 is one of the two climactic notes of this dramatic story. Thomas calls Christ "my Lord and my God" *(ho kyrios mou kai ho theos mou).* These words comprise the highest confession a human makes in the Gospel of John, and they are, of course, exactly what the Gospel has claimed all along about Jesus' identity. Thomas' words are both a confession and a proclamation. The combination of *kyrios* and *theos* could be an effort to join a Jewish-Hebraic title *(kyrios)* with a Greek title *(theos),* suggesting Christ's universal supremacy.

"My Lord" is a common Christian confession and perhaps a baptismal formula (for example, Rom. 10:9). The title is possibly a synonym for "God," since the lxx use *kyrios* to translate the personal name for God, yhwh. The title is also used in Christian liturgical settings (see *Marana tha,* "My Lord Come," 1 Cor. 16:22). Nor should it be overlooked that the caesars of the time—in particular, Domitian, who ruled 81–96, c.e.—were claiming to be "Lord and God." Christ is the Christians' Caesar! Moreover, naming Christ God at this point provides closures around the Gospel narrative, for it began by saying "the Word was God." The evangelist wants readers to see in these enclosures (*inclusio* or "ring composition"[27]) the essential message of this writing.[28] (See chapter 1.)

The Gospel could appropriately end with Thomas's words concluding the whole document, but there is another part of this final scene. Jesus responds to Thomas's confession by saying two things. First, he asks Thomas the reason for his faith. Is it because Thomas has "seen" him? Second, he issues a beatitude about seeing and believing: "Blessed are those who have *not* seen and yet have come to faith." We may think how blessed Thomas and the others were to have witnessed the risen Christ directly, to have seen and heard him, and even to have been invited to touch him. Many of us wish that we could have been with those first disciples; however, Christ says it is not they who are blessed but those who believe even without having seen the risen Christ.

What does this final beatitude mean? Clearly, it is directed toward all the future believers who follow. It offers us affirmation for the quality of our faith and emboldens us with confidence. John seems to say that genuine faith—"pure faith"—is belief that is not the result of direct and immediate sensation but that which arises from the proclamation of the Word. Indeed, faith at its best arises because of the witness of others to Christ. This final saying strengthens the suggestions through the Gospel that faith which arises from witnessing Jesus' signs is not yet authentic faith (e.g., 4:48).[29] Pure faith is trust in God through Christ *not because of the evidence for such trust but precisely in spite of the absence of such evidence!*[30] In our day there is much talk about the evidence for the truth of Christian faith, and our culture is captivated with a pseudoscientific mind-set. Christianity, as John understood it, stands at the opposite side of the issue: "Blessed are those who have not seen and yet have come to believe."

The First Conclusion (20:30-31)

If John wanted to diminish the role of signs—physical evidence for faith— why does the conclusion of the original Gospel begin with the statement that Jesus "did many other signs in the presence of his disciples?" Clearly, John had no desire to eliminate Jesus' acts as expressions of his and God's glory (see 2:11). It is to those of us beyond that historical period that he has Jesus speak his beatitude. The purpose of 20:31 is to disavow any appearance of having tried to tell everything Jesus had said and done. We will note that the second conclusion does the same sort of thing in 21:25.

What is important about this conclusion is the next verse in which the author seems to state the purpose for writing this document. That statement of purpose ("these [or these things] are written so. . . .") includes two parts. The first is "so that you (plural) may come to believe that Jesus is the Messiah, the Son of God. . . ." John claims that the goal is to bring readers to faith. As chapter 1 indicates, there is a troublesome textual variant that has caused much controversy. The verb "to believe" is spelled two different ways in the early manuscripts. The one that is translated in the RSV and NRSV is *pisteusēte* (second person, plural, aorist, subjunctive of *pisteuō*), meaning "that you may come to belief now (or become a Christian)." The second reading to which ancient manuscripts witness is *pisteuēte* (second person, plural, present, subjunctive of *pisteuō*), meaning "that you may continue to believe now (or be confirmed in your belief)."[31] The difference amounts to one single letter—a sigma, *s*—but has enormous consequences for interpretation. This raises the long-standing problem of whether John was written for evangelical purposes or to nurture readers who are already believers.[32] Probably the best solution is to say that both purposes can be found in the Gospel as a whole, whichever manuscript reading is taken as authority.

The second part of this conclusion is to nurture the gift of "life" in readers. Out of believing arises its benefit—a new life that roots in God's revelation in Christ. Gail R. O'Day writes about this verse, "These verses [30 and 31] suggest that an engagement with the biblical text, with its offer and interpretation of God, is vital to the life of faith. In preaching and teaching these texts, in meditating on them in prayer, it is, indeed, possible to believe without having seen."[33] The author invites readers into the narrative in order that they may live the story along with its characters and thereby discover what life is all about. In a real sense, what we all seek most avidly is a life that has meaning and is rooted in that which is the most important reality, that is, rooted in God.

The Appearance of the Risen Christ on the Sea of Tiberias (21:1-14)

There are two different ways of reading 20:30-31. The more popular has been to say that chapter 21 comprises some sort of appendix to the original Gospel, supposing that early in its circulation someone made an addition to the scroll. Hence, we take this first conclusion (20:30-31) as the original ending of the Gospel, and chapter 21 as an appendix.

The other way of reading 20:30-31 is as a conclusion—not to the whole of the Gospel—but to the resurrection stories told in chapter 20. In this case, the word "these" (*tauta*, "these things") in verse 31 refers not to the whole narrative but the stories of Christ's appearances, and the "signs" mentioned in verse 30 refer to the resurrection appearances as signs.[34] The newer literary critiques have also tended to treat the final chapter as a legitimate and important part of the Gospel.[35] Preachers may, I think, treat chapter 21 as integral to the whole Gospel, if for no other reason than the fact that the church has always done so, and the content of the chapter is generally harmonious with the previous twenty chapters, at least in major issues.

Moreover, chapter 21 is important for at least four reasons. First, it includes another appearance of the risen Christ, this time to seven of the disciples. Second, it tells of the conversation between Peter and Jesus, which in effect assures us that Peter was forgiven his denial of Jesus and reinstated as a leader of the disciples. Third, the remarks about the beloved disciple tell us something more about this mysterious figure. And, finally, in verses 24-25 we are told that the witness behind this writing is reliable.

In 21:1-14, the narrator first sets the stage. With "these things" *(tauta)* the storyteller links what is to follow with 20:30-31. The disciples are back in Galilee, and Peter declares to the others that he is going fishing. His companions are six other of Jesus' followers. Among them are "the sons of Zebedee," who we take to be James and John known to us from the Synoptic Gospels. This is the first mention of them in John, however. Perhaps the narrator wants us to think that the disciples have returned to their homes in Galilee and at least some to their professions. If that is the case, they are notoriously unsuccessful at their work. They fish all night without a catch.

Like the first resurrection appearance, this one occurs in the early hours of the morning. Jesus calls to the disciples, but they do not recognize him at first—again, as was the case in the first resurrection appearance. Jesus directs them in their fishing, and they are immediately successful—so successful that they can hardly handle the net. Then, in the face of this extraordinary turn of events, Peter recognizes Jesus and swims ashore to meet him. On shore, Jesus dines with the seven disciples. Strangely, the text claims they knew who Jesus was, yet did not dare to ask him who he was (21:12). Might this mean that Christ's appearance was changed in his risen body? Not accidentally, Jesus then feeds them bread and fish, as he had the crowd in chapter 6. The bread and fish may have Eucharistic meaning in this case, so that like Christ's appearance to the disciples on the way to Emmaus, his identity is made known when he breaks bread with them (Luke 24:30-31). The narrator tells us that this was the third resurrection appearance, but we count three already by the end of chapter 20. Did the author not regard Mary as a "disciple," or are the two appearances to the disciples in the locked room counted as one? The story reminds us of the great catch of fish narrated in Luke 5:1-11 and, in the same Gospel, the appearance to the disciples in which Jesus ate before them (24:36-42).

You will notice that I have carefully tiptoed around the "hundred and fifty-three" fish mentioned in verse 11, and for good reason. The exact number has stimulated the imaginations of interpreters for centuries, and its symbolism has been widely discussed. The proposals are numerous and need not detain us. The question is whether this number is symbolic and, if so, what does it symbolize? Could it be that there is no symbolism at all in this number? The fruitlessness of all the proposals of symbolic meaning leads some of us to think that the number is intended only to be large and exact, so as to suggest an eyewitness to the event.[36]

Preachers will note that this appearance story takes place in the context of the disciples' normal and "secular" life. They are at their work when Christ comes to them. But it is not always easy to recognize the risen Christ, not easy to distinguish his appearance from that of a mere stranger. So, we wonder how we can recognize the living Lord in our midst? Does he come disguised as an ordinary human?

The Conversation between Peter and Jesus (21:15-19)

If the Gospel ever circulated with chapter 20 as its ending, readers may have wondered whatever became of Peter. We would have last seen him denying Christ, even while Christ was bravely facing his opponents. Chapter 21 changes all of that. First, Peter is seen leaping into the water to swim to shore and meet the risen Christ, and now—in this conversation with Christ—he is reinstated. The story is written skillfully and filled with pathos. It has two major parts—verses 15-17 and 18-19.

First, Jesus addresses Peter, asking him three times if Peter loves him, and three time Peter replies he does. Yet there is a fascinating detail about this conversation that is lost in English translation, since we have only one word to translate two Greek verbs meaning "to love": *agapaō* and *phileō*. Still, there is another interesting variation in the questions and replies that needs to be mentioned. The conversation goes something like this:

Jesus' Question	Peter's Reply	Jesus' Response
"Do you love me?" (*agapaō*)	"You know that I love you" (*phileō*)	"Feed my lambs"
"Do you love me?" (*agapaō*)	"You know that I love you" (*phileō*)	"Tend my sheep" [Literally: "Shepherd my sheep"]
"Do you love me?" (*phileō*)	"You know that I love you" (*phileō*)	"Feed my sheep"

The first variation is that Jesus uses the verb *agapaō* twice, and each time Peter responds with the verb *phileō*. Then, finally, Jesus switches to Peter's word and asks if he loves him, using *phileō*. The question is whether a distinction between these two words is operative here, because that is not always the case in John. Does *phileō* mean to love in a "brotherly" or "sisterly" way and *agapaō* to love unconditionally and without any thought of return, that is, to love as God loves? If that distinction is at work here, Peter does not seem to get it—he sees no difference. Jesus is asking if he loves his Master without reserve and not for what's in it for him. Poor Peter never senses that and refuses to commit to that kind of love. Finally, Jesus accommodates Peter's understanding of love in his third question. The alternative is that Jesus intends to ask if Peter loves him fully, in every way, and hence asks his questions with two different verbs. This latter possibility, however, does not account for why Jesus asks twice using the stronger verb.

The other variation is what Peter is to do as a result of his love for Jesus:

- "Feed my lambs" *(Boske ta arnia mou)*
- "Tend my sheep" (or, "Shepherd my sheep," *Poimaine ta probata mou*)
- "Feed my sheep" *(Boske ta probata mou)*

Are these differences incidental, or do they mean something? We ought not be dogmatic in our response one way or the other. It is possible that the variation means that Peter is asked to care for others in every imaginable way. As he is to love others fully, so too should he devotedly look after the community of faith.

What impresses us about these verses is that Peter makes clear his devotion and affection for Christ, in spite of what he might have done earlier. He is, in other words, absolved of his sinful denials of Christ and once again assumes his role as a leader among the Christians.

In the second part of the passage (vv. 18-19), Jesus speaks of Peter's destiny. While Jesus sounds as if he is saying only how Peter will age and suffer the infirmities of aging, the narrator makes it clear in verse 19 that these words predict how Peter will die. He will be robbed of his independence, be led away, and be crucified with outstretched arms as Christ was. His death shall glorify God—reveal God's presence in the world. Jesus concludes the conversation with the simple words, "Follow me," as if he is asking Peter to accept his fate and nonetheless continue to be Jesus' disciple.

The preacher knows that the conversation between Peter and Jesus is one that goes on all the time between those who try to follow Christ but fail and must reaffirm their commitment. Christ's absolution of Peter's denials is our absolution as well for all the times and ways we may deny Christ. Peter's affirmation of his love is the affirmation that we make over and over again in our Christian journeys. Peter's story is our story, if we obey Christ when he commands us to "follow me."

Remarks about the Beloved Disciple (21:20-23)

These words of Jesus to Peter regarding the beloved disciple are far from clear. When Peter asks about him, Jesus says that does not concern Peter, and he should attend to his own discipleship. In verse 23, the narrator seems to be saying that Jesus' words have been misunderstood: "If it is my will that he remain until I come, what is that to you?" They have been mistakenly taken to mean that the beloved disciple would not die—at least before the *parousia*. What then do they mean? If the word "remain" (*menein*) is taken in its Johannine sense of being in a relationship with Christ, then Jesus is saying little more than that relationship will endure. Some think that Jesus' words are intended to say that, while Peter would have an illustrious career and end as a martyr, the beloved disciple's ministry would be quieter and less conspicuous.[37]

The Witness behind the Gospel (21:24-25)

In verse 24, "this" clearly refers to the beloved disciple of whom Jesus speaks in verse 23. The question, however, is what is meant by the two statements that he is "the one testifying about these things" and "the one having written these things" (my translation). What are "these things"— the whole Gospel or the preceding story (or perhaps the whole of chapter 21)? The very next phrase suggests that the author of the sentence is not the beloved disciple, since that person is referred to in the third person, "he." Scholarly opinions vary on the meaning of this verse, and we will not settle the debate here. "Has written" can mean that the beloved disciple actually penned the words, that he "caused these things to be written" (a causative meaning, like 19:19), or that he is responsible for the writing in a broader sense.[38] We cannot answer these questions with certainty, but I think it sounds as if the author is saying that the beloved disciple lies behind the Gospel as a whole. It is his witness that provides the primary source of the Gospel. Verse 25 sounds very much like 20:30 and seems to be no more than an admission that the Gospel is not complete in describing Jesus' ministry. It is the kind of confession most preachers want to make at the end of a sermon on a particular text!

Major Themes in Chapters 20–21

The stories of the appearances of the risen Christ in John are filled with subtle meaning and mystery. It would be a mistake to reduce these stories to a number of propositions and claim that we have thereby captured the meaning of the Easter events. Like so much in John, I find these stories endlessly stirring my imagination and evoking new possibilities of meaning. The most we can hope to do is isolate some themes that emerge throughout the stories.

Faith in the Resurrection Stories

Like all of the stories of Christ's appearance after his resurrection, John reports that only those who had had a prior relationship with Jesus and expressed faith in him see the risen Christ. The resurrection was not a marvelous event designed to convert the unbelievers. It was not a public show of divine might. Rather, it was the continuation and deepening of a relationship that had already been established. This is important for preaching the resurrection stories, because these stories are not going to win converts by overwhelming them with what God can do. Easter is a celebration of the community of faith—those already grasped by God's grace. They deepen and enhance faith but do not necessarily win faith.

Raymond E. Brown has suggested that the four stories in chapter 20 provide examples of different kinds of faith:

> The beloved disciple comes to faith after having seen the burial wrappings but without having seen Jesus himself. Mary Magdalene sees Jesus but does not recognize him until he calls her by name. The disciples (in the locked room) see him and believe. Thomas sees him and believes, but only after having been overly insistent on the marvelous aspect of the appearance. All four are examples of those who saw and believed; the evangelist will close the Gospel in 29b by turning his attention to those who have believed without seeing.[39]

The fourth evangelist has a complex understanding of faith, rooted in the complexity of the human personality. Hence, there are numerous levels of faith—none necessarily better than the other but slightly different. Like any human relationship, our relationship with Christ changes and grows, waxes and wanes. The Thomas story, I think, tells us something important about faith. Thomas's faith arises as a result of his doubt—his unwillingness to believe what others are telling him. Hence, even doubt is shown as an avenue toward new and more comprehensive faith, which brings us to another theme in these stories.

The Risen Christ Appears in the Midst of Human Difficulty

Interesting enough, each persons to whom the Johannine risen Christ appears is suffering some sort of trouble. Mary is in sorrow. The disciples in the locked room are fearful. Thomas is doubting. The fishermen in chapter 21 are notoriously unsuccessful. Christ appears to address these people in the midst of their difficulty. The suggestion is that Christ always comes to us amid our difficulties, our suffering, and our troubles. We might think just the opposite is true. That Christ comes when we get ourselves straightened out, when our faith and confidence is the strongest. Rather the risen Christ seeks to address us in our neediest times and in our moments of failure. Hence, we cannot program Christ's presence; it is free and unpredictable. In that context, Jesus' beatitude in 20:29 makes even more sense. Those who dare to believe against the evidence—in spite of the absence of Christ and of faith—are the ones who are most blessed among us.

The Gospel ends with the risen Christ unexpectedly appearing to his followers. This simple fact contradicts Luke's neat categorization of the divine presence. The resurrection appearances come to an end with Christ's ascension into heaven (Luke 24:50-53; Acts 1:6-11), and then, after a period of time at Pentecost, the Holy Spirit descends on the church (Acts 2:1-13). Luke clearly distinguishes between the presence of the risen Christ and the presence of the Holy Spirit. John, however, collapses these separate time periods into one. The risen Christ gives the Holy Spirit (20:22) but then sticks around to continue appearing to his followers. The Gospel ends with Christ still appearing among the disciples to surprise them with his presence.

We should not try to pour the Johannine reports into a Lukan mold, nor should we try to dismantle Luke's scheme to coincide with John's. The church has chosen to prefer Luke's scheme and constructed the liturgical year in large part around the Gospel of Luke. It is in this case, however, that each of our Gospels conceives the conclusion of the resurrection appearances differently. If we take the shorter end of Mark as the original, the Gospel story ends with the promise that Christ goes before us and awaits us elsewhere (Mark 16:1-8). Matthew never has Jesus ascend as does Luke but ends the story with Jesus' promise that he will be with the disciples "to the end of the age" (Matt. 28:16-20). In this regard, Matthew has something in common with John. Like the fourth Gospel, Matthew does not narrate an end to the resurrection appearances. In fact, Luke is the only Gospel that includes such a narrative.

The point is simply this: The resurrection appearances are not confined to the few days after the crucifixion. Christ arises suddenly among us and sometimes over against us. He is forever surprising us with his presence, keeping us off balance by making it impossible to know where and how he will appear. If this confuses the presence of the risen Christ with the presence of God's Spirit, then we are aided in remembering that some of our distinctions are not necessarily God's distinctions.

A Sermon Example

I hope that along the way in this discussion readers have discerned some of what is important and possible for our preaching. Surely, preachers ought not to divide the cross and the empty tomb any more than the fourth evangelist divides them. They are one event—Christ's glorification, his enthronement. We preach each one in its relationship with the other. John shares the basic Christian belief that the cross is the necessary path to the resurrection, and that we cannot leap over death to Easter. The importance of the risen Christ's identity as the crucified one is, as we have seen, important in John as it is in Matthew and Luke. However, the cross always points beyond itself just as the resurrection points back to the cross. The life God gives through Christ's death is linked with the life Christ exhibits in his conquest over death.

The Johannine accounts of appearances of the risen Christ are more prominent in the lectionary than is John's crucifixion scene. As a matter of fact, all four of the stories of Christ's resurrection appearances in John are prescribed in the RCL. I have tried to explore some of the themes preachers might use in preaching these stories and some of the individual features of each one about which we might say, "that'll preach!" It remains to offer you a sample of a sermon on one of these resurrection appearances.

This sermon was prepared for a congregation of moderate size at which I was a guest preacher. The occasion was the Third Sunday of Easter, C, and the assigned text was John 21:1-19. Note that I treat this passage in chapter 21 as continuous with the stories in chapter 20 and not as a "separate appendix."

～

Why fishing, Peter? Why go fishing? It doesn't make a whole lot of sense. Why would Peter want to go fishing? His master has been crucified, then unexpectedly he has appeared to him and the other disciples. He empowered them with the Holy Spirit and sent them out on their mission. *And Peter chooses to go fishing!*

Perhaps his head was swirling with the meaning of all of this. Perhaps he was confused and didn't know what to make of it all. Perhaps, perhaps, he was still haunted—still tormented by those three denials of his master. For whatever reason, Peter declares, *"I'm going fishing."* Peter seems to be returning to that which he knew best. Amid the confusion of the time, amid his uncertainty about his mission, amid his self doubts, he returns to what he knows best and to what he knows he can do—*fishing.*

So, afishin' they go, but what a disaster it was. All night these seven disciples fished, tending their nets in the bitter cold and darkness. All night they sit huddled in that little boat, bouncing here and there with the waves. And not a single fish to show for it. Not even a few small ones. Not even a good nibble. The fishing trip was a failure, a disaster, a fiasco. Professional fishermen! This was what they had been trained to do. Fishing was their livelihood. They grew up with the nets. *Yet, they fish all night without catching a thing.*

We know how you feel, Peter! We know how it feels to fail, even at that which we think we know the best. We know failure, and it haunts us like a ghost, lurking unseen around us, striking fear in our hearts. Many of us have had, at least, a good deal of experience with failure. Failures in business, failures in school, failures in marriage, failures in parenting, failures in friendship. We don't like to think about them, would rather not admit them, hate being reminded of them. But most of us know what it's like to fail, even as Peter and the others failed that night. Failure undermines our self-image. It cuts through our self-confidence. It rips down our facade of strength.

Oh, we try our best to ward off failure. We work hard to succeed and to avoid failure. And we have tried all the advice we have heard. We have tried making the lemons of life into lemonade. We have tried to learn some important lesson from our failures, just like mom taught us to do. But a failure is still a failure. It's still one of life's pits. It's still painful.

I have always thought of myself as a sensitive person. I have always tried to be aware of others and their situations. But on one occasion some years ago, just like Peter and the disciples, I failed miserably at what I thought I did rather well. It was lunchtime in the seminary's refectory. My dearest friend, Larry, is the seminary's Director of Development. He announced to the gathering the yearly telethon for the seminary's annual fund. He asked the members of the community to consider volunteering their time to be one of the callers needed for the project. After the announcement, he and I stood together in the line at the salad bar, and Larry asked, *"Well, Bob, will you be one of those callers?"* Without thinking, I allowed my big mouth to run its course. I launched into a tirade about how much I hate telephone solicitations. How I hate having my privacy interrupted by calls. How I despise those salespeople for intruding into the quiet of my evening at home. There in front of all those students, I denigrated my best friend's project. And suddenly the shock of what I had done hit me.

Later, I went to him to apologize, begging his forgiveness and received it. But the memory of that failure haunts me to this day. It continues to erode my spirits, each time I remember it.

We know how you feel, Peter! Right now most of us feel that we are part of a society that has failed. American society has failed at precisely those things in which we pride ourselves: equal justice for all, respect for life and property, equal opportunity for all. With the events of nearly each week, it is hard to avoid the conclusion that something is terribly wrong in America today. Our society seems to have failed. We have failed to free ourselves of racism. Failed to break the grip of poverty and hopelessness in our urban centers. Failed to win the war against drugs. Failed to nurture the value and dignity of human life. And because we have failed, injustice goes uncorrected, anger guts the lives of thousands, and our cities stand on the brink of chaos. Therefore, many of us this morning are feeling the pain and anguish of the failure of our society.

We know how you feel, Peter! We know how it feels to fail, to fail at what we know best, as individuals and as a society.

We know what failure can do to us. And we can imagine what it must have done to those disciples that night. There they are, wallowing in their failure, depressed that they had blundered again. Then a stranger appears on the shore. *"Children, you have no fish, have you?"*

What was he trying to do—rub it in, this stranger? Trying to rub their noses in their failure? *"No, we have no fish,"* they reply.

"Cast the net to the right side of the boat, and you will find some."

Now he's telling them how they should fish, this stranger, this land-loving stranger. Telling professional fishermen how to do their work. But they obey his instructions. What have they got to lose?

And, would you believe it? Their nets fill to the breaking point. Then one of them recognizes the stranger: *"It is the Lord!"* Peter jumps into the lake to swim to Jesus, leaving his colleagues to handle their full nets. It was not so much the marvelous catch of fish that motivated Peter. Not the success to which the stranger had directed them. What drove Peter into the cold waters of the lake was the presence of his master.

Jesus had come to them amid their failure. Appeared amid their disastrous efforts. Spoken to them amid their fiasco.

The story is typical of this Christ of ours. For so, too, does Christ come to us in our failures. In our hurt and discouragement, in our self-doubts and uncertainties, he appears on the shore of our lakes of failure. He appears not to turn our failures into successes, not to make us immune to failure, not to take away the danger of failure. He appears, rather, to be at our side in the hurt, to empower us in our discouragement, to strengthen us in our self-doubts.

There is an interesting similarity among the stories of the appearances of the Risen Lord in the Gospel of John. The Risen Christ is always popping up just when the disciples are in some kind of need or hurt. Of course, that is the nature of the coming of this Christ, isn't it? Humanity was in the dredges of failure, when God sent the divine son to live among us. Christ came into the world when we were lost and forsaken, beaten down and dead. Christ continues to appear when we are most in need, in our failures, in our hurts, in our hopelessness. Christ comes to us when we have recognized our failure to do what only he can do for us. When we finally admit that we have failed to save ourselves, he comes to our side to rescue us.

I thought that Christ had abandoned me in my failure. Where was the Risen Christ when I had so offended my dearest friend, Larry? He appeared to me, all right. But he appeared as a stranger on the shore. Christ came to strengthen me in my failure in the form of my spouse, Myrna, who offered me encouragement and solace. Christ came to forgive me in my failure in the form of Larry's own forgiveness. Christ appears to us as the stranger on the shores of our desolate lakes. He appears in the words and gestures of friends, in the comfort of a loved one, in the strength of another, in the guidance of a friend.

Like Peter and the other disciples, at first I did not recognize Christ in the other—in Myrna or in Larry. But he was there for me, as he is always there for us, when we give up on ourselves.

And he is there for us today as a society! Failures though we Americans may be, Christ appears to us. He comes offering us power to make changes. Power to right the wrongs of injustice. Power to transcend our old racist attitudes. Power to address poverty and hopelessness. This risen Christ appears on the shores of despairing America to say, *Cast your nets on the other side.*

Having recognized their master, the disciples hauled their catch ashore. And there on the shore, their master hosted an impromptu breakfast. Jesus took the bread and gave it to them and did the same with the fish. In their failure, the disciples are strengthened by the presence of their master in a meal.

In our failure, too, Christ strengthens us by his presence in a meal. Bread and wine. Words of promise. Surrounded by brothers and sisters in Christ. He is here for all of us failures. Here to forgive, to empower, to comfort.

⌇

6

Fragments of Texts:
John in the Lectionary

Unlike the Synoptics, the RCL makes no provisions for an extensive continuous reading of John. There is no year of John. Instead, we find passages from the fourth Gospel scattered throughout each of the three-year readings. The purpose of this chapter is to offer some help in terms of preaching John from the lectionary. First, however, it is necessary to make some general observations about the RCL and lectionaries in general. Then the chapter will survey what is included from John and where it is in the RCL, and what is excluded. Finally, we will pay special attention to passages that are prominent in the lectionary, including the Gospel's prologue (1:1-18), chapter 6, and the farewell discourses in chapters 14–17.

Preaching the Lectionary

The recent revival of the lectionary in the church is admirable. It is exciting to find clergy of so-called nonliturgical denominations using the RCL, if sometimes only as a guide. Furthermore, the efforts of the major church bodies to come to some agreement on a common lectionary is gratifying, even though we still do not all fully agree. In general, the lectionary provides a number of important benefits. First, preaching from the lectionary with some faithfulness imposes a rewarding and fruitful discipline on pastors and minimizes (but does not entirely eliminate) our tendencies to preach our favorite passages or themes over and over. Second, following the assigned readings enriches the congregation's life, providing the laity with a broad exposure to Scripture. Third, using the lectionary entails a commitment to the liturgical year, the value of which is self-evident.

Interpreting Lectionary Texts

There are at least two significant dangers in preaching the Lectionary, which can be avoided or minimized, provided pastors are sensitive to them. One such danger is exclusion. What has not been included in the lectionary? Naturally, when one begins to think about what can and should be read over a three-year period, the selections betray certain presuppositions and theological perspectives. There is, then, no way for a committee—however diverse and committed—to please everyone with its selections. The more inclusive such a committee becomes the more difficult is the task but all the better the results. The RCL does not include enough passages in which women have major and positive roles.[1] Second, it also tends to exclude passages that evoke difficulties and unpleasant reactions. The third type of passages that is sometimes excluded from the lectionary has to do with the Gospel of John itself. Very simply, to compensate for these omissions, preachers ought generally to feel free from time to time to depart from the assigned readings of the lectionary. We can become enslaved to the prescribed readings and feel that we dare not take liberties with them. But remember the lectionary was made for humans, not humans for the lectionary! It has its peculiar strengths and its obvious weaknesses, and we need to avail ourselves of the former and correct the latter.

Another important danger in preaching the lectionary is that we do not take seriously enough the fact that the lectionary creates and places passages within new contexts. Lections are in effect removed from their literary contexts in Scripture. (Of course, this is not so true when the lections are part of a continuous reading through some document.) The lectionary then places a reading in a new context comprised of two features. First, for better or worse, the lectionary readings are placed in the context of the liturgical year. In many cases the passages have been chosen to be read because of their appropriateness for a liturgical season or occasion. To varying degrees that fact prejudices readings. For instance, John 3:1-17 is the assigned Gospel for Holy Trinity Sunday, Year B. By virtue of its being read on this occasion, we attend to the Trinitarian implications of the passage, perhaps to the detriment of what may be the major messages in the reading.

The other dimension to the new context in which we read lectionary passages is the fact that each reading is associated with two other readings and a psalm. Invariably the juxtaposition of these fragments of Scripture provides an interpretative overlay on all of them. The most notorious result of this context is the tendency to pair a reading from the Old Testament with one from the New Testament. When that is done, the tendency may be to interpret the Old Testament passage in light of the New Testament, and in so doing we may distort the meaning of the passage from the

Hebrew scripture. That surely happens when Isaiah 7:10-16 is read along-side of Matthew 1:23 on the Fourth Sunday of Advent, A, and understood strictly in terms of Matthew's interpretation of the Old Testament passage.

What is a preacher to do to avoid distorting a passage with its liturgical setting and its relationship with three other selected passages? That question, however, assumes that the new context *always* distorts a passage, which is not the case. The liturgical setting is one in which the church has always found that Scripture speaks a new and living word. There is a logical and positive reason for the association of certain texts with certain seasons of the church calendar. Moreover, the association of one text with three others invites us to practice a kind of canonical reading. That is, every passage has a canonical context that illumines it.

Nonetheless, it is wise, I think, to be informed first of all of the literary context of a passage before seeing it through liturgical eyes. Moreover, it is wise initially to interpret a text within its own context without bringing other passages to bear on it. After having developed a foundational sense of the passage in its own context, then take up the spectacles of the liturgical year and the various lens of the other passages assigned along with the one on which we hope to preach. There are times when we would have to distort a passage to speak of some liturgical theme and/or to speak with other passages. We avoid doing that by first of all grounding ourselves in the literary sense of the passage.

John in the Lectionary

The appendix (see p. 223) lists the passages chosen from the Gospel of John and the occasion on which they are to be read. Skimming the two lists suggests some broad generalizations about the use of John in the RCL. The first of those is the appearance of the same passages from John for the days of Holy Week. This implies the importance of John's Passion story for the church, and one of the reasons this book devotes chapter 5 to that story. Regrettably, except for Holy Thursday and Good Friday, today few congregations schedule worship on the other days of Holy Week. The second observation is connected with the first, namely, the dominant use of Johannine passages during the Easter season. This is probably due to the fascinating Johannine episodes regarding Christ's resurrection and the way those episodes are told.

Third, note the simple fact that, with the exception of chapter 8, all the chapters of John appear in the lectionary. (Lutheran readers, however, are familiar with the use of 8:31-36 as the Gospel lesson for Reformation Day.) The omission of chapter 8 is interesting. Perhaps it is not irrelevant that this chapter contains what is probably the most vitriolic of the Johannine

Jesus' attacks on the so-called "Jews." The embarrassment of some of these passages (for example, 8:39-47) may account for their omission, but it is hard to understand why the famous "I am the light of the world" discourse (8:12) is not scheduled for reading. Notice also that portions of chapters 5 and 7 appear only as alternate readings.

Fourth, there are several clusters of readings given prominence in certain sections of the Gospel. The frequent use of the Gospel's prologue (1:1-18) does not surprise us, nor does the use of the report of Jesus' washing the feet of his disciples and his words commanding love in chapter 13. The selection of chapter 6 for such extensive study is fascinating and perhaps can be explained by the unique use of the bread imagery and the Eucharistic-sounding climax to the bread of life discourse (vv. 51-58). I commend the lectionary committee(s) for its use of chapter 12, even though it includes only the first eleven verses of the chapter. This is a pivotal chapter in the Gospel that provides the hinge between Jesus' public ministry in the preceding chapter and his private ministry with the disciples in chapters 13–17.

In general, an examination of the passages from John suggested for reading demonstrates that, even though there is no "year of John," a good deal of the fourth Gospel is read in the course of the three-year cycle and that by no means is the importance of the Gospel diminished by the lectionary. The scattered fragments of the fourth Gospel, however, require preachers to communicate the importance of the relationship of any one text with the whole of the Gospel. Unlike those times in a continuous reading of one of the Synoptics, we can seldom refer back to a previous Sunday's Gospel lesson for the context of the current one. (Happy exceptions include the Fifth and Sixth Sundays of Easter in Year A when 14:15-21 follows the week after we have read 14:1-14). So, preachers sketch the Johannine narrative on several occasions to help the congregation grasp a passage in its literary context. A good example is how a sermon on John 10:1-10 on the Fourth Sunday of Easter, A, needs to provide a summary of the narrative in chapter 9 so that the immediate reference of Jesus' words in 10:1-10 are those religious leaders in 9:40-41. It may help a bit that the narrative in chapter 9 is read on the Fourth Sunday of Lent in the same year (A).

We could make good use of a commentary on John that treated all of the assigned readings in their lectionary order, but such a task is too ambitious for this book. Instead, what we can do is look at some of the lectionary's Johannine favorites. Moreover, there are certain of these passages that are more difficult to interpret and preach than others, so they should be given special attention. The choices narrow down to discussions of the Gospel's prologue, chapters 6, 14, 15, 16, and 17. (While chapter 12 is assigned for the Monday and Tuesday of Holy Week, its only other appearance is in Lent, B and C. I also regret the necessity of having to eliminate chapter 13 from this chapter.) In dealing with some of these passages, I will need to refer you back to previous discussions in the book.

The Prologue (1:1-18)

The whole or some portion of 1:1-18 is assigned on Christmas 2, A, B, C, the third option for Christmas Day, A, B, C, and the Third Sunday of Advent, B (which focuses on John the Baptist). Particularly because of its place in the season of the Nativity and its role in systematic theology, interpreting the prologue is important for the preacher.

Homiletical Interpretation of 1:1-18

The prologue of the Gospel of John is one of those passages that the preacher would like simply to read and sit down. The poetry of 1:1-18 is so forceful that we may wonder what we can say about it without violating its integrity. A prosaic sermon pales alongside the hymn. So what are we preachers to do with this powerful passage?

While our sermons on the prologue in no way pretend to match its poetic power, these verses provoke an endless number of questions and stimulate a wide range of reflection. It is in keeping with the purpose of the prologue, then, to explore its meaning, to probe its possibilities, and to pursue the questions it raises. We need first to get the structure of the passage before us. There is a great deal of scholarly discussion of the source of the hymn and its original form. Some propose that we can identify an original poem within the present passage as well as the additions that have been made to it. There is little debate, however, regarding its present structure, which looks something like this.[2]

> Vv. 1-5: The nature of the *Logos*.
> The *Logos* is Divine, created all things, and is life and the light that "enlightens."
> Vv. 6-8: John's role.
> John is sent by God to witness to light in order to evoke faith.
> Vv. 9-14: The *Logos* and the World.
> 9: The true light came into the world.
> 10-11: But was rejected by the world and "his own."
> 12-13: Those who received him were reborn and became "children of God."

14: The *Logos* is made flesh and reveals God's glory as the
Son of the Father.

V. 15:   John's witness.
The incarnate *Logos* is greater than he and "before" him.

Vv. 16-18: Benefits of the presence of the *Logos* in the world.
The *Logos* was the source of "grace and truth" and by virtue
of his relationship with God made God known.

In this sketch we detect a process or journey: the divine *Logos* existed in the beginning, brought light to the world, was rejected by some, but accepted by others who then came to know God and received grace and truth. In the simplest of terms, it is the story of the revelation of God in the world by the one who was God.

There are, of course, a number of issues pertaining to the prologue on which we can beg off without weakening our preaching on this text. The most obvious of these are the questions of the passage's origin, intended purpose, and redaction at the hand of the evangelist or another. We need not decide if the evangelist wrote these words or whether they are a hymn (Christian or otherwise) that the author incorporated in the Gospel. The same may be said of the two portions of the prologue that speak of John the Baptist. Are they later insertions into the hymn by the evangelist or a later redactor? The question of the Gospel's portrayal of John as a whole is more important for us, since we first encounter that issue on the Third Sunday of Advent, B, where 1:6-8 is combined 1:19-28. The Baptizer is portrayed simply as a witness to Christ and as nothing more, although the function of witness is highly valued in the fourth Gospel.

Among the more significant questions for us is the meaning of *Logos*. As we saw in chapter 1, there are many different theories about the context in which the Gospel was written and consequently the context in which *Logos* is used. My simple proposal is that the hymn uses *Logos* in an inclusive way to suggest that Christ is all that the Hebraic tradition has said about *dahbar*, the Jewish tradition about Wisdom, and the Greek-Hellenistic tradition about *logos*. A simple but legitimate way of conceiving of *Logos* in this passage is God's self-expression. Like a truthful and deeply personal self-expression, the *Logos* is God's very self or person made public. The meaning of this term is best understood in the setting of communication in that one party seeks to express and convey herself or himself to another. (See chapter 3.)

Supposing that this helps us handle the key term of the prologue, we are next faced with the issue of the heart or climax of the hymn. That is, where does the hymn reach its highest point? Most would immediately say that verse 14 and fleshly incarnation of the *Logos* is the hymn's climax. R. Alan

Culpepper has successfully argued, however, both on a literary and conceptual basis that the climax (or "pivot" as he calls it) comes in verse 12. The goal of the *Logos*'s journey into the world is to provide humans with the possibility of a new parentage and family.[3] Actually these two proposals are not diametrically opposed to one another, since the transformation of humans into members of the divine family is a result equally of their perceiving God's *doxa* in the incarnate Word and of their believing response.

Third, the interpretation of the prologue is made richer if preachers understand the way in which these eighteen verses introduce and anticipate the Gospel as a whole. Apart from the hopelessness of seeking the prologue's author and origin, we can see that its presence at the beginning of the Gospel is entirely appropriate.[4] Among the various ways in which the prologue prepares readers for the Gospel's story is the fact that it informs the reader of the true identity of the Gospel's main character. While other characters in the narrative are struggling to learn Jesus' real identity and failing badly at it, the reader knows the secret ahead of time. As a consequence of the prologue, the implied reader then is in a position to appreciate the irony of the story (for instance, the charge that Jesus is the King of the "Jews") for what it is and experiences being an "insider" who knows what is really going on in the narrative. That experience is part of the new life the Gospel story offers. One who has accepted God's self-revelation in Christ is, in a sense, an insider who better understands what is really going on in the "narrative of life."

Less important, but equally true, is that the prologue forewarns us of how crucial the rejection of the central figure will be in the narrative. The implied reader knows that finally this story will take a tragic turn as the world fails to know the *Logos* and "his own people did not receive him" (1:11). The promises of receiving Christ are expressed in a number of key Johannine terms introduced on this first page. "Light," "darkness," "life," "world," "witness," "believe," "born," "truth," and "Father-Son." While the prologue does not serve as a glossary for the Gospel, it does put these key concepts before the readers—which is exactly what a "prologue" ought to do. Some have proposed that the role of this passage is that of the actor who appears on the stage of a Greek drama to introduce the theme of the play before the curtain goes up. Note, however, that the word *Logos* is not used as a title for Christ elsewhere in the Gospel and that the use of the word grace *(charis)* is found only in John 1:18.

A homiletical interpretation of the prologue often turns up more than a preacher can handle in any one sermon, which is all right because the lectionary takes us back to this passage on an annual basis. Some of the themes that arise are obvious, and the following paragraphs suggest only a few of them.

First, here we have one of the richest collections of the benefits Christ brings to us: power to become children of God, light, life, grace, and truth. The word translated "power" in verse 12 *(exousia)* also means "authority," "freedom to act," and "ability." Using only our own powers we cannot relate to God as children relate to a parent. That power and that option has to be given to us, as this verse says. However, the whole purpose of God's act in Christ is summarized here as the formation of a new human family. The gift of *exousia* promises to reform us not just as individuals but as a community. In a day when individualism in religion and spiritual quests is stressed, the prologue suggests that God's saving purpose is to form a new community. (See the sermon on the cross in chapter 5.)

Second, the words of 1:14 are, of course, enormously important and endlessly rich, so to pinpoint a single homiletical theme in the verse is dangerous. We contemporary Christians, however, may need to hear one of the implications of the incarnation, namely, how it honors and sanctifies human flesh and body. This implication takes us in two different directions. On one hand, it invites us to honor our fleshly existence in a new way because of God's act in Christ. We can no longer think that flesh is dirty and sinful, for God has used it to reveal God's own self. On the other hand, the implication of the incarnation is that the flesh becomes sacred in a way that should make it hard for us to abuse our physical bodies. This fleshly existence we share means that our bodies are the medium by which God reached the world, and hence God dignifies our bodies.

Third, and closely related to what has just been said, is the implication that ordinary, daily physical realities take on new potential because God has become incarnate among us. Just as it dignifies the fleshly body, so the incarnation hints that God appears among us in what we call the usual or mundane. God walked in the flesh of an ordinary Nazarene and so today may walk among us in other humans and the most common of realities. For this reason, of course, the enfleshment of God suggests the sacraments in which common and ordinary realities of water, bread, and wine become the means of our encounter with God.

Fourth, where do we see God? The effort to find God is incessant but today surfaces in the enormous interest in spirituality. The prologue states in clear terms the Christian conviction of where and how we find God. In the first case, it claims that we do see the divine presence (the "glory"— *doxa*) in our world. Then comes the outlandish claim that Christ—the very heart of God—makes God public. Interestingly the prologue does not direct us deep within ourselves to find our true identity. Rather, it points us outside ourselves to look for Christ both in the past and in the present. God becomes plainly known in Christ.

A Sermon Example

What follows is an abbreviated homily delivered as part of a service of morning prayer for a gathering of New Testament scholars from around the world. I then revised it for a Christmas Eve service in a congregation.

∾

"The light shines in the darkness, and the darkness did not overcome it."

We come here this evening because we believe that the Christmas light shines in the darkness. Once again, we come seeking that light and in praise of that light.

But today the darkness seems almost to have overcome the light. Everyday world news is filled with darkness. Ethnic wars and struggles. Bombs and threats of bombings everywhere. Corruption and scandal in high office. Attempts to solve international conflicts by returning violence for violence. Hunger and poverty and oppression. Human rights violations and abuse. *The darkness seems to prevail.*

In our own beloved Atlanta area, a newly elected sheriff is assassinated. A medical doctor drowns his two young children and then kills himself. The darkness seems to prevail.

When we look at ourselves, there too we see darkness. Many of us know the darkness of our lives. We know the professional jealousies and competitiveness. We know the subtle temptations of pride. We know the self-absorption that comes as a result of believing that we—and we alone—are all that matters. We know the comfort of hiding from the issues of our society and of our world within the womb of our homes.

Yes, the darkness seems to prevail. In our world and in our individual lives. The darkness seems to prevail. And so, we must ask again, does the light still shine in this darkness? Or, has the darkness finally overcome it?

It has always interested me that the prologue never claims that the darkness succumbs to the light. It has always interested me that these beginning words of the Gospel of John claim only that the light goes on shining amid the darkness, and the darkness does not overcome it—or master it. The author knew that we are a people in darkness. But a people, too, who claim that there is a light. A people not rescued from darkness. But a people given a glimmer of light.

Children are often afraid of darkness. For them the darkness holds dreaded possibilities. Terrible and unknown threats. So, they plead with their parents for light. "Please, Mommy, leave the light on!" The parents then provide a tiny night-light—a pitifully small light that only barely penetrates the darkness of the child's room. But the miniature light bulb proves enough. The child feels secure, knowing that there is some light, some light that the darkness does not overpower. The child trusts because there is some glimmer of light. The monsters will not emerge from under the bed or out of the closet. And because there is some glimmer of light, the powers of the darkness cannot prevail.

So it is for us. God provides "light that the darkness cannot overcome." A tiny beam of light, discernible only in faith. And because there is some glimmer of light, we can trust. We trust God that the powers of the darkness cannot prevail. We believe in that light in spite of the darkness.

There have been many times when a thunderstorm has caused us to lose electricity in our home. When that happens, we cannot see in the darkness, and I go looking for thé flashlight. Fumbling about our home, crashing into furniture and walls, hitting my shins. But finally I find the flashlight. But, like so many other times, the batteries in the flashlight are dead! It's useless against the darkness. So my loving wife gave me one of these new flashlights with rechargeable batteries. You plug the whole flashlight into the electrical wall socket. It is always charged and ready for use.

Not long ago, the lights in our house again went out during a thunderstorm. Again I groped my way through the darkness toward the flashlight. But this time I was confident that it would be charged and ready for use. I was confident that its batteries would not be exhausted. With its light, I could penetrate the darkness.

The darkness seems to prevail, but we know there is a source of light that does not fail us. And we pray and grope for the faith to discern its light amid the darkness.

This day is no different than that day in which the prologue of the Gospel of John was written. The darkness remains even today. But amid the darkness a glimmer of light. Amid the darkness a light from a manger many years ago. Amid the darkness a Christmas promise that this light still shines in the darkness. Amid the darkness, the light of the word made flesh for our salvation in a tiny baby. And we trust that glimmer!

"The light goes on shining in the darkness! And the darkness does not overcome it."

✍

Chapter 6—The Heavenly Bread

With the possible exception of the prologue, chapter 6 is arguably the most discussed and debated of the Gospel of John. Moreover, the series of lessons from this chapter for Propers 12–16 during Year B may be among the most difficult preaching assignments of the entire lectionary. One of the reasons for the difficulty is simply that essential themes seem repeated over and over without much clear advance of thought, and this leaves the preacher struggling by Proper 15 with what to say that has not already been said. Still this is, as we have said, the longest of the continuous readings from John in the RCL. The lectionary readings from chapter 6 are as follows: 1-21 (Proper 12), 24-35 (Proper 13), 35 and 41-51 (Proper 14), 51-53 (Proper 15), and 56-69 (Proper 16), with 6:25-35 assigned for Thanksgiving Day, C.

Homiletical Interpretation of Chapter 6

The chapter is divided among a narrative of the feeding of the crowd (vv. 1-15), Jesus' walk on the water (vv. 16-21), and a discussion between Jesus and the crowd that followed him from the site of the feeding. We should then treat each of these in order, since they each have their own integrity however closely they are related in this chapter.

John's Story of the Feeding of the Multitude (vv. 1-15)

We have investigated this passage in some detail in chapter 4 under the topic of the symbolic features of some of the Johannine narratives, and I invite you to review that discussion. Here only a few other features of this story merit mention. Notice, first, that the fourth Gospel makes it clear that this act is one of Jesus' "signs" *(sēmeia);* that is, wondrous acts that reveal Jesus' identity.[5] Beyond that, one is struck by the detail in the Johannine narrative, for example, the green grass, the barley loaves, and "small fishes." Dating the event near Passover may be no more than the narrator's chronological marker, or it may indicate that the meaning of the event hinges on the Passover and/or Jesus' own Passover on the cross. The use of the Greek word *eucharisteō* ("give thanks") has often been taken as an indication that the feeding anticipates the Eucharist, which then leads the interpreters to see a Eucharistic meaning in the discourse that follows. Some even think that this *is* John's account of the institution of the Eucharist. The author or tradition placed it here so that it stands at the center of Jesus' ministry and not at its end.[6] In the story, Johannine Christology gets expressed in Jesus' quizzing Philip and the narrator's comment in verse 6. Jesus already knew exactly what he would do. The tragic conclusion in verse 15 indicates how drastically the crowd misunderstands Jesus, while at the same time it ironically points the reader toward that occasion on which Jesus is enthroned, namely, his crucifixion.

The crowd's misunderstanding in verse 15 should interest preachers. A wondrous event—and especially one that feeds our physical hunger—leads us to want to enthrone the wonder-worker and make him a celebrity. Jesus, however, has no desire to be received solely because of the physical benefits of believing. In fact, he flees from just such an effort. All the emphasis on Jesus' wondrous deeds is not a basis for genuine faith, as the treatment of "signs" in John clearly suggests. Jesus feeds us out of his compassion for the needy but not as a means of wooing us to him. At the very surface of this wonder story is the invitation to feed the hungry of the world today as Jesus fed the multitude. That obvious point ought not to get lost in our search for deep symbolic meaning.

The metaphorical force of some of the details in the story demonstrates how much Christ is able to do with the smallest and most insignificant of gifts. The "little boy" *(paidos)* furnishes nothing more than two small fish and two barley loaves, the cheapest bread available. The fourth Gospel's version of the story stresses how much Christ makes out of so little. We may often feel that we have little to offer Christ, especially in contrast to the problems of our world and the difficulties of discipleship. Christ feeds a multitude with two small fish and a couple of cheap loaves of bread, and there are still twelve baskets of leftovers! As individuals and as a congregation, we may have little abundance, few gifts, and too little commitment. Nonetheless, Christ accepts them and multiples them in his ministry.

The Walk on Water (vv. 16-21)

The lectionary reading for Proper 12, B, joins this episode to the feeding of the multitude. We need briefly to compare this story with the Synoptic tales found in Matthew 14:22-33 and Mark 6:45-52. (Luke curiously does not relate this wondrous story. It is a part of Luke's "great omission," which includes Mark 6:45—8:26.) A cursory comparison of the Johannine and Synoptic stories yields several interesting differences.[7] John's story is far shorter than even Mark's, which Matthew expands. John gives no motive for the disciples' movement across the sea to Capernaum (v. 16). Neither does the fourth evangelist show any interest in the darkness of night and the difficulty the disciples were having in the hard wind but does say they have "rowed about three or four miles" (v. 19). The disciples have no trouble identifying Jesus, as do those in the Synoptic stories, but their reaction is fright (v. 19). Jesus' word to them does not include the command "take heart" *(thareite)* but only the self identification, "It is I" (actually *egō eimi*, "I am"), and the admonition, "do not be afraid" *(mē phobeisthe).* This is the only place in the Synoptics where we find the Johannine *egō eimi*. John says nothing of the cessation of the wind but speaks of a sudden "wondrous landing" (v. 21). The narrator in the fourth Gospel does not say that Jesus actually got into the boat with the disciples, only that they "wanted" or "were willing" *(ēthelon)* to take him aboard.

The preacher must take care not to read the Johannine account of the walk on water as if it were exactly like the Synoptics. The disciples are neither brought to a confession of faith (as in Matt. 14:33) nor to astonishment and confusion (as in Mark 6:51-52). As a matter of fact, nothing is said of them except that they welcomed Jesus, and who would not in those circumstances! What is clear is that Jesus comes to rescue them from the wind (as is also the case in the Synoptics) and to bring them immediately to their destination. What is striking is that in this context the Lord who strolls across the sea and then wondrously brings the boat to its destination is so very much unlike what the crowd had thought he was when they sought to make him king. This is more than an earthly king. This is God's own presence coming to the disciples (as the *egō eimi* means in John's case) and not just a candidate for royalty. We really do not need a king! We need God's presence! Like the crowd, however, we may not know what it is we really need.

The Bread of Life Discourse (vv. 22-71)

The discourse, or better, the discussion seems to move without clear order and repeats itself time and time again. So, we need to place our discussion in the context of an overview of 6:24-71, and none is better than that of Raymond E. Brown (which I have used here with only slight modification).[8] We will, however, note where the assigned readings begin and end. The lectionary does not include the rather confusing story of the crowd's search for Jesus and the crossing of the Sea of Tiberius, so we will proceed to the beginning of the introduction to the discourse at verse 24.

The preface to the discourse (vv. 24-34) moves through several stages. (1) The initial encounter between Jesus and the crowd and the issue of "food that endures for eternal life" (vv. 24-27). (2) The discussion of the "works of God" (vv. 28-29). (3) The crowd's request for a "sign" and their invocation of Moses' feeding of the people manna in the desert as the sign that allowed their ancestors to believe (vv. 30-31). (4) Jesus responds by saying that God—not Moses—fed the people and that "the bread of God is that which (or he who) comes down from heaven and gives life to the world." The people naturally ask Jesus to give them that bread (vv. 32-34).

The lectionary readings for both Proper 13, B, and Thanksgiving, C, add verse 35, which is Jesus' response to the people's request in verse 34. He himself is the bread that fills all hunger and thirst. However, Brown correctly begins the first major section of the discourse itself with verse 35.

A number of themes leap out at us as we contemplate preaching on 6:24-35. Among them is the troubling question of why people "follow Jesus." Is it because they are drawn to him by his indications of who he is and whom he reveals (that is, the "signs"), or are there other motives that are less pure? Jesus questions the crowd's motives for seeking him out as he is always pushing us to examine our own reasons for faith. Today we know how complicated motives can be and how difficult it is to discern one's true motives. The crowd is going to be offered something as a result of faith in Christ, but it is not simply self-satisfaction. In this brief exchange, Jesus calls into question all claims that we should believe because of "what's in it for us." Today that includes the frantic search for a peace of mind in a hassled world.

Our motives are called into question by this passage but so too are the "works" we think we must do in order to receive God's gifts. We must be careful not to read a Pauline view of "works of the Law" into this discourse, yet the people are asking an important question: "What may we do that we may work the works of God" *(Ti poiōmen hina ergazōmetha ta erga tou theou)?* God's singular work or *ergon* is bringing humans to faith in Christ. What does that mean today? Certainly it means more than we have sometimes narrowly defined as "evangelism." God's redemptive will among humanity is designed to free humans from all that prevents their being truly human. Bringing humanity to faith entails social as well as spiritual concerns. But the works of God center in the divine effort to recreate a relationship with humanity.

Part one of the discourse (vv. 35-40) begins with the first of the *egō eimi* sayings in the discussion. (But see 6:20.) Another is found in verse 48 and then expanded in verse 51: "I am the living bread that came down from heaven." Note that a simple emphatic like "I myself am" may be all that is needed here for a translation, although more may indeed be implied. Jesus speaks in a metaphor. He claims that he is what heavenly bread is. The metaphor picks up the feeding of the multitude and links it with manna. It is at once both a metaphor derived from the universal need for nourishment and from the peculiar history of the Jewish people. As a metaphor, its suggestive quality expands with all of the other ways in which we use the word and concept "bread."

Jesus follows this *egō eimi* saying immediately with a challenge to the crowd, which the lectionary truncates by omitting verses 36-40. Nonetheless these verses pose some interesting issues. Jesus claims the crowd does not yet believe. That introduces a rather lengthy description of Christ's mission in the world. With the ideas of what (and who) the Father gives Jesus (v. 37) and doing the Father's will (v. 38), Jesus stresses his authority as God's Revealer. If there are those whom the Father "gives" to the son, then by implication there may be those whom the Father has *not* given the son. The opposite of "losing" is "raising up on the last day." The resurrection at the final day, of course, was thought to be strictly God's prerogative, so Jesus' promise that he will raise the believers claims he has been given divine roles.

Here are examples of two of the great paradoxical tensions on John's theology (see chapter 2). The first is the tension, on the one hand, between a kind of predeterminism with regard to who will believe and who will not and, on the other hand, a human freedom to believe or reject belief. I think an honest reading of John necessitates that we maintain this tension and recognize a paradoxical combination of divine and human responsibility for belief and unbelief. Or, to put it another way, both God and humans have roles in the birth of faith.[9]

The other tension is less clear but nonetheless discernible, namely, the paradox of a realized (or present) eschatology and a futuristic one. The expression "eternal life" in John seems to refer to that quality of life here and now in which the believer participates. Hence, the Gospel can claim, as it does here, that the believer *has* eternal life. (See 3:36; 5:24; and 6:47 for other examples, but also 12:25, which can be interpreted as a reference to the life of the believer beyond death. See also chapter 2 and the sermon under the topic of salvation in that chapter.) On the other hand, resurrection of the dead here is still clearly an event reserved for "the last day." In fact this reference to Christ's raising the Christians at the last day is nearly a refrain in the discourse, occurring at verses 39, 40, and 44. The tension between having eternal life now and being raised on the last day is not as difficult to resolve as the one between human and divine responsibility for faith. Nonetheless, the two positions placed side by side makes it impossible for us to generalize that the fourth Gospel teaches only a present eschatology, as is sometimes done. Or, is it the case that the "last day" is the moment of encounter with Christ in this life and that resurrection is the transformation that occurs when one is brought from unbelief to faith?[10]

The bold preacher might effectively take one of these two conceptional tensions in thought as a sermon theme. The heart of the passage, however, suggests that preachers undertake a discussion of the hunger and thirst that bread and water cannot fulfill—the restlessness for something that sustains a meaningful and rich life. Jesus' words in verse 35 offer this focus. Needless to say, there is today still an unsettled search among many for something that transcends the material, the secular, and the immediate. How is Christ the bread that satisfies that hunger? Is it the gift of love? Is it the revelation that the heart of the universe—the ultimate reality—is caring and compassionate? How would you say this to the inquirer? (One warning: if we use the bread metaphor here and relate it to the Eucharist, we still have to deal with the text assigned for Proper 15, B.)

Part Two of the Discourse (vv. 41-51) moves in a new direction. Verse 41 presents a narrative anomaly. Suddenly those to whom Jesus speaks are referred to as "Jews." The discourse began with the "crowd" that followed Jesus after the feeding of the multitude (v. 22), and there is no indication that they do not continue to be the discussion partners in the discourse. Notice, too, that the crowd has not been hostile in their attitude toward Jesus. Quite the opposite, they are presented as serious inquirers. Now there is hostility and opposition, and it is attributed to the "Jews." (See the discussion of "the Jews" in chapter 1.) These opponents experience, first, a cognitive dissonance between Jesus' words about himself and the fact that they know him to be "the son of Joseph, whose father and mother we know." Quite simply it is the scandal of the incarnation that arouses their complaining. Their grumbling recalls the "murmuring" of the people in the desert (Exod. 15:22—17:7), and the Greek verb *(goggyzō)* is better translated "murmur."

Jesus responds that believing in him requires a prior drawing of the individual to him (v. 44)—another indication of the divine role in the origin of faith. That drawing is coupled with or identical to the necessity of being taught by God. Without a clear logical relationship, Jesus' words then proceed through a series of self-claims. He has seen God (v. 46) and is the "bread of life" who gives eternal life (vv. 47-48). Moreover, Jesus for the first time identifies the bread from above with his "flesh" (v. 51b). With that startling claim the conversation takes a radical turn, which is developed in the third part of the discourse.

Verses 41-51b provide a chance to address the scandal of the incarnation outside of the festive settings in which we read and preach John 1:14. Can this Jesus be both the bread from heaven and the kid down the street whose parents we know very well? The fourth evangelist convinces us that the incarnation is a scandalous idea, but it may be that some of us today would rather dodge that scandal. Furthermore, as the idea of the incarnation becomes too common, it loses its shock for us. This may be a preacher's opportunity to revive it. To do so, I think, we need to contemporize the fact that God meets us in the materiality of the world. The neighbor who shows compassion when we need it; the Christian colleague who demonstrates an openness and honesty that makes us reevaluate our own lives; and the terminally ill who minister to us rather than we to them by their courage and endurance. Only with something concrete and contemporary can we begin to feel the offense those so-called "Jews" felt. What is essential, too, I think, in this sort of a sermon is the recognition that the characters who are portrayed as Jesus' antagonists ironically are models for us in the sense that we ought, in all honesty, always be offended by the idea of God inhabiting flesh and blood.

Another theme tucked away in this reading is our trust of our own knowledge. Those who are offended by Jesus think they know who he is and who his parents are. In fact they are wrong. And these are religious folk. They have allowed their religious views to become dogma and thereby blind them to the presence of God in Christ. This is not to denounce the Jews. Rather, the "Jews" represent any of us when we allow our religious faith to become so certain that we think we know exactly how God must work. "Watch Out for the Known" is a sermon possibility by which preachers could raise the question of when our own certainty blinds us to God's presence.

Part three of the discourse (vv. 52-59) is the most debated and radical part of the discourse. The debate wages around both what this section means and how it found its way into the Gospel. On the latter issue, scholars have long argued that these verses seem to stand out like a sort thumb and that it is likely they were an addition made to the Gospel by a later editor.[11] We will put that question aside and be content with the fact that they are in our Gospel as it now stands. The former question of meaning is far more important for us. It has to do with whether or not the primary reference of these words is to the Sacrament of Holy Communion. There is little doubt that in the church they were very soon interpreted as references to the Eucharist; but is that their first and major reference?[12] I think it is best to assume that the reference is primarily to Jesus himself, but that the church was entirely correct in reading them Eucharistically.

The new turn in the discussion of the bread from heaven begins right away in verse 51, where Jesus identifies himself with the "living bread" and then the bread with "my flesh." The Greek word is *sarx* as it is in 1:14 and not *sōma* ("body"), which occurs in the passages that recount the institution of the Eucharist (for example, 1 Cor. 11:24). His opponents object to Jesus' words, and he elaborates in verse 53. He immediately adds "his blood" to the equation and makes a series of claims:

1. Eating his flesh and drinking his blood are required to have "life" and "eternal life."
2. His flesh and blood are *true* "food" and "drink."
3. One who eats his flesh and drinks his blood "abides" (*menō*) in Jesus and he in them.
4. "This is" the heavenly bread that assures life as opposed to the manna, which does not.

The word for "eat" is *phagein* in verses 51-53 but then changes to *trōgo*, which means "gnaw" or "gobble" as when an animal consumes food.[13] The change of the verb suggests a desperate and eager consumption, as if one's life depended on it. Hence, the discourse intensifies in its insistence that Jesus must be taken into oneself.

Obviously, it is hard to read this portion of the discourse without thinking of the bread and wine of Holy Communion. Yet on a first level of meaning, the passage seems to express radically the necessity of believers' taking Christ into themselves and making him part of their very essence. A Eucharistic reading simply transfers this to the sacramental bread and wine. Most important is to note how the discourse intensifies through these three parts, becoming more and more radical and offensive. As if readers might be tempted to dismiss the whole discourse as a "simple metaphor," the text drags us into it with hyperbole of the highest form. (Of course, a metaphor is never just "simple.")

The lectionary reading for Proper 15 includes verses 51-58, and the geographical location of the teachings stated in verse 59 is connected with 60-69. Looking ahead to verses 60-70 we find how repulsive these words prove to be, and once again we are brought back to the scandal of the incarnation. Preachers might explore what it means for Christians today to "ingest Christ." How does one go about "eating his flesh and drinking his blood?" Is it still true what we used to say—"you are what you eat"? Yes, to be sure, to take Christ into our very essence demands a sacramental life, but beyond that how does Christ become the center of human existence, even as flesh and bone are central to our physical lives? This text points us to a sacramental view or life that seeks the divine reality in everything physical, but most especially in other human beings. The sacraments of Baptism and Eucharist model for us how physical and mundane things convey divine love. Such a view denies us the leisure of superficial perception and will not allow us to avoid the divine encounter with the Word incarnate still today. Moreover, ingesting Christ surely means that our relationship with God is all the more intimate. God is as close as the food that nourishes us. Finally, let us cautiously venture to add a Pauline dimension to this passage for the sake of preaching. Remember that the body of Christ is the church and—whatever else ingesting Christ may mean—it means founding one's life on and in the confessing community.

Reactions to the bread of life discourse (vv. 60-71) are both dramatic and tragic. The reading for Proper 16, B, repeats verses 56-58, perhaps in order to remind hearers of the setting of the rest of the reading, which includes verses 59-69. The omission of verses 70-71, however, seems clearly an effort to avoid two "unpleasant" ideas: First, it avoids Jesus' claim that he chose the disciples, not they him (as Peter's words might seem to suggest), and, second, it dodges Jesus' reference to Judas and the fact that the betrayer was also "chosen." Those last two verses, it seems to me, are essential for understanding the whole of the discourse and most especially verses 51b-65.

The offended ones are now the disciples. The discourse shifts attention from the crowd to "the Jews" and now finally to the disciples. Here we have one of the clearest indications that the Gospel does not equate "disciples" *(mathētēs)* with the "twelve" and that "disciple" seems to be synonymous with believer. This passage narrates how believers fall away because of Jesus' offensive words and thereby reveal their inauthentic and superficial faith. As Jesus said to the believing Nathanael in 1:50-51, he now says to the apostate disciples: "You ain't seen nothing yet!" Unlike the Gospel of Luke, in the Gospel of John Christ's ascension is the crucifixion. Consequently, Jesus is saying that the offense of his words will only be intensified by his death.

Verse 63 is none too clear, particularly in light of what has just been said in the discourse. The point seems to be that believers must see through the flesh to perceive the "spirit" and that flesh alone is without power. The difficulty hinges on the ambiguity of the word *pneuma* in John. Suffice it to say, spirit here refers to the divine presence and, while flesh contains the spirit, the spirit is the more important. Therefore Jesus can say that his words give both the divine presence and true life. However, it is not the case, I think, that spirit-flesh constitutes a human duality (like body and soul). What is clear is that God (Spirit) can inhabit flesh.

The omniscient Jesus of the fourth Gospel is not surprised that some of his followers are unreliable, and he again insists that faith is a gift and not an achievement. Bultmann puts it rather well: "Faith is exercised in the abandonment of one's own certainty; a [person] therefore can never achieve it as a work of his [or her] own purposeful action, but experiences it only as something effected by God. In the hour of decision it is shown whether faith was one's own work or the gift of God"[14] (see the sermon on pp. 66–70).

Now Jesus asks the "twelve" if they will decide to leave him. This surely implies that, while faith is a gift from God (granted by the Father), humans can *at least* abandon faith and become unbelieving. At this point Simon Peter has his golden moment in the fourth Gospel, comparable in some ways to his confession at Caesarea Philippi (Mark 8:27-30 and parallels). He says the following: (1) There is no other source of life; (2) Jesus' words provide eternal life; and (3) Jesus is the Messiah.

The lectionary reading ends at verse 69, but look at 70-71. Over against what might be an affirmation of the role of human decision in faith in verses 67-69, Jesus now assures the Twelve that *he chose them, not they him.* The initiative is with God. Since Jesus is portrayed in this Gospel as all-knowing, we are not surprised that the chapter comes to an end with Jesus' acknowledgment of Judas and what he will do. Along with verse 62, this recognition of Judas among the Twelve ties the whole chapter—feeding, sea walk, and discourse—with the cross. All of what this chapter has to say points toward and is fulfilled in Jesus' death.

The preacher is again invited to discuss faith in the context of this last reading from chapter 6. Here you might say it is all pulled together—faith, apostasy and opposition, revelation, and eternal life. Peter's words, however, are a good summary of what discipleship is all about.

First, disciples of Christ believe as they do because there is no other source of life and meaning. Some of us have searched high and low for the key to existence and have ended up at Christ's feet. Perhaps true disciples need to experience for themselves that, so far as we know, God's revelation in Christ is the only source of authentic life and meaning—what John calls "eternal life." Second, Peter's words indicate a path of growth regarding the disciple's grasp of the identity of Jesus. We believe and through believing come to the confident knowledge about Christ's role as the revealer of the ultimate reality. Faith and knowledge are closely related to one another in the fourth Gospel and thereby imply that the two are not opposites but tandem processes in the life of faith.

As a whole the dominant theme in chapter 6 is simply food. From the feeding of the crowd, through the discussion of why the crowds followed Jesus, on to the discussion of bread and manna, and finally to eating Christ's flesh and blood—everything clusters around the word food in both its ordinary meaning and broader metaphorical implications. And there is no other metaphor that is more inclusive and universal than food.

A Sermon Example

The following sermon uses Peter's response to Jesus' invitation that the Twelve are free to leave him, if they wish. It was an effort to use this text to address the frantic search for meaning and purpose that pervades our society. It is titled, "To Whom Shall We Go?" and was preached on Proper 16, B.

∼

To whom might we go to have our dryer fixed? It has been giving us trouble lately. Do you know someone who could repair it?

To whom might I go to have this spot on my skin looked at? It has been changing color lately, and I'm worried about it. Do you know a doctor I could trust to give me a competent analysis?

To whom might we go for help with our daughter? She has been acting strangely lately. We are worried about her. Do you know someone who could help us?

To whom shall we go? It's a question we often ask—and ask about a multitude of matters. Where is a source of help? Who is able to assist us with this or that need?

The question is most serious when we ask it with regard to life's meaning and purpose. To whom shall we go to find out what life is all about? To whom shall we go to get the clue to life's puzzles? To whom shall we go to discover a center for our lives? Sometimes some of us have asked that question in frantic depression. Then it's a matter of life and death. Sometimes some of us have spent years looking for the answer to the question. To whom shall we go to find the key to a meaningful life?

Our society seems especially preoccupied with trying to make life *exciting*. Think of all the new sports and other forms of entertainment designed to provide excitement. I marvel at the so-called "extreme sports," which involve life-threatening dangers of the worst kind. I marvel at the number of people who seek escape from boredom through drugs and alcohol. But I also understand them. I understand the quest to make life interesting through adventure—through excitement. (After all, I ride a motorcycle for a hobby.) However, excitement by itself cannot make life totally meaningful. It can transform a few minutes of life; but when the buzz of excitement is over, we are right back where we started.

But neither can other easy, quick-fix answers work. Years ago my brother sent me a rather unusual birthday card. It features Ziggy, that woeful character whose life seems always to be going wrong. In this case, the outside of the card read: "For your birthday we thought that you would like to know the secret of eternal life." You open the card to find a bearded guru-type figure sitting in his mountain cave. He says to Ziggy, "The secret of eternal life is to live forever."

At times the church may be prone to give that kind of glib and evasive answer to our questions about the meaning of life. Jesus is the answer to all of life's problems! Just pray long enough and everything will be fine. Have faith! That sort of answer will not suffice. Platitudes will not do. Not for those who are sincere and even desperate in their search for the meaning of life.

Yet our Gospel lesson seems to give that sort of simple answer. His followers are bolting right and left. So, Jesus asks the twelve disciples if they too would leave him. Peter speaks for the group, "Where else shall we go? We have no alternative. You have the words of eternal life."

What kind of answer is this? Well, we need first of all to understand what "eternal life" means in this case. (Here the preacher summarizes the meaning of the phrase in the Gospel of John.) So eternal life is that quality of life right now—here and now—that has meaning and purpose.

But that's not enough. Understanding what Peter means by eternal life does not solve our problem. We must ask *how* Jesus' words lead us to a meaningful life? How can life become purposeful because of Jesus' teachings? It becomes a matter of discerning in Christ something that transforms life and makes it worth living.

Some years ago the movie *City Slickers* was popular. It was the movie that hooked us on Billy Crystal and what a fine actor he is. Some of you will remember the story. A group of urban businessmen seek some new meaning for their lives. These city slickers fly out west and become cowhands for a few weeks. They think that in doing this tough, manly work they will find a new depth and significance for their lives.

On one occasion, the old, tough trail boss gives the confused city slickers some sound advice. They ask him what he thinks the meaning of life is. In response, he simply holds up one finger. It is one thing. But what one thing, the crew wants to know? The trail boss claims, however, that everyone of them must find out for themselves. It takes the city slickers the rest of the movie and a series of difficulties for them each to discover the one thing in their lives to which they must commit themselves. The one thing that makes their lives meaningful, provided they are committed to it. For me at least, the message of the movie is that the meaning of life is found in *one single commitment.*

In some ways our Gospel lesson agrees with that message. Peter's response to Jesus is similar to the advice of the trail boss. There is one person to whom we must be committed. But in another important way our Gospel lesson disagrees with the movie's message. The movie suggests that we must discover a single commitment for ourselves. We must mold something around which we can center our whole lives. Peter also claims that meaningful life is found in a single commitment. But that commitment is not discovered by us humans. We do not create it out of the hodgepodge of our lives. God give us that single commitment in what God has done in Christ.

Christ is the bread sent down from God to feed us confused and starving humans. In Christ, God gives us the glue that holds our lives together. God provides us a direction for our lives—a map that leads us out of our confused, excitement-seeking search.

Oh, it is not that simple, I suppose. A gift is no good to us unless it is accepted. The bread of life is not nourishing unless it is eaten. The promise of eternal life requires our trust. It demands that we embrace it as our own commitment.

Notice that in our Gospel lesson the disciples have a chance to leave Jesus. Like the others, they are free to junk this whole Jesus thing and go off in search for some new purpose for their lives. Christ does not prevent them. He does not bind them to their commitment. Here they must reaffirm it. That one single commitment, however, requires something of us. God has given us the gift of a meaningful and purposeful life. But we are asked to appropriate it for ourselves. Like Peter and the others, we need to follow Jesus in trust that in doing so life comes together around him.

"Lord, to whom shall we go? You have the words of eternal life."

～

Chapters 14, 15, and 16—The Farewell

These three chapters comprise what has been called the farewell discourses, because they represent Jesus' final teachings for the disciples and deal in large part with Jesus' departure from this world. They are very important, since they contain the largest amount of teaching about discipleship to be found in the Gospel. Elsewhere in the Gospel, Jesus most often deals with conflicts with his opponents, but in these last discourses attention is focused on how the disciples are to live and what they are to believe. In chapters 1–12 Jesus' ministry is a public affair; in 13–17 he is in private with the disciples.

Chapters 14–16, however, are notoriously difficult to interpret and consequently to preach, as our earlier discussion suggested. (See chapter 4.) The language is thick and hard to understand, and logical order of thought is nearly impossible to discern. There are themes that appear and then are dropped, only to reappear again. In these chapters we experience firsthand what we said earlier about discourses moving in cyclical fashion or even like a flow of consciousness. For those reasons, these chapters are worth our attention, and in particular those portions that appear in the lectionary.

In many ways these chapters need to include chapter 13, because that chapter sets the context for the discussion that follows in the next three chapters. Moreover, the teachings in chapter 13 sound like Jesus' farewell words to his disciples and introduce some of the themes that will surface again in chapters 14–16. Before we undertake interpretation of any of the passages from chapters 14–17, we should probably first reread chapter 13.

According to some scholars, the "farewell discourses" are composite and betray the presence of several discussions welded together at various times in the history of the Johannine Christian community. That history of composition explains why there are some contradictions and so many repetitions in the chapters. The most glaring of the problems is at the end of chapter 14, where Jesus commands the disciples to get up and go (v. 31). Then the discussion goes right on, ignoring what Jesus has asked the group to do. The detection of different "layers" of discourse is interesting but not that helpful for the preacher. It is finally more important for us to have a grasp of the whole of the chapters, in spite of their composite nature.[15]

Eight passages from chapters 4–16 are included in the lectionary, and we will discuss them in their order in the Gospel. At the conclusion, there is a sample sermon on one of the eight passages. Before beginning, however, we should note that the disciples to whom Jesus speaks are never named, and it is important to assume that they were comprised of a broader group than the "twelve." For that reason, I think we need to consider the possibility that those women who appear at the foot of the cross might well have been present for these discussions.

Easter 5, A, 14:1-14

This lesson is familiar partly because it is often read at funerals; however, the passage has a larger role to play. It begins with a kind of dialogue between Jesus and the disciples. Jesus speaks, and Thomas responds. Then Jesus speaks again, and Philip responds. Each of the speeches from Thomas and Philip is only important for what they solicit from Jesus.

Three parts comprise the passage: (1) Jesus' departure and the promise of abiding (vv. 1-7); (2) the relationship between Jesus and the Father (vv. 8-11); and (3) the greater works of the disciples (vv. 12-14). This is a good example of how various themes are related in portions of these discourses. In this case, Jesus' departure necessitates that the disciples understand his relationship with the Father and be assured of the value of their ministries after his departure.

Clearly one of the themes in this passage is the "rooms" Jesus promises in verse 2. (See the discussion of this theme in chapter 3 and the sermon fragment at the end of that chapter.) The word is actually a noun, *monai*, which is related to the verb *menein* (to abide). So, the places prepared for the disciples are relational, as the verb *menein* speaks of a relationship of an intimate sort. Preachers may deal with this promise as one to be fulfilled in the future, and even beyond death. There is a possibility, too, that the "rooms" and the "place" are present in the believers' relationship with God and Christ.[16] The relationship with God established through Christ is a reality in the present and continues through and beyond death. In other words, this is another way of speaking of "eternal life." Such an interpretation is invited by the ambiguity of the promise, "I will come again. . . ." To what coming does this promise refer? The appearance of the risen Christ after the crucifixion, the coming of the Spirit, or a reappearance at the end time? Once again, I suggest preachers preserve the ambiguity of the promise so that it might refer to all three.

Jesus' response to Thomas's question suggests that Jesus is both the goal and the means by which one travels toward the goal. "Truth" and "life" are prominent Johannine themes, both identifying the gift of life in relationship with God made possible by Christ. "Way" is a standard Hebraic concept for the lifestyle one chooses to live. Verse 6b becomes more difficult as our global consciousness grows. You will have to interpret these harsh words in the light of your own theological convictions. There is, however, a possibility of saying that this is not a universal statement but a confessional one. That is, those who have been brought into a relationship with God through Christ can do nothing else but affirm that for them Christ is the only way.

Verses 8-11 simply affirm the relationship between Jesus and God that runs throughout the whole Gospel. Here the preposition "in" *(en)* describes the intimacy of that relationship, even as the verb "abide" *(menein)* does elsewhere. The final part of this reading is actually the beginning of a new section. It is problematic only if one fails to understand the importance of the church's ministry in John. This promise of "greater works" does not diminish the redemptive work of Christ but emphasizes the church's mission (see also 5:20). The point, however, is that once Christ ascends to the Father's side and transfers his power to the world through the disciples, "greater works will be done."[17] That's a promise the church needs to hear again and again, especially in this day when its power seems diminished.

Easter 6, A, 14:15-21

This lesson explains both the content of those "greater works" and how they are done. Like Christ's work, they are works of love (in this case *agapē*), and they are accomplished through Christ's presence in the Spirit. As the reading is carved out, it begins with the theme of love and ends with it (v. 21). The question-response pattern established in verses 1-14 continues in verses 22-24, but those verses are excluded from this reading. (John 14:23- 29, however, is the assigned reading for Easter 6, C, so it is only Judas's question that is entirely excluded.) Truncated as it is, the reading deals first with the promise of the Paraclete (vv. 15-17) and then with the related promise that Christ will come again to his believers (vv. 18-21).

This is the first of the four passages that speaks of the gift of the *paraklētos* (see also 14:25-26; 15:26-27; 16:7-15). The Johannine community (or the evangelist) conceived of the Holy Spirit as One who is closely related to Jesus and who serves both to strengthen believers and judge the world. The Greek word *paraklētos* is used only in these passages and in 1 John 2:1 but nowhere else in the New Testament. Its sister noun *paraklēsis* is relatively common (see, for example, 1 Cor. 14:3; Phil. 2:1; and Heb. 6:18) and means "encouragement," "exhortation," "appeal," "consolation," or "comfort." From the association of these two nouns, the King James Bible drew the title "Comforter" to translate *paraklētos*. Actually, its meaning can be "consolation in the gospel," but it can also mean one who comes to the side of another in her or his defense (hence the RSV and NRSV translations). What is startling is that these passages use what apparently was a fresh, new word to speak of the Spirit, as if the evangelist or the tradition before the Gospel wanted to evoke new thought about and faith in the work of the Spirit. The Greek word has juristic as well as religious associations, with the result that none of the various English translations are entirely adequate—advocate, counselor, comforter, and so on. The Paraclete continues the work Christ has begun and serves as the divine presence in the world after Christ's departure.[18] The four passages concerning the Paraclete should provide a context within which we interpret each individual one.

The passage begins as a conditional statement: "If you love me. . . ." When that condition is met, two things follow: The disciples will be obedient to Jesus and will receive the Paraclete. Jesus speaks three times in the farewell discourses of "keeping" his "commandments" (14:15, 21; 15:10), and each time the word *commandment* is plural. Yet if we ask what those commandments are, we find only one—to love one another (13:34; 15:12). It might be argued that belief is commanded (for example, 8:24; 14:1, 11; 20:27). But whether or not each of these passages actually orders belief is debatable. The Johannine Jesus does not offer moral injunctions beyond the simple invitation to "love one another." Still, obedience might be correctly construed in John to mean belief as well as love.

Note several things said about the Paraclete in this passage: God sends the Paraclete in response to Jesus' request. The passage speaks of the Paraclete as "another" Paraclete, suggesting that Jesus is the first. Unlike Jesus, however, the Paraclete remains in the world "for ever." This figure is called the "Spirit of truth." Since the word *truth* usually means the revelation of God in Christ, the Spirit continues to convey that revelation to the world. The world is blind to the Paraclete's presence, who both "abides" with the disciples and is "in" them. The presence of God through the Paraclete thus distinguishes the Christian community from the world and assures the community that it has God's self-revelation.

In the light of the promised advent of the Paraclete, Jesus can say that he will not "orphan" his believers but through the Spirit will come and remain with them (v. 18). The final verses are thick with meaning. Jesus' departure means that the disciples will no longer experience him physically ("see" him) but, unlike the world, will nonetheless perceive his presence. This means that Jesus will live beyond his departure and will sustain life through the disciples. That life consists of the reciprocal relationship between Jesus and God, as well as between believers and Christ. Finally, obedience expresses the disciples' love of Christ and will in turn insure that Christ loves them and reveals himself to them.

Whether or not preachers decide to focus on the gift of Paraclete here or save that for one of the other passages that speak of the Spirit, the treatment of the topic in the pulpit calls for a careful preaching plan. The other passages about the Paraclete are assigned for Easter 6, C, Pentecost, B and C, and Holy Trinity Sunday. Except for Holy Trinity, the present passage is the only place one of the Paraclete passages is read in Year A. (See below for suggestions on preaching on the Paraclete.)

Christ's promise not to abandon the disciples (v. 18) is continually important for the Christian community. On the individual level, tragedy often brings a sense of abandonment; and on the community level, the seemingly endless fractionalization of the church evokes a similar kind of feeling. The disciples feel threatened by the loss of Jesus and the loss of that relationship. Like them Jesus invites us to cling to the promise of Christ's presence solely on the basis of who has promised it. Christ's presence cannot depend on our emotions—"feeling the presence of God"—nor can it depend on our ability to manipulate Christ's presence either through the sacraments or through righteous living. We believe Christ will not abandon us because Christ has promised not to, and he keeps his promises! Promises have been cheapened today by the advertisers and politicians, and the process shows no signs of subsiding. So the church needs to make clear that the divine promise is dependable. On the basis of the promise of Christ's presence through the worse of times, a shower of other gifts result (as verses 19-21 suggest). Moreover, Christ's presence in the community is what continues to distinguish the church from the world—even in a time when it sometimes looks as if the distinction is blurred. Preachers need to affirm Christ's presence but also to suggest ways in which Christ is present (for example, through Christian consolation.) Otherwise, for some the affirmation becomes hollow and meaningless.

Easter 6, C, 14:23-29

This passage continues the discussion that begins in 14:1 but in the lectionary it appears in another cycle (see chapter 4). The reading has three discernible parts: verses 23-24, 25-26, and 27-29.

Verses 23-24 are framed as a response to Judas's (not Iscariot) question as to why Christ will not manifest himself to the world, and they repeat some of the essential themes of 14:1-21. Verse 23 parallels verse 15, except that the one who loves Christ keeps his "word" (as opposed to "commandments" in v. 15). If the condition is fulfilled, two things happen. First, God loves those who love Christ and, second, God and Christ come to them and make their "home" with them. Here the coming of God and Christ to the believer parallels the coming of the Paraclete in verse 15, which suggests that the Paraclete is the specific presence of the divine after Christ's ascension. The word "home" translates *monē,* the singular of the word used in 14:2, but is translated in that verse as "rooms." God and Christ choose to make their dwelling place with believers, and that "home" is the intimate relationship implied by the verb *menein.* God and Christ do not dwell in some remote "heaven" but are among us. Verse 24 presents the opposite of verse 23, "whoever does not love me. . . ." This is an incident of simple Hebraic poetic parallelism (in this case, antithetical parallelism).

Verse 25 names the Paraclete the "Holy Spirit." The function of the Paraclete is to "teach . . . all things" and "remind" the disciples of Jesus' teachings. Clearly, the Spirit is a continuation but also an expansion of Jesus' ministry. The theological implications is that while God's revelation in Christ is definitive, more will be revealed through the Paraclete. If we were to take this promise seriously, the work of the Spirit might enable the contemporary church to hold a more progressive and open view of change.

Peace *(eirēnē)* introduces the third section of the passage, verses 27-29. The verses attempt to console the disciples as they face their master's departure. Peace, fearlessness, and rejoicing are the features of the time that we would call the "postresurrection" church. Jesus prepares the disciples for their loss by telling them these things now. The statement in verse 28, "the Father is greater than I," complicates Johannine Christology. While God and Christ are "one" (10:30, 38; 17:1, 22), there is a distinction between them (even as 1:1 suggests). This leads many of us to believe that the Johannine community was not thinking so much in terms of a oneness of God and Christ in "substance" or being as in action and will. God and Christ are one in terms of will and love, but God is greater.[19]

In the context of the Easter season, this passage suggests a sermon on "God's home." In our insistence that God transcends our world and experience, perhaps we need a corrective to the sense that God is too distant to be reached. The popularity of angels today in North American culture suggests that very assumption, namely, that God is so distant that divine agents must serve as intermediators. Yet Christ promises that he and God will make their "home" with the community of believers. The Trinity is "at home" among us! It is in the community of faith that God and Christ have promised to dwell.

Easter 5, B, 15:1-8

The passage contains the metaphor of the vine and the branches. This is one of the seven times in the Gospel that Jesus speaks, using *egō eimi* with a predicate nominative. In these cases, Jesus identities himself with another reality of some sort: "the bread of life" (and "living bread, " see 6:35 and 51), "the light of the world" (8:12 and 9:5), "the door of the sheep" (10:7 and 9), "the good shepherd" (10:11 and 14), "the resurrection and the life" (11:25), "the way, the truth, and the life" (14:6), and "the true vine" (15:1 and 5). These sayings are often treated as allegories, but I prefer to think of them as metaphors that shock the mind and tease the imagination. They are not meant to be reduced to simple propositions; for example, Jesus is the source of our Christian lives as a vine is the source of life for the branches. To do so attempts to eliminate the poetic quality of such sayings. Through the centuries the church has allowed these sayings to work on the consciousness of believers, which invites new and rich meanings.[20]

Go through this passage and find all of the uses of the word "abide" in the NRSV or *menein* in the Greek, and you will get in touch with the heart of the metaphor. This word works to build the closeness of the believers and Christ. If the passage is a metaphor, we ought not to worry too much about specific details. For instance, John gives us little idea just what is meant by "fruit" in verses 1 and 2 (see also 4:36 and 12:24), except in the next passage, 15:9-17. Matthew clearly uses the word to speak of righteous deeds, but we must not strictly impose that on the fourth Gospel. Nor should we try to build a concept of hell out of verse 6.

What is evident is that this relationship means everything to the church and believers. It is a relationship that is close but not simply warm and fuzzy, since something grows out of it in terms of responsible living. Most of all the passage suggests an absolute dependence on Christ and God. One of the ideas is that our life flows from this relationship, but other ideas are spawned as well. A sermon that sets the congregation thinking about all the possible meanings they might draw from this metaphor might be a bit

unusual but would certainly be productive. We might invite our congregations to think of their own individual Christian lives and their own Christian community in the light of this metaphor. Our sense of dependence
may wither with too much attention to money and buildings or to popularity and appeal and even growth in numbers. A congregation finds its
strength from being rooted in the presence of Christ in its midst.

Easter 6, B, 15:9-17

This passage, coupled with the preceding reading, allows us to read two
sections of chapter 15 one Sunday after the other. The first section is the
metaphor of the vine and the branches, and in the subsequent section
Jesus speak of one of the "fruits" the relationship yields, namely, love. The
passage spirals through a series of affirmations about love, which include
the following:

> • Love is an essential feature of the relationship between God and Christ.
> • Jesus' love of the disciples is one that goes to extremes.
> • Obedience arises from love.
> • Jesus commands the disciples to love "one another."
> • The disciples are Jesus' friends and not his servants.
> • Christ has chosen the disciples to bear the fruit of love.

Note that the command to love one another brackets all that is between
verses 12 and 17.

Scholars worry that in the fourth Gospel the love commandment is
restricted to "one another" and is thereby weaker than the command to
love your "neighbor" (see Mark 12:30-33) and even your "enemy" (Matt.
5:43-44; Luke 6:27-35). Indeed, the restriction of this commandment is
one of several indications of a sectarianism in the Gospel of John. It seems
to qualify the mission of the church, and these days nurtures a parochial-
ism. There is truth in this interpretation, although it may not be the whole
story. On the negative side is the sectarianism implicit in the command,
but on the positive side is the centrality of love as the defining characteristic of the Christian community. Can the church express the positive ele-
ment of the command without slipping into its negative possibilities?
Preachers have an obligation to lessen the negative sectarianism by stressing other parts of this Gospel and the rest of the New Testament, while
emphasizing the positive aspect of the commandment.

Surely the most startling part of this passage, however, is the claim that
Christ names us "friends" *(philoi)*. The classical distinction between the
two Greek words *agapē* and *philos* crumbles in this passage, since Christ's

declaration that he loves the disciples with an *agapē* is butted up against his calling us *philoi*. The contrast between friend and servant is powerful in several ways, not least of all in the difference Jesus points out: the servant does not know what the master is doing, and by implication a friend knows what the other is doing. Friendship held a place of honor in the Greco-Roman world, and the passage should be read in that light. This does not mean that Christ is our buddy, "who walks and talks with us"; however, divine love tears down the usual stereotypes of the God-human relationship. If friendship is the essence of the love Christ has for us, how then does that fact impact our human friendships? Does it not sanctify them, even implying that through friendships we may experience God's love for us?[21] (See the sermon below.)

Pentecost, C, 14:8-17 (25-27)

This passage is one of the two readings from John for Pentecost. Its content is discussed above under Easter 5 and 6, as well as Easter 6, C.

Pentecost, B, 15:26-27 and 16:4b-15

These passages connect the Paraclete saying in 15:26-27 with the longer one in 16:4b-15. We will focus on the latter, which is by far the most difficult of the four sayings about the Paraclete. Like the other Paraclete sayings, John 16:4b-17 begins with an announcement of Jesus' forthcoming departure. He then complains that no one has asked where he is going, even though that seems to be the substance of Thomas's question in 14:5. (This problem is one of the reasons some believe that portions of the farewell discourses were written at different times and then patched together without careful editing to hide the "seams.") Two other features of the introduction to the topic of the Paraclete (16:4b-7) are worth noting. First, Jesus acknowledges that his departure causes the disciples sorrow (16:6), and, second, that his departure is to the advantage of the disciples.

The Paraclete can come only if Jesus departs, intimating that the Spirit's presence is one of the results of Jesus' death and resurrection. Indeed, John associates the bestowal of the Spirit with the appearance of the risen Christ (20:19-23). In 16:7b Jesus states that he will send the Paraclete, although in the previous two passages he says God will send the Paraclete (14:16, 26). The function of the Spirit in this passage is to "convince the world" (RSV) or "prove the world wrong" (NRSV). The Greek word *(elegchō)* is difficult to translate. I find the NRSV translation helpful, since I think Christ promises that the Spirit will assure believers through proving them right and the world wrong. The world is wrong about sin, and righteousness and judgment. The three "because" *(hoti)* clauses following each of these three topics are not clear. The point is that the Paraclete's function is to assure believers of their views, even though the world opposes those views.

Verses 12-15 are sometimes considered a continuation of the saying in 4b-11 and sometimes a separate saying. Here the Paraclete's roles are to repeat Jesus' teachings and guide the church "into all truth." Moreover, the Spirit glorifies Jesus; that is, the Spirit makes clear who Jesus is and how to honor him. The dependence of both the Son and the Spirit upon God closes this passage.

In the simplest of terms, the reading promises that the Holy Spirit will assure, teach, and guide the church. The church's witness and ministry in the contemporary world is harder and harder to define. The changes of our culture force the church to change, and hence we find ourselves walking the narrow precipice that drops off on one side into accommodation and on the other into isolation from the world. Furthermore, we don't know how to stand on thorny issues, even though there are many who look to their church for guidance on matters such as the death penalty, abortion, and homosexuality. The Spirit helps us know what is faithful and what is perfidious, where we should change and where we should not.

The tougher question is how do we discern the Paraclete in our midst. In the Gospel lesson Jesus addresses the disciples as a group—a single community. It is not so much that the Paraclete is given to the individual as that it is given to the body of believers. The contemporary church needs to take that simple fact seriously and look for the work of the Paraclete in our gathering. Perhaps we ought to test claims to the guidance of the Spirit within the community of believers, so that corporate perception takes authority over individual perception.[22] Finally, the church would do well to understand consolation and assurance from one another as the consolation and assurance of the Spirit. In other words, let's look to our community for the guidance and teaching of the Holy Spirit.

Holy Trinity, C, 16:12-15

This passage simply puts a portion of the lesson for Pentecost, B, in another liturgical context. This passage is one of the few places where we find the three persons of the Trinity mentioned together in the course of four verses. Some preachers are put on the spot trying to determine whether to interpret these verses in the context of the church's later doctrine of the Trinity or in the context of the Gospel of John itself. We must be clear that John does not have an orderly and logical view of the three persons of the Father, Son, and Holy Spirit. What we find in the fourth Gospel, however, might be deemed the ingredients out of which the church fashioned the doctrine.

These verses articulate the communal nature of God. The three figures—Father, Son, and Holy Spirit—comprise a team working to accomplish a common goal. Or, to put it more properly, the three form a community. The communal nature of God is one of the most important features of the doctrine of the Trinity and one which has immediate relevance for our lives together today as a society of faith. Community is formed out of relationships, so that relationship too has to do with the divine being. Paul helps us understand the church by speaking of it as a body with different parts and functions (1 Corinthians 12). Is it helpful to think of God as a single body composed of different members, each with a valuable contribution? Some such view of the Trinity invites us to value our community life and the unity of that life even though it may involve members very different from one another but bound together by common commitment and goal.

A Sermon Example

This is a sermon on John 15:9-17 preached on the Sixth Sunday of Easter, B and entitled simply "Friends"; however, it was prepared and preached for a very special occasion. It was a farewell sermon to a congregation for whom Myrna had served as pastor, but with which I had become intimately related and of which I was very fond. It may seem unduly personal and even corny, but I include it here because it was my honest interpretation of the passage in a very specific occasion. The sermon was part of a Eucharistic service.

~

I have little claim to fame! Except for the fact that I am married to Myrna. (And that's quite enough fame for me!) I do, however, have one other possible claim to some fame. As some of you know, during my last year at Emory University before my retirement, my neighbor in the office next door to mine was none other than Archbishop Desmond Tutu. Here I was, a simple Idaho potato picker, with Desmond Tutu as my neighbor. A Noble Prize Laureate, a major force in the dismantling of Apartheid in South Africa, chair of that nation's "Truth and Reconciliation Commission," a figure known throughout the world, and residing in the office adjacent to mine!

A first I was terribly intimidated by the archbishop. Who wouldn't be? But gradually his warmth and concern dissolved my intimidation. He is such a kind and compassionate man! And within a few weeks of meeting him, he was calling me *friend!*

Me! A friend of Desmond Tutu's? Impossible! Incredible! Unbelievable! (Oh, if only Mom could see me now!) I will always cherish that friendship.

I was amazed that the archbishop would call me friend. How much more amazed those disciples must have been when Jesus said to them: "I do not call you servants any longer, because the servant does not know what the master is doing; but I have called you friends. . . ."

I have called you friends! Not servants! Not disciples! Not children! But friends! What an astounding declaration. Christ, the revelation of God on earth. Christ, God's own self in human form. Calling those of us who follow him *his friends! God calls us friends.*

These words come at a pivotal point in the narrative of the Gospel of John. Jesus is having his last conversation with his disciples—the last one before he would be arrested and executed. He is preparing them for his death. Summing up the meaning of his ministry. In that context he speaks of love. The love God has for him. The love he has for the disciples. The love we should have for one another. And then suddenly he says it: "I have called you friends!'"

Of course, Jesus is violating all the rules! Masters aren't supposed to be friends with their servants. Corporation executives shouldn't make friends with those under their supervision. Pastors aren't even supposed to be friends with parishioners—at least in the view of some. Certainly, the Creator ought not be friends with creatures. Jesus breaks down another human barrier by becoming friends with his disciples.

So, what does this mean for us? What does it mean that Jesus calls us—you and me—friends?

Friendship is very popular these days. There's even a popular and award-winning television show called simply, "Friends." Everyone wants friends, needs friends. But human friendship is not always so great. Sometimes friendships can be superficial—a kind of buddy-buddy relationship. A friendship based on only some shared interest you have with the other. And sometimes so-called friends can be manipulative. It can be friendship only for the sake of what's in it for me.

Years ago, Cat Stevens recorded a song called "Hard-Headed Woman." (My apologies to all women for that title.) The lyrics are about seeking a true friend among so many who are not really interested in being your friend. Stevens complains about these phoney friends whom he calls "fine-feathered friends"—the ones who exploit you and use you for their own purposes. They know all the ways to find the sucker to pay for their drinks, for example. Stevens is right of course, there are a lot of "fine-feathered friends." And there are some who fail us, who betray our friendship, who let us down.

Still, not all human friendships are false. Not all of them are superficial or manipulative or unreliable. There are friendships that are deep, faithful, and self-giving.

As some of you know, I went through a divorce many years ago. I learned in that experience what Cat Stevens means by "fine-feathered friends." Some of my so-called friends wanted nothing to do with me—not after it was public that I was in the process of a divorce. But I also learned the meaning of true friendship. Other of my friends came rushing to my side to support and care for me. I don't know how I would have survived those years without Jim and others. True friendship entails being with another through the pains and hurts of life.

And Christ's friendship is of that kind. Christ isn't our friend for the sake of what he might gain. What could he possibly gain from our friendship? And his friendship is dependable through the worst of times.

But what does this mean for true friendship? If Christ is our true friend, what does that tell us about our own friendships? By calling his disciples friends, Christ elevates friendship to the highest level. He lifts up ordinary human friendships and makes them special, makes them experiences of God.

Christ calls us friends, and that means *you and I can know God through friendships with others.* Through our relationship with friends who love us and we them, we come to know about God's love. Friends are like channels for God's love and grace. In my own experience, I have found God most often in relationships with other people. And most often in relationships with friends. Not least of all, I have found God's love and grace for me in my relationships with many of you.

The reason Christ Lutheran Church has meant so much to me is simple. Some of you have been little Christs to me. Being my friend. Lifting me up when I was down. And rejoicing with me when I was up. I find it hard therefore to tell you goodbye. Because among you I have been nourished and strengthened

There is another old song by another now-old singer, but one that fits what I want to say. But more important, I think the song expresses the meaning of the Gospel for today. Anne Murray made famous the song she entitled "You Needed Me." And it won her a Grammy Award. Let these words be our prayer to God. And let these words be our statement to all our friends: [Here the sermon includes the lyrics of the song, but expense prohibits our reprinting them.]

Jesus even called us friends. And like a good friend he seems to need us; he cares for us and lifts us to see eternity. And now, our friend Jesus invites us to have lunch with him.

∾

Jesus' Prayer in Chapter 17

Unlike Luke, John pays little attention to Jesus' prayer life. The fourth Gospel assumes such a close relationship between God and Christ that formal prayer seems unnecessary. However, following the lengthy farewell discourses of chapters 14–16, John includes Jesus' prayer as he prepares himself to face his death and execution. Chapter 17 plays roughly the role that the Garden of Gethsemane scenes play in the Synoptics but without Jesus' personal agonizing. (For that agony, see John 12:27.) It is a far more inclusive prayer than those attributed to Jesus in the garden.[23] Jesus begins by speaking of his relationship with God (vv. 1-5). Then in verses 6-23 he expresses his concern for the disciples—all believers—and finally brings these two subjects (his relationship with God and the disciples) together with special attention to the disciples' lives in the "world."[24]

The prayer is presented as a conclusion to Jesus' final private ministry with the disciples. More specifically, 16:33 provides an interesting transition to the prayer. In the first part of that verse, Jesus claims his reasons for saying what he has to his disciples is that they might have peace. Verse 16b invites the disciples to be cheerful in a world that presents them with tribulation because "I have conquered the world." The theme of the church's life in the world figures prominently in Jesus' prayer.

On three successive years, the Gospel lesson for the Seventh Sunday of Easter takes a portion of chapter 17 with the result that going through the whole cycle of readings exposes a congregation to the whole the prayer.

Easter 7, A, 17:1-11

This reading includes the entirety of the first part of the prayer (vv. 1-5). The prayer's second major part (vv. 6-23) appears to have two subsections, verses 6-11 and 12-23. This reading begins with the first major section (vv.

1-5) and continues through the first subdivision of the second major part (vv. 6-11). It opens with Jesus' declaration that his "hour" has come. A number of places in the earlier narrative contribute to a reader's anticipation of this decisive hour (for example, 2:4; 7:30; 8:20), and the first announcement of its arrival occurs in 12:23. The hour is the time when God reveals the divine self in Jesus' death and resurrection. (See chapter 5.)

The first five verses concentrate on the themes of "glory" and "glorify" *(doxa and doxazō),* which we discussed when we considered the meaning of Christ's death in the fourth Gospel (see chapter 5). Jesus prays that his death might reveal God's presence in him and that he himself might be shown to be one in whom God is present. His prayer leads us to ask, Where in our world today do we find God's glory?

In verse 6 Jesus begins to speak of his disciples, beginning by saying that they belong to God and have been given to Jesus by divine will and action. Jesus has provided them with God's self-revelation, which affords them "knowledge" and faith. The essential character of their faith and knowledge is that they know God sent Christ into the world (vv. 3 and 8). Through them, Jesus declares, he is glorified. Note that the prayer begins by asking God to glorify Jesus and now the glorification is said to be accomplished through the believers (that is, the church). This is part of the church's task in the world. Christ is no longer "in the world" except as the body of believers makes the presence of God in Christ clear to the world. This anticipates the mission of the church, which appears again later in the prayer (see v. 18).

The reading concludes with the petition that God keep the disciples in the divine name and make them one, as God and Christ are one (v. 11). Again the unity of the disciples is only introduced here and will be mentioned again later (see vv. 21-22). This is an occasion, however, to speak of the unity of the church. The unity John has in mind here is surely not ecumenical unity—a merger of denominations in polity and doctrine (although that's desirable in every sense). It is rather the unity of will and mission modeled after the unity of God and Christ in will and mission (see 10:30). Moreover, this sort of unity is not a human accomplishment but a gift from God. To be sure, we are called to unite ourselves with all other Christians in a common mission and commitment, but just as faith cannot be thought of as simply an act of the human will, neither can this unity. What is striking about Jesus' petition is that the divine relationship (of the Trinity!) is the pattern for our unity. As they are one, so shall we be one.

The preacher might take this opportunity to discuss the unity of the church and a specific congregation. It is natural that we confuse unity with same-mindedness, shared social class and values, and mutual traditions (often ethnic). Hence, the presence of people who differ from the majority challenges a congregation. Some of us have learned that in many ways it is more difficult to integrate a congregation of persons of different economic classes than it is to integrate a congregation racially. Yet we don't open a congregation to new and different people by haranguing them about their lack of openness, but perhaps a sermon that helps us think about unity and how it comes about is a good beginning. Particularly important might be praying for the gift of unity.

Easter 7, B, 17:6-19

The reading repeats verses 6-11 but by doing so selects what seems clearly to be a full unit in the text itself. What figures more prominently in verses 12-19 is the theme of the world. Jesus prays that believers will be protected in the world, for they stand in opposition to the bulk of society, wherever that may be. "World" *(kosmos)* in this case means that realm or those powers that are opposed to God's revelation in Christ. (See chapter 2.) Notice several of the themes that occur in these verses. First, Jesus is in the world and his ministry takes place there (v. 13). Second, believers do not belong *to* the world anymore than Christ does. (The phrase is literary: "they are not of [or out of] the world" *[ouk eisin ek tou kosmou].*) That is, their fundamental loyalties and perspectives are at odds with the dominant society. Third, Jesus prays not that the disciples might escape the world—be taken out of the world—but that God would protect them in the world "from the evil one" (or "from evil"—*ponēros*). The church's proper place is in the world, amid the culture of its time, and engaged with the secular.

Fourth, Jesus prays that believers be sanctified *(hagiazō)* in the world. It is not easy to determine what this word means in John, since the verb is used only here and in 10:36. However, 10:36 and 17:19 indicate that God sanctified Jesus, so now Jesus is asking that God do for the disciples what God did for him. Of course, the verb does not refer primarily to a moral transformation, but it indicates that immersion in the truth of God's revelation that distinguishes one from the whole of society. It is perhaps the matter of the totality of life given over to and shaped by God's self-revelation in Christ. (Unfortunately, the RSV translates *hagiazō* "to consecrate" in verse 19 but as "sanctify" in v. 17, thus giving the impression that different words are used in vv. 19 and 17. However, "consecrate" might be a better translation for this passage, provided that we recognize that the act is done by God and not by us.)

The fifth and final theme is the climax of the section and the reading (v. 18). Jesus has sent the disciples into the world as God sent him into the world. This petition anticipates the actual sending of the disciples by the risen Christ in 20:21. (See chapter 5.) As the unity of the church is modeled after the unity of God and Christ, so the church's mission is modeled after Christ's mission. God and Christ "send" the church. The church's life in the world is a result of God's commissioning us to be servants in the world. Moreover, the motive and purpose of our mission as a church are the same as God's motive and purpose for sending Christ. God sent Christ out of love (3:16) and now Christ sends us out of love. That makes love—and love alone—the church's reason for being in the world.[25]

Easter 7, C, 17:20-26

The final section of the prayer constitutes the last of the assigned Gospel lessons drawn from chapter 17. Jesus widens his prayer to include "those who will believe in me through their (the first disciples') word." These words exhibit the concern of the fourth Gospel for those who were not eyewitnesses to Jesus but who came to belief as a result of the church's proclamation of the gospel. (The risen Christ's word to Thomas in 20:29 is another example of this concern for later disciples [see chapter 5].)

Jesus prays that these later believers will be included in the unity of the first ones (which may suggest that such a unity was a problem for the Johannine church). Then Jesus declares that he has given to the church the *doxa* he received from God. That gift of glory, he claims, will unite believers as one. If one thinks of the *doxa* as the presence and revelation of God, then Christ is asking that the community of believers become the means of God's self-manifestation in the world. With Christ's departure, the divine presence is now found within the church (that is, the community of faith, and not necessarily an institutional structure). This is a startling and terrifying idea, as well as a dangerous one. Taken up with intentions of power and repression, it destroys the true church; however, when it is taken in the context of the Gospel as a whole, it provides the church with both its responsibility and its mission. John's view can flesh out Paul's concept of the body of Christ.

Jesus goes on to pray for the future of the church and believers when he asks that they be where he is and see his glory there (v. 24). Yet the conclusion of the prayer puts everything else in perspective. Jesus makes the divine name known "so that the love with which you have loved me may be in them, and I in them" (v. 26). The whole life of faith and the church are patterned after divine relationships, especially the relationship between God and Christ. Now the love that creates the relationship pulls the prayer to its conclusion. When God's revelation in Christ allows us to know who God is ("name") and what God has done, we are grasped by the same divine love that occasioned the sending of Christ (3:16). The final word of the prayer—Jesus' last petition—is that God's love fill our lives. If and when it does, then Christ will fill our lives as well.

The Gospel narrative proceeds from this point to make that divine love concrete and specific. Love in the abstract is meaningless, but Jesus is not interested in abstract love. He goes to the cross to demonstrate the love with which God loves the whole of humanity, and he shows that true love when one lays downs her or his life for friends. If there is any doubt that the unity of the church is the unity of will and commitment, this final petition clarifies it. Our unity with one another—and I would say with the whole of humanity—is love itself. God's love in Christ is the glue that binds us with one another and with others.

A Sermon Example

This sermon, written and preached by the Reverend Dr. Myrna Kysar, is entitled simply "That They May Be One" and was used on the Seventh Sunday of Easter, B, which in that case happened to be "Mother's Day."[26] At the time the sermon was prepared, the Gospel lesson for the Sunday assigned in the Lutheran lectionary was 17:11b-19. Using a metaphor of a jigsaw puzzle, the sermon employs petitions for unity as a means of helping a suburban congregation reconceive themselves and their mission. The inspiration for the sermon's basic metaphor came from a meditation by Martin Bell entitled "Life Is Like a Card Game."[27]

◠

There it was: a box of 500 pieces of cardboard. On one side of each piece, there was a bit of color and just a tiny bit of design. On the other side, all the pieces were the same bland tan color. Five hundred pieces that were supposed to all fit together—each in its own unique place—to form the beautiful picture on the outside of the box. My task? Join all these pieces together. Make them one. I was not sure I was up to the task, but what else is there to do on a cold, wintry Sunday afternoon in northern Minnesota? I think of that experience as I read the Gospel lesson for today.

It is the last few hours before his arrest, trial, and crucifixion, and Jesus prays for his disciples. On his lips is this strange sounding petition: "Holy Father, protect them in your name that you have given me, so that they may be one as we are one."

That they may be one! Why would Jesus pray for the oneness of his disciples? Why would he desire above all else that those of us who follow him share a unity among ourselves? Fit all the pieces together into one beautiful picture of Christian unity!

It is not a very realistic prayer, is it? Look around you. Look at all the different pieces there are. Look at the variety of people gathered here in this place to worship. There are young and old, male and female. There are pieces who are healthy and pieces who are ailing. There are some who have a good deal of financial security and some who are not sure they will be able to pay the mortgage next month. Some are well educated, some are not. There are married pieces in the puzzle and single pieces. Some are happy, some depressed, some joyful, some mourning. Some speak with one accent, some with another.

How is it that the pieces might be brought together to produce that ideal picture on the cover? How is it all we Christians might be one?

But there are still other pieces to this particular puzzle—far more than 500. Imagine now all the Christian people in the world. Imagine, if you can, the mixture of persons who claim Christ as their Lord. These pieces speak a variety of languages, live in a variety of cultures, worship in a variety of ways. They represent the entire spectrum of the human race.

How is it we might be one? No way! Never! Impossible! Forget the puzzle, Jesus! Leave us to live our isolated separate lives as individual pieces.

Why some of us don't even want to be one with one another! Remember how, when you are doing a picture puzzle, there are often certain pieces that you are sure should fit together. But, try as you may, you cannot get them to fit. They stubbornly resist union with other pieces. They stubbornly maintain their distinct individuality.

We don't want to be one with one another. We value our individuality. We have been taught to cultivate our own individual distinctiveness. Our differences are what make us who we are. We are not about to surrender that for oneness with others.

Moreover, I'm not sure I want to be one with some. I've got all the problems I can handle without taking on the problems of another. I don't want to have to become one with some who are wrestling with addiction, depression, poverty, broken marriages, and so on. Spare me sharing the life of some who are caught up in prejudices and bad judgments. I don't want to join my color and design with yours!

Thanks but no thanks! This business of being one seems quite undesirable, quite impossible! Leave the puzzle in the box! Go read a good book!

And yet he prayed, *"That they may be one!"*

A strange prayer, indeed! Yet it is the prayer that arose from that loving heart on the night before he went to the cross. And not just once in passing, as in our Gospel lesson for today, but again and again throughout his final prayer. We have no choice but to take it seriously. If Jesus prayed it, then surely the puzzle pieces will fit together.

What could Jesus have meant by this plea to God that we be made one? What kind of oneness did he have in mind?

In the Gospel of John the oneness that Jesus and God shared was a mutual love. God loves Christ; Christ loves God. That love makes them one. That mutual affection unites them into a single being. So, the mystery of the oneness Christ seeks for us seems to reside in the oneness of love. In the unity that results from mutual love. The mystery of the picture puzzle resides in the way mutual care and concern for one another can unite the individual pieces.

Love can bind us together into one.

What binds parents and children? On this Mother's Day, like others of you, I too think about my own Mother and what she has meant to me. But I cannot think of mom without realizing again how very different we are. When we have occasion to visit together, our differences are so evident. We hold different values, different political and social views. We like different foods, different forms of entertainment. Even our religious faiths are different, in spite of the fact that we both call ourselves Lutherans. Ironically, Mom helped me learn independence of thought and action. She taught me well! And now that independence has yielded the result that her youngest daughter is very different from her. Mom has produced a unique piece to the puzzle—a piece very different from her.

Yet amid all of our differences, Mom and I are strangely bonded. It is not just the biological bond of parent and child. It is the bond of love. In spite of the fact that we have differences, we share a respect and love of one another that transcends our differences. A respect and a love that allows these two distinct pieces to fit together.

It is that kind of unity I think Jesus had in mind when he prayed that we Christians might be one, even as he and his God were one. *A unity of love. A unity in love.*

But the unity love produces is a peculiar unity. The puzzle is a quaint one. The picture it produces is not what we might expect. Indeed, it is a unity—a single picture—that some might not see, might not even recognize. For it is a unity that does not annihilate our differences but transcends them. It does not seek to destroy differences but to celebrate them. It does not mix us together to produce a bland sameness among us. Imagine mixing all the colors of the rainbow together to destroy the uniqueness of each of them in favor of one single color. Imagine a picture puzzle that reduced all of the uniqueness of each individual piece to one design. No, not that kind of oneness. The unity of Christian love means that individuality exists within the context of a shared respect and mutual affection.

Yet our initial fears of this kind of unity were not far off. The pieces do not go together easily. This unity is costly. To share a mutual love is, indeed, to share one another's burdens, problems, and peculiarities. To enter into this oneness of love with other Christians is going to be expensive. Because I am bound to others in the unity of Christian love means that I'm going to rejoice with the others in their joys, but also I'm going to suffer with them in their suffering. While this oneness celebrates our individuality, it also expands our individuality. I can no longer live my life as an isolated person. My world of experience is extended to embrace the experience of other Christians. The boundaries of my individual life are moved out to encompass all of you and other Christians as well.

When one piece of our picture puzzle is fitted into its place in the total picture, it participates in the whole. One single piece shares its design with all the others, and all the others share in the design of each particular piece. No single piece is unaffected by the context of the total picture.

That they may be one!

On the one hand, it sounds so strange. On the other hand, it seems so simple. But it is a profound request Jesus makes of God.

Indeed, our lives are like the individual pieces of the unsolved picture puzzle. Yes, each has its individual color and design. But each means little or nothing without the whole picture—without all the other pieces. Each of us is a confused blur of color and design without one another.

But the one who prayed that prayer—the one who asked of God *"That they may be one"*—he has pulled us together into a single picture. With his love he has welded us into a whole. He has given birth in each of us a love that joins us with all other Christians into one beautiful picture.

∾

Conclusion:
Preaching John
in the Roundtable Church

Homiletics (the study of preaching) has been in a transition, even revolution, for nearly three decades now. The so-called "new homiletics" has stimulated a continuous process of reexamination and revision of preaching. That movement doubtless began with the seminal work of Fred Craddock[1] and was accelerated by the rise of "narrative preaching."[2] It is not important here that we explore in detail these new movements in preaching. What is important, however, is that we take note of how some features of contemporary homiletics might impact preaching John and most particularly what Lucy Atkinson Rose has called "preaching in the roundtable church."[3] My goal is only to suggest a number of connections between features of the Gospel of John and this new way of thinking about preaching. These are three of the future directions of preaching, in my opinion, but they are not necessarily features I have succeeded in incorporating into my own preaching. However strongly I endorse these, I leave it to the next generation of preachers to put them into practice.

The first of these is *conversational preaching*. By conversational preaching, I do not mean only a style of the delivery (the way the preacher strikes a conversational tone), although that is surely one result of a more thorough conversational mode. A definition of the sort of conversational preaching I have in mind might go something like this: Conversational preaching occurs when the preacher engages the congregation in genuine dialogue, inviting and stimulating thought without trying to persuade or coerce listeners.[4] The preacher witnesses to her or his own interpretation of a passage of Scripture and asks listeners to weigh the interpretation for themselves.

The most striking thing about this movement in contemporary preaching is the way it construes pastoral authority. The goal is to abandon all pretense of hierarchical authority and trust the "authority of the community." That is, any authority in the church resides within the gathered community as a whole. There are clearly issues to be discussed and assessed in this sort of preaching, and not all would agree that the authority of the gospel resides in the congregation's reading of Scripture and not the clergy's. Rose suggests, however, that we imagine the preacher sitting at a roundtable with the rest of the congregation and offering a message for discussion. The preacher has no more authority than any single member of the congregation but does have some training that enables her or him to lead the discussion.

The Gospel of John would seem to be an exact opposite of what Rose and others propose. The Jesus of John speaks with an absolute authority given him by his heavenly Parent. The difference between truth and falsehood, above and below, and the rest of the Johannine dualistic structure, would seem to mitigate against anything like a democratic consideration of the revelation. At least from one perspective, that is a correct reading of John, I think; however, there is another dimension to the message of the fourth Gospel that needs also to be recognized.

Ernst Käsemann has argued that the Johannine church that we discern through the pages of the fourth Gospel was a democratic community without authoritarian leadership. As evidence of this view, he cites 15:14 as an indication that the community regarded everyone equally a "friend."

> The relationship to the Lord determines the whole picture of the Johannine Church to such an extent that the differences between individuals recede, and even the apostles represent only the historic beginnings of the community. Perhaps the most interesting feature of this connection is the role in the Gospel of John of women. . . .[5]

Käsemann's view, of course, has met with considerable opposition, but I still think he is right. The Gospel seems effectively to undermine the authority of Peter and the Twelve and leaves no room for the sanctioning of official leaders, such as elders, deacons, and so on.[6] It indirectly elevates women to an equal place in the church—even claiming that Mary was the first "apostle." Beyond the Paraclete, if there is a "leader" among the community of followers as it is portrayed in the Gospel, it would be the "beloved disciple," and that figure is either a founder of the community in the distant past or (more likely) a symbolic representation of any believer. The Johannine church is a gathering of equals who believe that the Paraclete leads them to the truth.

The point is that "preaching in the roundtable church" would seem to be precisely the way in which the Gospel was (or might have been) proclaimed in the Johannine church. If we take this view and if we believe that John does indeed teach us how to preach as well as what to preach, then a conversational mode is the most appropriate way of preaching John.

Another of the features of "preaching in the roundtable church," Rose suggests, is an inclusiveness in which no one is denied a place at the table or their voice ignored. Everyone is heard and respected, even those who have at times been at the margins of the church and society.[7] Whether Rose's vision of preaching in the future is ever realized or not, there is little doubt that contemporary preaching has worked hard at being inclusive. Two of the obvious indications of this is the use of gender-inclusive language in the pulpit and the growing appreciation for a variety of preaching styles, especially ones often characteristic of the Black church. Beyond that, some of us have tried to insist that preachers become sensitive to the diversity of situations represented in a congregation. One cannot use a story of a married couple to speak about the gospel without being sensitive to the increasing number of single adults in our congregations. One cannot demean any group of people from the pulpit, since members of that group are likely in our congregation. A growing edge of this inclusiveness has to do with the respect with which we regard those of other cultures and religions. In the global society of today, the church's inclusive ministry becomes more and more important.

Once again, inclusiveness is not the first word that comes to mind when we think of the fourth Gospel. Indeed, its radical exclusiveness seems a polar opposite. The feature that we have called sectarianism necessarily demeans those outside the group in favor of those in the group. The nasty way in which "the Jews" are treated in this Gospel is surely neither respectful nor caring. It would seem that preaching the fourth Gospel would exclude any sense of inclusiveness.

The truth is not that simple. To be sure, there is a strong and disturbing sense of Christian exclusiveness in the fourth Gospel. Yet if you ask about the inclusive quality of the Christian message, John makes a persuasive case for inclusion—at least on one level. John's story of Jesus makes clear that women are gathered around the Johannine table. The treatment of Samaritans and their willingness to believe is unparalleled in the four Gospels, with the possible exception of Luke. The receptiveness of Gentiles is represented in the story of the royal official in 4:46-54, who models belief on the basis of Jesus' word alone. The Gentiles are mentioned again when they come to see Jesus, and their arrival brings "the hour," or so it would seem (12:20-23. See also the reference to "those who will believe in me through their [the disciples'] word" in 17:20).

The apparent openness of the Johannine Jesus and community to these groups does not by any means prove that the gospel presents an inclusive Christian message. While it may say something about the universal relevance of the Gospel in John, it does not minimize the exclusive quality of the Johannine community. But the church can choose the inclusive feature and put aside the exclusiveness of John in its preaching and teaching. That is, we can denounce the implicit anti-Jewish stance while endorsing the story's openness to women and members of other ethnic groups and cultures. In fact, I would say that the Gospel of John challenges us on precisely this point. Shall we become a sect group in the world or shall we open ourselves to the world and those who dwell therein? Shall we highlight the inclusive rather than the exclusive feature of the Gospel and contribute to a roundtable church?

The final feature of preaching John in a roundtable church is the imaginative use of images. The birth (or rebirth) of images in homiletics is exciting. Throughout the whole range of different styles of preaching, different preaching traditions, and even those who think preaching is a thing of the past, there is a common appreciation for the way in which images (verbal pictures) work to communicate and produce change in human lives. The gradual passing of the era of literacy in favor of the new age of visual images in the media has certainly helped to propel imagery and imagination to the forefront of preaching. In the years since I was in seminary, the shift from what we called "illustrations" to the imaginative use of language has been dramatic, and the literature on the subject is now overwhelming.[8]

What we have come to learn—or at least have come to think is likely true—is that humans learn through and are most often changed by images. Preaching needs to reach the imaginations of a congregation if it hopes to have any impact on their lives. So, homileticians vigorously propagate the use of images. David Buttrick, for instance, argues that each of the sermon's "moves"—those discernible fragments of a sermon—must "image" the major theme of the move.[9] More importantly, others have spoken of the way in which images enable listeners first to picture something as true for them and then embrace that truth.

While the imagery of the fourth Gospel is worn and tattered from use, nonetheless it offers us rich possibilities for imaginative preaching. I have already argued for the tactic of treating Johannine language as metaphorical, so as to enliven its possibility for enticing the imagination. All the way from the elaborate metaphors (the vine and the branches) to the simple playful use of language (the word *menein*), John offers us almost endless opportunities to exploit a Johannine passage for the sake of its imagery. One might say that the incomparable poetic style of John (that we find so difficult to interpret) ought to be read as if it were a verbal picture for the imagination and that this style ought to encourage the poet-preacher.[10]

There is, however, that dreadful tendency, of which we have spoken earlier, to define an image with a proposition and file it away in our theological dictionaries. That is, preachers have the chance with the Gospel of John to preach imaginatively by rekindling the provocativeness of its language.

Can we, for instance, give the good shepherd new vitality in an age when shepherds are more and more only a thing of the past? Or, shall we deaden its language with stale propositions?

To be sure, the creative use of imagery and imagination in preaching is not limited to Rose's "roundtable church," even though she shows how the newer understandings of language have influenced current trends in preaching. Imagery is appropriate for the congregation that seeks to deal with the sermon as a provocative discussion starter because (among other reasons) imagery invites participation. The preacher can seldom use a metaphor or image of some kind in a sermon without someone later suggesting another metaphor or image that occurred to her or him as a result of the preacher's sermon. Such is the "conversational" quality of imagery, which I believe the fourth Gospel readily encourages.

Whether or not we learn to preach in a roundtable church and whether or not such a preaching style becomes the common mode of preaching, I believe that faithful proclamation of the gospel might very well move us in that direction. My hopes for the impact of this book are far more modest than a revolution in preaching style. If this book does no more than stimulate a few readers to think new thoughts about the Christian message of John and venture new kinds of sermons to speak of John, I will be more than pleased.

Appendix

The Gospel of John
in the Revised Common Lectionary

The numbers in brackets ([-]) refer to the readings based on the Roman
Lectionary and are used by the Roman Catholic and Anglican Churches.

1:(1-9), 10-18	Christmas 2	A, B, C
1:1-14	Christmas Day 3	A, B, C
1:6-8, 19-28	Advent 3	B
1:29-42	Epiphany 2[2]	A
1:43-51	Epiphany 2[2]	B
2:1-11	Epiphany 2[2]	C
2:13-22	Lent 3	B
3:1-17 (Alt.)	Lent 2	A
3:1-17	Trinity Sunday	B
3:13-17	Holy Cross	A, B, C
3:14-21	Lent 4	B
4:5-42	Lent 3	A
5:1-9 (Alt.)	Easter 6	C
6:1-21	Proper 12 [17]	B
6:24-35	Proper 13 [18]	B
6:25-35	Thanksgiving	C
6:35, 41-51	Proper 14 [19]	B
6:51-58	Proper 15 [20]	B
6:56-69	Proper 16 [21]	B
7:37-39 (Alt.)	Pentecost	A
9:1-41	Lent 4	A
10:1-10	Easter 4	A
10:11-18	Easter 4	B
10:22-30	Easter 4	B
11:1-45	Lent 5	A
11:32-44	All Saints	B

12:1-8	Lent 5	A
12:1-11	Holy Monday	A, B, C
12:12-16 (Alt.) (palms)	Palm / Passion Sunday	B
12:20-33	Lent 5	B
12:20-36	Holy Tuesday	A, B, C
13:1-17, 31b-35	Holy Thursday	A, B, C
13:21-32	Holy Wednesday	A, B, C
13:31-35	Easter 5	C
14:1-14	Easter 5	A
14:8-17, (25-27)	Pentecost	C
14:15-21	Easter 6	A
14:23-29 (Alt.)	Easter 6	C
15:1-8	Easter 5	B
15:9-17	Easter 6	B
15:26-27; 16:4b-15	Pentecost	B
16:12-15	Trinity Sunday	C
17:1-11	Easter 7	A
17:6-19	Easter 7	B
17:20-26	Easter 7	C
18:1—19:42	Good Friday	A, B, C
18:33-37	Reign of Christ [34] (Christ the King)	B
19:38-42 (Alt.)	Holy Saturday	A, B, C
20:1-18 (Alt.)	Easter (Resurrection of Our Lord)	A, B, C
20:19-23 (Alt.)	Pentecost	A
20:19-31	Easter 2	A, B, C
21:1-19	Easter 3	C

Notes

Introduction: The Problem and Promise of Preaching John

1. Eugene L. Lowry, *The Sermon: Dancing the Edge of Mystery* (Nashville: Abingdon, 1997), 62–74 and 94–100.

2. Eugene L. Lowry, *The Homiletical Plot: The Sermon as Narrative Art Form* (Atlanta: John Knox, 1980), 29–35.

3. See, among others, Robert H. Hughes and Robert Kysar, *Preaching Doctrine in the Twenty-First Century*, FRP (Minneapolis: Fortress Press, 1997), especially chapter 4. See also the work of Richard A. Jensen on story in preaching, namely, *Telling the Story: Variety and Imagination in Preaching* (Minneapolis: Augsburg, 1980) and *Thinking in Story: Preaching in a Post-Literate Age* (Lima: C.S.S., 1993).

4. See David Ourisman, *From Gospel to Sermon: Preaching Synoptic Texts* (St. Louis: Chalice, 1999).

5. D. Moody Smith, *John*, Proclamation Commentaries, 2nd ed. (Minneapolis: Fortress Press, 1986), 107.

6. See Gail R. O'Day's excellent commentary on the Gospel of John, *NIB* 9 (Nashville: Abingdon, 1995), 491–865, especially p. 852.

7. Adele Reinhartz has done a fascinating study of what I am calling "the world" in *The Word in the World: The Cosmological Tale in the Fourth Gospel*, SBLMS 45 (Atlanta: Scholars, 1992).

8. As early as 170 C.E., Tatian created a harmony of the Gospels to which Eusebius gave the name "Diatessaron"(*Historia ecclesiastica* 4.29.6). It was widely used until the fifth century, when church leaders spoke against it and confiscated copies. Other harmonies of the four canonical Gospels were also used even by prominent leaders such as Justin Martyr. See William L. Petersen, "Diatessaron," in *ABD* (New York: Doubleday, 1992),2:189–90.

9. See Jack Dean Kingsbury, *Jesus Christ in Matthew, Mark, and Luke*, Proclamation Commentaries (Minneapolis: Fortress Press, 1981).

10. See the excellent commentary by Raymond E. Brown, *The Epistles of John*, AB 30 (Garden City: Doubleday, 1982).

11. See the helpful discussion in D. Moody Smith, *The Theology of the Gospel of John*, New Testament Theology (Cambridge: Cambridge Univ. Press, 1995), 77–78;

and Smith's essay "The Presentation of Jesus in the Fourth Gospel," in *Johannine Christianity: Essays on Its Setting, Sources, and Theology* (Columbia: Univ. of South Carolina Press, 1984), 175–89. This issue became a point of contention between Rudolf Bultmann and his student, Ernst Käsemann. See Käsemann, "The Structure and Purpose of the Prologue to John's Gospel," *New Testament Questions of Today,* trans. W. I. Montague (Philadelphia: Fortress Press, 1969), 138–67; and Bultmann, *The Gospel of John: A Commentary,* trans. G. R. Beasley-Murray (Philadelphia: Westminster, 1971), 60–72.

12. For a fuller discussion of the difference between the Synoptic and Johannine portrayals, see Robert Kysar, *John, the Maverick Gospel,* rev. ed. (Louisville: Westminster John Knox, 1993), 3–14.

13. See the provocative but controversial work by J. Massyngbaerde Ford, *Redeemer, Friend and Mother: Salvation in Antiquity and in the Gospel of John* (Minneapolis: Fortress Press, 1997).

14. See as examples the Roman Catholic, Luke Timothy Johnson, *Reading Romans: A Literary and Theological Commentary* (New York: Crossroad, 1997), 6–10; and the Lutheran, Krister Stendahl, *Final Account: Paul's Letter to the Romans* (Minneapolis: Fortress Press, 1995), 1–7.

15. As examples, see Krister Stendahl, *Paul among Jews and Gentiles* (Minneapolis: Fortress Press, 1976); and more recently Hendrikus Boers, *The Justification of the Gentiles: Paul's Letters to the Galatians and Romans* (Peabody, Mass.: Hendrickson, 1994). A more radical proposal is offered by Mark D. Nanos, *The Mystery of Romans: The Jewish Context of Paul's Letters* (Minneapolis: Fortress Press, 1997).

16. This is an oversimplification of Martin Heidegger's treatment of understanding. See *Being and Time* (New York: Harper and Row, 1962), especially pp. 285–90. For a discussion of understanding as it is conceived in postmodern thought by A. K. M. Adams, see *Making Sense of New Testament Theology: "Modern" Problems and Prospects,* StABH 11 (Macon, Ga.: Mercer Univ. Press, 1995), 170–81.

1. A Tangle of Theses: Understanding Johannine Research

1. This is the view of Raymond E. Brown, S.S., in his splendid commentary, *The Epistles of John,* AB 30 (New York: Doubleday, 1982). See also Robert Kysar, *I, II, III John,* ACNT (Minneapolis: Augsburg, 1986).

2. On the history of the interpretation of the Gospel of John, see Robert Kysar, "John, Gospel of," in *Dictionary of Biblical Interpretation* (Nashville: Abingdon, 1999), 1:609–19.

3. For an example of a late dating, see Francis J. Moloney, S.B.D., *The Gospel of John,* SP 4 (Collegeville. Minn.: Liturgical, 1998), 2–3. The last published scholarly work of Bishop John A. T. Robinson exemplifies the argument that John may have been the first of the four canonical Gospels written. See *The Priority of John* (London: SCM, 1985).

4. Scholarship on the question of the relationship of John and the Synoptics is masterfully summarized and critiqued in D. Moody Smith, *John among the Gospels: The Relationship in Twentieth-Century Research* (Minneapolis: Fortress Press, 1992). Smith concludes that the question simply cannot be answered.

5. For a general overview of recent Johannine scholarship, see Gerard S. Sloyan, *What Are They Saying about John?* (New York: Paulist, 1991).

6. J. Louis Martyn, *History and Theology in the Fourth Gospel*, rev. ed. (Nashville: Abingdon, 1979); and Raymond E. Brown, S.S., *The Gospel according to John*, AB 29 and 29A (Garden City: Doubleday, 1966 and 1970); and idem, *The Community of the Beloved Disciple* (New York: Paulist, 1979). In his original proposal, Martyn had argued that the Rabbinic Council at Jamnia in the 90s C.E. ordered synagogues to pronounce the Benediction Against the Heretics (the *Birkath ha-Minim*) and to expel those who would not do so. Subsequent historical research, however, has not sustained Martyn's first thesis, and he was forced to modify it in the second edition of *History and Theology in the Fourth Gospel*. Now many of us contend that the separation of the Christian Jews from the synagogue was a purely local matter and had no official Rabbinic endorsement.

7. See Martyn's work in the previous footnote. My own view of the matter is that it is likely the separation occurred in a local synagogue or group of synagogues. The Christians felt they were "expelled" but probably the separation came about as a result of the behavior and attitudes of both groups. I think we have no evidence on which to assume that the Jews of the synagogue were any more hostile toward the Christian Jews than the Christian Jews were toward their Jewish sisters and brothers in the synagogue.

8. There is a good deal of literature on the Gospel's view of Jews and Judaism as well as early Christianity and Judaism in general. Among them are D. Moody Smith, "Judaism and the Gospel of John," in *Jews and Christians: Exploring the Past, Present, and Future*, ed. James H. Charlesworth (New York: Crossroad, 1990), 76–99; John Koenig, *Jews and Christians in Dialogue: New Testament Foundations* (Philadelphia: Westminster, 1979); Stephen G. Wilson, ed., *Anti-Judaism in Early Christianity* (Waterloo: Wilfrid Laurier Univ. Press, 1986); and Robert Kysar, "Anti-semitism and the Gospel of John," in *Antisemitism and Early Christianity: Issues of Polemic and Faith*, ed. Craig A. Evans, and Donald A. Hagner (Minneapolis: Fortress Press, 1993), 113–27.

9. See Luke Timothy Johnson, "The New Testament's Anti-Jewish Slander and the Conventions of Ancient Polemic," *JBL* 108 (1989): 419–41; and Evans and Hagner, eds., *Anti-Semitism and Early Christianity*.

10. Norman A. Beck offered this proposal in his book, *Mature Christianity: The Recognition and Repudiation of the Anti-Jewish Polemic in the New Testament* (Selinsgrove, Pa.: Susquehanna Univ. Press, 1985), 267–68.

11. An example of one psychological approach is Gerd Theissen, *Psychological Aspects of Pauline Theology*, trans. J. P. Galvin (Philadelphia: Fortress Press, 1983). See also D. Andrew Kille, *Psychological Biblical Criticism*, GBS (Minneapolis: Fortress Press, 1999).

12. A good general introduction to this movement is Carolyn Osiek, R.S.C.J., *What Are They Saying about the Social Setting of the New Testament*, rev. ed. (New York/Mahwah: Paulist, 1992). A recent example is K. C. Hanson and Douglas E. Oakman, *Palestine in the Time of Jesus: Social Structures and Social Conflict* (Minneapolis: Fortress Press, 1998).

13. This is my overly simplistic summary of the study done by John G. Gager,

Kingdom and Community: The Social World of Early Christianity, Prentice-Hall Studies in Religion Series (Englewood, N.J.: Prentice-Hall, 1975), chap. 2. Gager's book was for many of us the first taste of the social-science method in biblical studies.

14. A contemporary classic study is Wayne A. Meeks, *The First Urban Christians: The Social World of the Apostle Paul* (New Haven: Yale Univ. Press, 1983).

15. The incredibly insightful work of Vernon K. Robbins is an example. His most accessible volume is *Exploring the Texture of Texts: A Guide to Socio-Rhetorical Interpretation* (Valley Forge, Pa.: Trinity Press International, 1996).

16. In 1981, when I tried to summarize contemporary research on the Gospel of John, I entitled my essay, "Community and Gospel: Vectors in Fourth Gospel Criticism," because it seemed that Johannine scholarship was focused on the community behind the Gospel. The essay appears in *Interpreting the Gospels*, ed. James Luther Mays (Philadelphia: Fortress Press, 1981), 265–77.

17. R. Alan Culpepper, *Anatomy of the Fourth Gospel: A Study in Literary Design*, Foundations and Facets: New Testament (Philadelphia: Fortress Press, 1983), 199. Actually, Culpepper's study is strictly literary; but the fact that literary analysis yields this sort of social function for language demonstrates how persuasive it is in the fourth Gospel.

18. Bruce J. Malina and Richard L. Rohrbaugh, *Social-Science Commentary on the Gospel of John* (Minneapolis: Fortress Press, 1998), 4. Malina's and Rohrbaugh's introduction to their commentary provides a concise and clear summary of one social-scientific approach to John.

19. Malina and Rohrbaugh draw from the work of the anthropologist Michael A. K. Halliday, for example, *Language as Social Semiotic: The Social Interpretation of Language and Meaning* (Baltimore: University Park, 1978). This practice of borrowing insights from "secular" social-scientific studies and applying them to the Bible is typical of this contemporary movement in biblical studies.

20. A singularly important study that ignited the study of the Johannine church as sectarian is the 1972 article by Wayne A. Meeks, "The Man from Heaven in Johannine Sectarianism," in *The Interpretation of John*, ed. John Ashton, Studies in New Testament Interpretation, 2nd ed. (Edinburgh: T. and T. Clark, 1997), 169–206.

21. See, for instance, Jerome H. Neyrey, S.J., *An Ideology of Revolt: John's Christology in Social-Science Perspective* (Philadelphia: Fortress Press, 1988).

22. Two books related to this approach to John are David Rensberger, *Johannine Faith and Liberating Community* (Philadelphia: Westminster, 1988); and Richard J. Cassidy, *John's Gospel in New Perspective: Christology and the Realities of Roman Power* (Maryknoll: Orbis, 1992).

23. For the best examples of the fruits of the literary study of John, consult Culpepper, *Anatomy of the Fourth Gospel*; and Jeffrey Lloyd Staley, *The Print's First Kiss: A Rhetorical Investigation of the Implied Reader in the Fourth Gospel*, SBLDS 82 (Atlanta: Scholars, 1988).

24. One of the best narrative-critical studies of John is Mark W. G. Stibbe, *John as Storyteller: Narrative Criticism and the Fourth Gospel*, SNTSMS 73 (Cambridge: Cambridge Univ. Press, 1992). See also Fernando F. Segovia, "The Journey(s) of the Word of God: A Reading of the Plot of the Fourth Gospel," *Semeia* 53 (1991): 23–54.

25. This is the view of R. Alan Culpepper, "The Pivot of John's Prologue," *NTS* 27 (1980): 1–31.

26. See Moloney, *The Gospel of John*, 23.

27. Paul D. Duke, *Irony in the Fourth Gospel* (Atlanta: John Knox, 1985), 17.

28. See Gail R. O'Day, *Revelation in the Fourth Gospel* (Philadelphia: Fortress Press, 1986).

29. For example, Sandra M. Schneiders, *The Revelatory Text: Interpreting the New Testament as Sacred Scripture* (New York: HarperCollins, 1991), 180–97; and Culpepper, *Anatomy of the Fourth Gospel*, chap. 5.

30. Jeffrey L. Staley, "Stumbling in the Dark, Reaching for the Light: Reading Character in John 5 and 9," *Semeia* 53 (1991): 55–80.

31. David R. Beck, *The Discipleship Paradigm: Readers and Anonymous Characters in the Fourth Gospel*, BibIntSer 27 (Leiden: Brill, 1997).

32. See Rudolf Schnackenburg, *The Gospel according to St. John*, vol. 3 (New York: Crossroad, 1982), 375–88.

33. See Schneiders, *The Revelatory Text*, chap. 5; and Norman R. Petersen, *The Gospel of John and the Sociology of Light: Language and Characterization in the Fourth Gospel* (Valley Forge, Pa.: Trinity Press International, 1993).

34. Culpepper, *Anatomy of the Fourth Gospel*, 4–5.

35. Robert G. Hughes and I explore this idea a bit further in *Preaching Doctrine for the Twenty-First Century*, FRP (Minneapolis: Fortress Press, 1997), 68–69.

36. One of the few books on preaching the Gospel of John is Gail R. O'Day's volume, *The Word Disclosed: John's Story and Narrative Preaching* (St. Louis: CBP, 1987), which takes the Gospel's narrative seriously as a basis for preaching John with sermons that are narrative in character.

37. I use the word "ambiguity" to speak of polyvalence or multi-meaning. Some reserve the word for those situations in which readers know a word can mean one of two or more things but that only one of those possibilities is the intended meaning. Hence, the reader should determine which is the more likely. By ambiguity, I mean multiple meanings are suggested without one necessarily being the "true" or intended meaning. Readers are left to struggle for themselves over the possible meanings and all remain viable options.

38. The theory of an expulsion from the synagogue needs to be reexamined. It has been so widely taken for granted during the last forty years that we are liable to forget that it is *only* a theory (and a very speculative one at that) and that other proposals need to be considered.

2. Theological Themes: The Heart of Johannine Thought

1. A very good overview of Johannine theology is found in D. Moody Smith, *The Theology of the Gospel of John*, NTT (Cambridge: Cambridge Univ. Press, 1995).

2. See Kysar, *John, the Maverick Gospel*, rev. ed. (Louisville: Westminster John Knox, 1993), chap. 1.

3. This posed the classic conflict between Rudolf Bultmann and Ernst Käsemann. See Käsemann, "The Structure and Purpose of the Prologue to John's Gospel," in *New Testament Questions of Today*, trans. W. I. Montague (Philadelphia:

Fortress Press, 1969), 138–67, and Rudolf Bultmann, *The Gospel of John: A Commentary,* trans. G. R. Beasley-Murray (Philadelphia: Westminster, 1971), 60–72.

4. See Paul N. Anderson, *The Christology of the Fourth Gospel: Its Unity and Disunity in the Light of John 6* (Valley Forge, Pa.: Trinity Press International, 1996).

5. See note 3.

6. See Robert Kysar, *Stumbling in the Light: New Testament Images for a Changing Church* (St. Louis: Chalice, 1999), chap. 5.

7. Rudolf Bultmann, *Theology of the New Testament,* vol. 2, trans. K. Grobel (New York: Scribners, 1955), 27.

8. Bultmann, *Gospel of John,* vol. 2, 348 n. 2.

9. For the variety of uses of the preposition *eis,* see William F. Arndt, F. Wilbur Gingrich, and Frederick W. Danker, *A Greek-English Lexion of the New Testament and Other Early Christian Literature,* 2nd ed. (Chicago: Univ. of Chicago Press, 1979), 228–30.

10. Robert Kysar, "The Dismantling of Decisional Faith: A Reading of John 6:25-71," in Critical Readings of John 6, BibIntSer 22 (Leiden:Brill, 1997): 161–81.

11. See Thomas H. Naylor, William H. Willimon, and Magdalena R. Naylor, *The Search for Meaning* (Nashville: Abingdon, 1994); and the older classic by Viktor Frankl, *Man's Search for Meaning: An Introduction to Logotherapy,* 4th ed. (Boston: Beacon, 1992).

12. G.B. Caird, *New Testament Theology,* completed and edited by L. D. Hurst (Oxford: Clarendon, 1994), 118–22.

13. This way of preaching theological themes is described and illustrated in some detail in Robert G. Hughes and Robert Kysar, *Preaching Doctrine for the Twenty-First Century,* FRP (Minneapolis: Fortress Press, 1997).

14. Leonora Tubbs Tisdale, *Preaching as Local Theology and Folk Art,* FRP (Minneapolis: Fortress Press, 1997), uses the expression "exegeting the congregation" as the title for her third chapter and provides a method for doing such an exegesis. For the best description of an exegetical method for interpreting a biblical text for preaching, see Stephen Farris, *Preaching That Matters: The Bible and Our Lives* (Louisville: Westminster John Knox, 1998).

3. The Word and Words: Johannine Language

1. See Raymond E. Brown, *The Gospel according to John (1–12),* AB 29 (Garden City: Doubleday, 1966), cxxii–cxxv, 23–36, and 519–24. The classic study of the intellectual environment for the Gospel is C. H. Dodd, *The Interpretation of the Fourth Gospel* (Cambridge: Cambridge Univ. Press, 1963); see especially pp. 263–85.

2. D. Moody Smith, *John,* ANTC (Nashville: Abingdon, 1999), 50.

3. See Terence Fretheim, "Word of God,"in *ABD* 6, 961–68; and Hugh C. White, ed., *Speech Act Theory and Biblical Criticism, Semeia* 41 (Atlanta: Scholars, 1988).

4. See Gail R. O'Day, "The Gospel of John: Introduction, Commentary, and Reflections," *NIB* 9 (Nashville: Abingdon, 1995), 852.

5. An example of such a discussion is found in Paul Ricoeur, *Figuring the Sacred: Religion, Narrative, and Imagination,* ed. Mark I. Wallace, and trans. D. Pel-

lauer (Minneapolis: Fortress Press, 1995), esp. pp. 53 and 143. See also Ricoeur, *The Symbolism of Evil*, trans. E. Buchanan, Religious Perspectives 17 (New York: Harper and Row, 1967).

6. Craig R. Koester, *Symbolism in the Fourth Gospel: Meaning, Mystery, Community* (Minneapolis: Fortress Press, 1995), 4.

7. Thomas L. Brodie, *The Gospel according to John: A Literary and Theological Commentary* (Oxford: Oxford Univ. Press, 1993), 175–76.

8. See the discussion of the symbolism of the passage in Brown, *Gospel according to John*, 109–10.

9. For a discussion of the interpretations of this passage, see George R. Beasley-Murray, *John*, WBC 36 (Waco: Word, 1987), 355–58.

10. For a fuller discussion of my understanding of metaphor and its function, see my book, *Stumbling in the Light: New Testament Images for a Changing Church* (St. Louis: Chalice, 1999), chap. 2.

11. For example, Joachim Jeremias says Palestinian shepherds were "reckoned among the *hamartōloi* [sinners]" (*The Parables of Jesus*, 2nd ed., trans. S. H. Hooke [New York: Scribner, 1972], 133).

12. Ricoeur, "*Paul Ricoeur on Biblical Hermeneutics*," *Semeia* 4 (1975), 80, italics in original.

13. Lucy Atkinson Rose, *Sharing the Word: Preaching the Roundtable Church* (Louisville: Westminster John Knox, 1997). Actually Rose pursues the fuller implications of the view of preaching espoused by her teacher, Fred B. Craddock. See Craddock's *Overhearing the Gospel: Preaching and Teaching the Faith to Persons Who Have Heard It All Before* (Nashville: Abingdon Press, 1978). See the conclusion.

14. See Robert G. Hughes and Robert Kysar, *Preaching Doctrine for the Twenty-First Century*, FRP (Minneapolis: Fortress Press, 1997), 29–32, who are indebted for the concept of "relanguaging" to Sandra M. Schneiders, *The Revelatory Text: Interpreting the New Testament as Sacred Scripture* (New York: HarperCollins, 1991), 69–71.

15. See Brown, *Gospel according to St. John*, 510–12.

16. On Johannine dualism see Kysar, *John, the Maverick Gospel*, rev. ed. (Louisville: Westminster John Knox, 1993), 60–67.

17. See my discussion of 20:19-23 in *John*, ACNT (Minneapolis: Augsburg, 1986), 302–5.

4. Words and Stories: Johannine Discourses and Narratives

1. Peter F. Ellis, *The Genius of John: A Composition-Critical Commentary on the Fourth Gospel* (Collegeville, Minn.: Liturgical, 1984), 90, italics in original. Ellis argues the Gospel as a whole is structured as a chiasm, so that one has chiastic parallelism within a larger chiasm (13–16). For a chiastic analysis of Jesus and the Samaritan woman, see Charles H. Talbert, *Reading John: A Literary and Theological Commentary on the Fourth Gospel and the Johannine Epistles* (New York: Crossroad, 1992), 120.

2. Raymond E. Brown, *The Gospel of John (13–21)*, AB 29A (Garden City: Doubleday, 1970), 667.

3. See also James Limburg, "Psalms, Book of," in *ABD* 5 (1992): 528–30.

4. C. H. Dodd, *The Interpretation of the Fourth Gospel* (Cambridge: Cambridge Univ. Press, 1963), 401–20. For other proposals for the structure of these chapters, see also Fernando F. Segovia, *The Farewell of the Word: The Johannine Call to Abide* (Minneapolis: Fortress Press, 1991).

5. For examples of parallels to the farewell discourses, see also Talbert, *Reading John*, 200–202.

6. The task of discerning which of Jesus' sayings in the Gospel of John actually come from the historical Jesus, or are rooted in the earliest Christian tradition, and which are the evangelist's interpretations of the words of the living Christ is impossible. I am convinced, however, that there are remnants of traditional sayings that have been expanded, elaborated, and developed probably for homiletical reasons. There is little reason for preachers to become encumbered with this distinction. For a rather conservative statement of the question, see Barnabas Lindars, *The Gospel of John*, NCB (London: Oliphants, 1972), 54–56.

7. Kysar, *John*, ACNT (Minneapolis: Augsburg, 1986), 219–54.

8. For other similarities and the unique themes of each of the three discourses, see also Kysar, *John*, 235.

9. See John Ashton, "*Paraclete*," in *ABD* 5 (1992): 152–54; Brown, *Gospel of John (13–21)*, 1135–44; and Rudolf Schnackenburg, *The Gospel according to John*, vol. 3 (New York: Crossroad, 1982), 138–54.

10. For a full discussion of the theories of disarrangement and rearrangement, see also Wilbert Francis Howard, *The Fourth Gospel in Recent Criticism and Interpretation*, revised by C. K. Barrett (London: Epworth, 1955), 95–127.

11. See Bultmann, *The Gospel of John: A Commentary*, trans. G. R. Beasley-Murray (Philadelphia: Westminster, 1971).

12. Culpepper, *Anatomy of the Fourth Gospel: A Study in Literary Design* (Minneapolis: Fortress Press, 1983), 231, 234.

13. I use the category "pronouncement stories" as proposed years ago by Vincent Taylor (see also *The Formation of the Gospel Tradition* [London: Macmillan, 1957]). In his book on form criticism, Martin Dibelius includes these stories under "paradigms" (*From Tradition to Gospel*, trans. B. L. Woolf [New York: Scribners, 1934]). Rudolf Bultmann labels this form "apophthegms" (*The History of the Synoptic Tradition*, trans. J. Marsh [Oxford: Basil Blackwell, 1963]). While form criticism is a method that is somewhat outdated, the recognition of these literary forms in the Gospels is still valuable.

14. This is particularly the case in J. Louis Martyn's construction of a hypothesis that the Gospel was written soon after the Christian community was expelled from their synagogue. Martyn argues that in a number of places in the narratives of the Gospel the author betrays two levels of reference, the "back there" and the "here and now" of the church (see *History and Theology in the Fourth Gospel*, 2nd ed. [Nashville: Abingdon Press, 1979]). See also Martyn, *The Gospel of John in Christian History: Essays for Interpreters*, Theological Inquiries (New York: Paulist, 1978), 90–121.

15. I try to develop this understanding of preaching in my article "Preaching as Biblical Theology: A Proposal for a Homiletical Method," in *The Promise and Practice of Biblical Theology,* ed. John Reumann (Minneapolis: Fortress Press, 1991), 143–56.

16. Brown, *Gospel according to John (1–12),* 463.

17. Craig R. Koester, *Symbolism in the Fourth Gospel: Meaning, Mystery, Community* (Minneapolis: Fortress Press, 1995), 5.

18. In Mark's account of the feeding of the four thousand (8:1-10), the narrator says Jesus gave "thanks" (the verb, *eucharisteō*) for the loaves and "blessed" (the verb, *eulogeō*) the fish (Mark 8:6-7). In Matthew's telling of the same story (15:32-39), Jesus gives "thanks" for both the loaves and the fish (Matt. 15:36). However, in the story of the feeding of the five thousand that word *eucharisteō* is not used. Instead we are told that Jesus "blessed" both the loaves and the fish.

19. Brown, *The Gospel according to John (1–12),* 247–49. See also John Marsh, *Saint John,* Pelican Gospel Commentaries (Baltimore: Penguin, 1968), 284; and Thomas L. Brodie, *The Gospel according to John: A Literary and Theological Commentary* (Oxford: Oxford Univ. Press, 1993), 262–63.

20. See also Kysar, *John, the Maverick Gospel,* rev. ed. (Louisville: Westminster John Knox, 1993), 122–26; and idem, *The Fourth Evangelist and His Gospel* (Minneapolis: Augsburg, 1975), 249–59. An older assessment of the problem is found in Howard, *The Fourth Gospel,* 195–212 and 304–5.

21. My suggestion in many of these cases are efforts to apply the idea that the form of the sermon should follow the form of the text. For discussions of this method, see also Thomas G. Long, *Preaching and the Literary Forms of the Bible* (Minneapolis: Fortress Press, 1988); and Don M. Wardlaw, ed., *Preaching Biblically: Creating Sermons in the Shape of Scripture* (Philadelphia: Westminster, 1983).

22. Eugene L. Lowry, *How to Preach a Parable: Designs for Narrative Sermons* (Nashville: Abingdon, 1989). For Lowry's sermon and an analysis, see pp. 115–41.

23. Paul does this very thing in a number of his letters. In Romans, for instance, he asks questions of what he has just said much as an opponent would. See, for example, Romans 6:1. Paul can help teach us how to preach using the dynamic exchange with another.

24. The precise reference of the word "Greeks" *(hellēnes)* is uncertain. The word is sometimes used to refer to Gentiles and other times to Gentile proselytes to Judaism and/or perhaps the so-called "god-fearers" of the Hellenistic synagogues.

25. Dodd, *Interpretation of the Fourth Gospel,* 384.

26. Mark W. G. Stibbe, *John as Storyteller: Narrative Criticism and the Fourth Gospel,* SNTSMS 73 (Cambridge: Cambridge Univ. Press, 1992), 17–18, italics added.

27. Re-reading in biblical studies is a new critical concern with little written about it. The study from which I gained the most insight about this process has unfortunately not yet been translated into English, and its purpose is to show how the farewell discourses were written to be re-read. Andreas Dettwiler, *Die Gegenwart des Erhöhten: Eine exegetische Studie zu den johanneischen Abschiedsreden (John 13:13—16:33) unter besonderer Berücksichtigung ihres Relecture-Charakters,* FRLANT 169 (Göttingen: Vandenhoeck & Ruprecht, 1995).

28. Culpepper, *Anatomy,* 56–70.

5. The King Is Enthroned: The Johannine Passion Story

1. Some of the following discussion reflects my earlier work on chapters 18–21 in my commentary, *John*, ACNT (Minneapolis: Augsburg, 1986), 265–322. None of the previously published material is repeated verbatim here.

2. See the older but useful study by A. E. Harvey, *Jesus on Trial: A Study in the Fourth Gospel* (Atlanta: John Knox, 1976); and the more recent study by Andrew T. Lincoln, *Truth on Trial: The Lawsuit Motif in the Fourth Gospel* (Peabody, Mass.: Hendrickson, 2001). The theory that the Gospel was written in the aftermath of the expulsion of the Johannine Christians from the synagogue (see chapter 1) supposes, too, that the whole of the Gospel narrates how the leaders of the synagogue accused the Christians and how they defended their faith. As I have said, however, such a theory for the origin of the Gospel is very speculative.

3. See especially Gail R. O'Day, "The Gospel of John: Introduction, Commentary, and Reflections," in *NIB* 9 (Nashville: Abingdon, 1995), 805–10.

4. Matthew and Mark report a "false charge" brought against Jesus to the effect that he declared, "I am able to destroy the temple of God and to build it in three days" (Matt. 26:61), or "I will destroy this temple that is made with hands, and in three days I will build another, not made with hands" (Mark 14:58). John, of course, attributes nearly the same words to Jesus in 2:19, but they have no role in Jesus' trial before the religious leaders.

5. Raymond E. Brown, *The Gospel according to John (13–21)*, AB 29A (Garden City: Doubleday, 1970), 858–59, quotation on p. 858.

6. Rudolf Bultmann, *The Gospel of John: A Commentary*, trans. G. R. Beasley-Murray (Philadelphia: Westminster, 1971), 653–57, quotation on p. 653.

7. Unfortunately, John concludes the trial before Pilate by having the narrator say, "Then he [Pilate] handed him over to *them* to be crucified" (19:16, italics added; contrast Mark 15:16). The antecedent of "them" is either the "chief priests" of verse 15 or (worse) "the Jews" in verse 14. The narrative leaves the clear impression that the Jews or their leaders actually crucified Jesus, even though that impression is corrected in 19:25. This suggestion that the Jews were responsible for Jesus' death has aided and abetted anti-Semitism among Christians for centuries and must be corrected and denounced. (See n. 9 in chapter 1.) In the context of John's symbolic use of the "Jews," however, the message is that the forces of evil are responsible for Jesus' execution.

8. Rudolf Bultmann says, "John's passion-narrative shows us Jesus as not really *suffering* death but *choosing* it—not as a passive victim but as the active conqueror." Bultmann, *Theology of the New Testament*, vol. 2, trans. K. Grobel (New York: Scribners, 1995), 53, italics in original.

9. I try to show the place of Jesus' "hour" in the structure of the whole Gospel narrative in *John, the Maverick Gospel*, rev. ed. (Louisville: Westminster John Knox, 1993), 18.

10. See also Sverre Aalen, "Glory, Honour," in *The New International Dictionary of New Testament Theology*, vol. 2, ed. Colin Brown (Grand Rapids: Zondervan, 1981), 44–48. Aalen says about the use of glory in John, "Here too glory is to be understood as a revelation of God, or as the intervention of his [*sic*] power in his-

tory (John 1:14; 2:11; 11:4; 12:41)" (48). Also helpful is the article on *doxa* found in Ceslas Spicq, *Theological Lexicon of the New Testament*, trans. and ed. James D. Ernest, vol. 1 (Peabody, Mass.: Hendrickson, 1994), 362–79.

11. For a discussion of honor and shame in the Gospel of John, see also Bruce J. Malina and Richard L. Rohrbaugh, *Social-Science Commentary on the Gospel of John* (Minneapolis: Fortress Press, 1998), 121–24. Commenting on 17:1-3, Malina and Rohrbaugh say, "Both [Jesus'] own honor ('glorify your Son') and that of the Father ('so that the Son may glorify you') are at stake. Given the fundamental importance of honor in ancient Mediterranean life, Jesus asks for that which is of the highest value" (244).

12. This is related to Bultmann's famous slogan, "Jesus as the Revealer of God *reveals nothing but that he is the Revealer*" (emphasis Bultmann's). See also, for example, Bultmann, *Theology*, vol. 2, 66–69.

13. See Kysar, *John, the Maverick Gospel*, 49–54.

14. The best study of this theme as the theology of the cross in John is J. Massyngbaerde Ford, *Redeemer, Friend, and Mother: Salvation in Antiquity and in the Gospel of John* (Minneapolis: Fortress Press, 1997).

15. For a lengthy discussion of the character of the beloved disciple in John, see Rudolf Schnackenburg, *The Gospel according to St. John*, vol. 3 (New York: Crossroad, 1982), 375–88.

16. For a clarification of the relationship between the chronologies of the Synoptics and John, see Gail O'Day, "The Gospel of John," 704–5.

17. Whether or not the killing of the Passover lambs may have had some sacrificial meaning is not clear, and historical evidence limits our knowledge. However, Paul refers to the sacrifice of the "pascal lamb" (1 Cor. 5:7). See John R. Miles's helpful article on "Lamb" in *ABD* 4 (1992): 132–34.

18. Bultmann, *Theology*, vol. 2, 56.

19. Daniel J. Harrington, S.J., *The Gospel of Matthew*, SP 1 (Collegeville, Minn.: Liturgical, 1991), 408.

20. For my view of the treatment of women in the Gospel of John, see *John, the Maverick Gospel*, 147–54.

21. Brown, *Gospel according to John 13–21*, 1012–13. As is usually the case, I am most indebted to Brown's treatment of the resurrection appearances.

22. Brown credits J. A. Jungmann, *The Mass of the Roman Rite* (New York: Bensizer, 1950), 470, n. 55 for this expression. Brown, *The Community of the Beloved Disciple* (New York: Paulist, 1979), 190. In the same discussion of "Roles of Women in the Fourth Gospel," Brown writes, "It is clear that John has no hesitation in placing a woman in the same category of relationship to Jesus as the Twelve who are included in the 'his own' in 13:1" (192). In the 1970s this was a bold statement for a Roman Catholic priest-teacher to make! Brown was not afraid to confront the church with the biblical witness.

23. Bultmann thought that Paul used *psychē* in the sense of "vitality" or "life essence," much as the Hebrew Scriptures used *nephesh* (for example, Gen. 2:7) and which the LXX translated with *psychē* (*Theology of the New Testament*, vol. 1, 204).

24. Robert Kysar, "'As You Sent Me': Identity and Mission in the Fourth Gospel," *Word and World* 21 (2001): 370–77.

25. See Eduard Schweizer, *The Good News according to Matthew*, trans. D. E. Green (Atlanta: John Knox, 1975), 373; and David E. Garland, *Reading Matthew: A Literary and Theological Commentary on the First Gospel* (New York: Crossroad, 1995), 192–93.

26. Carl Schneider has a long article on the Greek words related to witness in *Theological Dictionary of the New Testament*, ed. Gerhard Kittel (Grand Rapids: Eerdmans, 1967), 4:497–502.

27. Mark W. G. Stibbe, *John as Storyteller: Narrative Criticism and the Fourth Gospel*, SNTSMS 73 (Cambridge: Cambridge Univ. Press, 1992), 19.

28. See Brown, *Gospel according to John (13–21)*, 1046–48; and C. K. Barrett, *The Gospel according to St. John: An Introduction with Commentary and Notes on the Greek Text*, rev. ed. (Philadelphia: Westminster, 1978), 572–73.

29. Kysar, *John, the Maverick Gospel*, 80–86.

30. This is the view of faith, as I understand it, advocated by Paul Tillich in his classic work, *The Dynamics of Faith* (New York: Harper, 1957).

31. The United Bible Societies rank different manuscript evidence for a single passage with letters: "A" being the most certain choice among alternative readings, "B" for one that is nearly certain, and so on. The Societies use the aorist reading ("that you may believe") in their construction of the Greek text, but rank the choice with a "C," meaning there is "a considerable degree of doubt as to whether this or that alternative reading is to be preferred." Barclay M. Newman, and Eugene A. Nida, *A Translator's Handbook on the Gospel of John*, Helps for Translators (New York: United Bible Societies, 1980), 620.

32. Contrast Barrett, *Gospel according to St. John*, 575; and D. A. Carlson, *The Gospel according to John* (Grand Rapids: Eerdmans, 1991), 661–63. Although his argument does not apply to Barrett, Carlson is correct in saying that the scales of interpretation of this verb have tilted toward taking it to mean "to continue in your faith," in part because of the prominence of the theory that the Gospel was written to a congregation recently separated from the synagogue. Although I have reservations about that theory, I still think the Gospel as a whole makes more sense if it is read as a document intended to confirm rather than create initial faith.

33. O'Day, "Gospel of John," 853.

34. Ibid., 850–52. On this matter, she follows Edwyn Clement Hoskyns, *The Fourth Gospel*, 2nd ed. (London: Faber and Faber, 1947), 549–50.

35. See, for example, Mark W. G. Stibbe, *John*, Readings: A New Biblical Commentary (Sheffield: Sheffield Academic Press, 1993), 206–8.

36. Again, see Brown, *Gospel according to John (13–21)*, 1074–76.

37. For example, see George R. Beasley-Murray, *John*, WBC 36 (Waco: Word, 1987), 410–11. For a discussion of the eschatology implicit in this passage, see also D. Moody Smith, *John*, ANTC (Nashville: Abingdon, 1999), 397–401.

38. See Brown, *Gospel according to John (13–21)*, 1123. For assigning this verb a causative meaning, see J. H. Bernard, *The Gospel according to St. John*, ICC 2 (Edinburgh: T. and T. Clark, 1928), 713.

39. Brown, *Gospel according to John (13–21)*, 1046.

6. Fragments of Texts: John in the Lectionary

1. See Marjorie Procter-Smith, "Feminist Interpretation and Liturgical Proclamation," in *Searching the Scriptures*, vol. 1: *A Feminist Introduction*, ed. Elisabeth
Schüssler Fiorenza (New York: Crossroad, 1997), 316–17.

2. For a good discussion of the poetic structure of the passage, see Charles H.
Talbert, *Reading John: A Literary and Theological Commentary on the Fourth Gospel
and the Johannine Epistles* (New York: Crossroad, 1992), 66–68.

3. R. Alan Culpepper, "The Pivot of John's Prologue," *NTS* 27 (1981): 1–31.

4. See Robert Kysar, "Christology and Controversy: The Contributions of the
Prologue of the Gospel of John to New Testament Christology and Their Historical Setting," *CurTM* 5 (1978): 348–64.

5. For a discussion of the function of signs in the fourth Gospel, see Kysar,
John, the Maverick Gospel, rev. ed. (Louisville: Westminster John Knox, 1993),
80–86.

6. For example, Raymond E. Brown, S.S., *The Gospel according to John*, AB 29
(1966), 287–91.

7. See ibid., 253–54, for a full comparison.

8. Ibid., 260–95.

9. This issue has preoccupied me for several years. My present position is
expressed in *John, the Maverick Gospel*, 70–74; and "The Dismantling of Decisional
Faith: A Reading of John 6:25-71," in *Critical Readings of John 6*, ed. by R. Alan
Culpepper, BibIntSer 22 (1997), 161–81.

10. See *John, the Maverick Gospel*, 99–106; and "The Eschatology of the Fourth
Gospel—A Correction of Bultmann's Redactional Hypothesis," *Perspectives* 13
(1972): 23–33.

11. The most famous of the theories that 6:51b-59 is a redactional addition was
advanced by Rudolf Bultmann, who argued that the original Gospel included
nothing about the sacraments and that a later "ecclesiastical redactor" added references to the sacraments to make the document more palatable to the church. You
will find this theory scattered through *The Gospel of John* (Philadelphia: Westminster, 1971), especially pages 443–51; and *Theology of the New Testament*, vol. 2 (New
York: Scribners, 1955), 58–59. For a clear summary and critique of Bultmann's
view, see D. Moody Smith, *The Composition and Order of the Fourth Gospel* (New
Haven: Yale Univ. Press, 1965).

12. The various positions on this question are discussed in Kysar, *The Fourth
Evangelist and His Gospel: An Examination of Contemporary Scholarship* (Minneapolis: Augsburg, 1975), 249–58. My current view, however, is best expressed in
the second edition of *John, the Maverick Gospel*, 122–26.

13. For a discussion of the debate over the significance of these two verbs, see Francis J. Moloney, S.D.B., *The Gospel of John*, SP 4 (Collegeville, Minn.: Liturgical, 1998),
224.

14. Bultmann, *The Gospel of John*, 447.

15. See Fernando F. Segovia, *The Farewell of the Word: The Johannine Call to
Abide* (Minneapolis: Fortress Press, 1991).

16. See Gail R. O'Day's discussion of this passage in *The New Interpreter's Bible*,

where she writes, "To turn Jesus' promise here into language about Jesus' coming to the individual believer at the believer's death is to misconstrue the eschatological significance of this promise" (*NIB* 9 [1995]): 741.

17. Rudolf Schnackenburg, *The Gospel according to St. John*, vol. 3 (New York: Crossroad, 1982), 71–72.

18. See *John, the Maverick Gospel*, 106–12.

19. For a fuller discussion of this relationship and the church's interpretation of 14:28, see Schnackenburg, *The Gospel according to St. John*, vol. 3, 85–86.

20. See my discussion of metaphor in *Stumbling in the Light: Images for a Church in Change* (St. Louis: Chalice, 1999).

21. J. Massyngbaerde Ford argues in a most provocative way that friendship constitutes the understanding of redemption in the Gospel of John. *Redeemer, Friend and Mother: Salvation in Antiquity and in the Gospel of John* (Minneapolis: Fortress Press, l997).

22. I am well aware that such a view of the discernment of the Spirit threatens the role of the individual prophet in the community. Yet I am also convinced that the prophetic voice against the community nearly always forms a new community, so that the question then becomes not whether the individual or the community but which community is right.

23. See the classic study of chapter 17 by Ernst Käsemann, who really summarizes a theology of the whole Gospel from this single chapter. *The Testament of Jesus according to John 17*, trans. G. Krodel (Philadelphia: Fortress Press, 1966).

24. Kysar, *John*, ACNT (Minneapolis: Augsburg, 1986), 254–55.

25. I have made this point in several of my writings, but I believe it is important enough to be said again here. For an example of another expression of it, see my commentary, *John*, 261 and 304.

26. For another sermon on John 17, see chapter 2 and the sermon entitled, "What's Eternal About Life?"

27. Martin Bell, *Nenshu and the Tiger: Parables of Life and Death* (New York: Seabury, 1975), 24–25.

Conclusion: Preaching John in the Roundtable Church

1. Fred B. Craddock, *As One without Authority: Essays on Inductive Preaching*, rev. ed. (Enid, Okla.: Phillips Univ. Press, 1974); idem, *Overhearing the Gospel* (Nashville: Abingdon, 1978); and idem, *Preaching* (Nashville: Abingdon, 1985).

2. Especially, Eugene L. Lowry, *The Homiletical Plot: The Sermon as Narrative Art Form* (Atlanta: John Knox, 1980). For a brief history of this new movement in preaching see David Buttrick, *Homiletic: Moves and Structures* (Philadelphia: Fortress Press, 1987), 483–84.

3. Lucy Atkinson Rose, *Sharing the Word: Preaching in the Roundtable Church* (Louisville: Westminster John Knox), 1997.

4. See my modest effort to nurture this sort of preaching, "The Renaissance and Demise of the Listener: Empowering the Laity through Preaching," *Lutheran Partners*, 13/6 (November/December, 1997), 18–21.

5. Ernst Käsemann, *The Testament of Jesus according to John 17*, trans. G. Krodel (Philadelphia: Fortress Press, 1968), 31.

6. This democratic structure seems to have been repressed by the time 2 and 3 John were written, since both purport to be the words of "the elder." It is possible, however, that *presbyteros* in this case means only a "senior citizen" and not the name for an official position in the congregation. Still, the authors of all three of these so-called Johannine epistles seem to assert a special authority over the community that is not discernible in the fourth Gospel.

7. Rose, *Sharing the Word*, 127–30.

8. Among the books I most value on this subject are these: Patricia Wilson Kastner, *Imagery for Preaching*, FRP (Minneapolis: Fortress Press, 1989); Richard L. Eslinger, *Narrative and Imagination: Preaching the Worlds That Shape Us* (Minneapolis: Fortress Press, 1995); and Eslinger, ed., *Intersections: Post-Critical Studies in Preaching* (Grand Rapids: Eerdmans, 1994).

9. Buttrick, *Homiletic*, 113–70.

10. Walter Brueggemann, *Finally Comes the Poet: Daring Speech for Proclamation* (Minneapolis: Fortress Press, 1989).

Bibliography

The Gospel of John

Anderson, Paul N. *The Christology of the Fourth Gospel: Its Unity and Disunity in the Light of John 6.* Valley Forge: Trinity Press International, 1996.

Ashton, John. "Paraclete." In *ABD* 5 (1992): 152–54.

Barrett, C. K. *The Gospel according to St. John: An Introduction with Commentary and Notes on the Greek Text.* Rev. ed. Philadelphia: Westminster, 1978.

Beasley-Murray, George R. *John.* WBC 36. Waco: Word, 1987.

Beck, David R. *The Discipleship Paradigm: Readers and Anonymous Characters in the Fourth Gospel.* BibIntSer 27. Leiden: Brill, 1997.

Brodie, Thomas L. *The Gospel according to John: A Literary and Theological Commentary.* Oxford: Oxford Univ. Press, 1993.

Brown, Raymond E. *The Gospel according to John.* AB 29 and 29A. Garden City: Doubleday, 1966 and 1970.

———. *The Community of the Beloved Disciple.* New York: Paulist, 1979.

———. *The Epistles of John.* AB 30. Garden City: Doubleday, 1982.

Bultmann, Rudolf. *Theology of the New Testament.* Translated by Kendrick Grobel. Vol. 2. New York: Scribners, 1955.

———. *The Gospel of John: A Commentary.* Translated by G. R. Beasley-Murray. Philadelphia: Westminster, 1971.

Carlson, D. A. *The Gospel according to John.* Grand Rapids: Eerdmans, 1991.

Cassidy, Richard J. *John's Gospel in New Perspective: Christology and the Realities of Roman Power.* Maryknoll: Orbis, 1992.

Culpepper, R. Alan. "The Pivot of John's Prologue." *NTS* 27 (1980): 1–31.

———. *Anatomy of the Fourth Gospel: A Study in Literary Design.* Foundations and Facets: New Testament. Philadelphia: Fortress Press, 1983.

Dodd, C. H. *The Interpretation of the Fourth Gospel.* Cambridge: Cambridge Univ. Press, 1963.

Duke, Paul D. *Irony in the Fourth Gospel.* Atlanta: John Knox, 1985.

Ellis, Peter F. *The Genius of John: A Composition-Critical Commentary on the Fourth Gospel.* Collegeville, Minn.: Liturgical, 1984.

Ford, J. Massyngbaerde. *Redeemer, Friend and Mother: Salvation in Antiquity and in the Gospel of John.* Minneapolis: Fortress Press, 1997.

Harvey, A. E. *Jesus on Trial: A Study in the Fourth Gospel.* Atlanta: John Knox, 1976.

Hoskyns, Edwyn Clement. *The Fourth Gospel.* 2nd ed. London: Faber and Faber, 1947.

Howard, Wilbert Francis. *The Fourth Gospel in Recent Criticism and Interpretation.* Revised by C. K. Barrett. London: Epworth, 1955.

Käsemann, Ernst. *The Testament of Jesus according to John 17.* Translated by Gerhard Krodel. Philadelphia: Fortress Press, 1968.

———. "The Structure and Purpose of the Prologue to John's Gospel." In *New Testament Questions of Today.* Philadelphia: Fortress Press, 1969, 138–67.

Koester, Craig R. *Symbolism in the Fourth Gospel: Meaning, Mystery, Community.* Minneapolis: Fortress Press, 1995.

Kysar, Robert. *The Fourth Evangelist and His Gospel.* Minneapolis: Augsburg, 1975.

———. "Community and Gospel: Vectors in Fourth Gospel Criticism." In *Interpreting the Gospels,* edited by James Luther Mays, 265–77. Philadelphia: Fortress Press, 1981.

———. *John.* ACNT. Minneapolis: Augsburg, 1986.

———. *I, II, III John.* ACNT. Minneapolis: Augsburg, 1986.

———. "Antisemitism and the Gospel of John." In *Antisemitism and Early Christianity: Issues of Polemic and Faith,* edited by Craig A. Evans and Donald A. Hagner, 113–27. Minneapolis: Fortress Press, 1993.

———. *John, the Maverick Gospel.* Rev. ed. Louisville: Westminster John Knox, 1993.

———. "The Dismantling of Decisional Faith: A Reading of John 6:25-71." In *Critical Readings of John 6,* edited by R. Alan Culpepper, 161–81. BibIntSer 22. Leiden: Brill, 1997.

———. "John, Gospel of." *Dictionary of Biblical Interpretation,* edited by John H. Hayes, 609–19. Vol. 1. Nashville: Abingdon, 1999.

———. "'As You Sent Me': Identity and Mission in the Fourth Gospel." *Word and World* 21 (2001): 370–77.

Lincoln, Andrew T. *Truth on Trial: The Lawsuit Motif in the Fourth Gospel.* Peabody: Hendrickson, 2001.

Lindars, Barnabas. *The Gospel of John.* NCB. London: Oliphants, 1972.

Malina, Bruce J., and Richard L. Rohrbaugh. *Social-Science Commentary on the Gospel of John.* Minneapolis: Fortress Press, 1998.

Marsh, John. *Saint John.* Pelican Gospel Commentaries. Baltimore: Penguin, 1968.

Martyn, J. Louis. *The Gospel of John in Christian History: Essays for Interpreters.* Theological Inquiries. New York: Paulist, 1978.

———. *History and Theology in the Fourth Gospel.* Rev. ed., Nashville: Abingdon, 1979.

Meeks, Wayne A. "The Man from Heaven in Johannine Sectarianism." In *The Interpretation of John,* edited by John Ashton, 169–206. Studies in New Testament Interpretation. 2nd ed. Edinburgh: T. and T. Clark, 1997.

Moloney, Francis J. *The Gospel of John.* SP 4. Collegeville, Minn.: Liturgical, 1998.

Newman, Barclay M., and Eugene A. Nida. *A Translator's Handbook on the Gospel of John.* Helps for Translators. London: United Bible Societies, 1980.

Neyrey, Jerome H. *An Ideology of Revolt: John's Christology in Social-Science Perspective.* Philadelphia: Fortress Press, 1988.

O'Day, Gail R. *Revelation in the Fourth Gospel.* Philadelphia: Fortress Press, 1986.

————. *The Word Disclosed: John's Story and Narrative Preaching.* St. Louis: CBP, 1987.

————. "The Gospel of John: Introduction, Commentary, and Reflections." In *NIB* 9, 491–865. Nashville: Abingdon, 1995.

Petersen, Norman R. *The Gospel of John and the Sociology of Light: Language and Characterization in the Fourth Gospel.* Valley Forge: Trinity Press International, 1993.

Rensberger, David. *Johannine Faith and Liberating Community.* Philadelphia: Westminster, 1988.

Robinson, John A. T. *The Priority of John.* London: SCM, 1985.

Schnackenburg, Rudolf. *The Gospel according to St. John.* 3 vols. Translated by Cecily Hastings. New York: Crossroad, 1968, 1980, 1982.

Segovia, Fernando F., "The Journey(s) of the Word of God: A Reading of the Plot of the Fourth Gospel." *Semeia* 53 (1991): 23–54.

————. *The Farewell of the Word: The Johannine Call to Abide.* Minneapolis: Fortress Press, 1991.

Smith, D. Moody. *The Composition and Order of the Fourth Gospel.* New Haven: Yale Univ. Press, 1965.

————. *Johannine Christianity: Essays on Its Setting, Sources, and Theology.* Columbia: Univ. of South Carolina Press, 1984.

————. *John.* Proclamation Commentaries. 2nd ed. Minneapolis: Fortress Press, 1986.

————. "Judaism and the Gospel of John." In *Jews and Christians: Exploring the Past, Present, and Future,* edited by James H. Charlesworth, 76–89. New York: Crossroad, 1990.

————. *John among the Gospels: The Relationship in Twentieth-Century Research.* Minneapolis: Fortress Press, 1992.

————. *The Theology of the Gospel of John.* NTT. Cambridge: Cambridge Univ. Press, 1995.

————. *John.* ANTC. Nashville: Abingdon, 1999.

Sloyan, Gerard S. *What Are They Saying about John?* New York: Paulist, 1991.

Staley, Jeffrey Lloyd. *The Print's First Kiss: A Rhetorical Investigation of the Implied Reader in the Fourth Gospel.* SBLDS 82. Atlanta: Scholars, 1988.

————. "Stumbling in the Dark, Reaching for the Light: Reading Character in John 5 and 9." *Semeia* 53 (1991): 55–80.

Stibbe, Mark W. G. *John as Storyteller: Narrative Criticism and the Fourth Gospel.* SNTSMS 73. Cambridge: Cambridge Univ. Press, 1992.

————. *John.* Readings: A New Biblical Commentary. Sheffield: JSOT Press, 1993.

Talbert, Charles H. *Reading John: A Literary and Theological Commentary on the Fourth Gospel and the Johannine Epistles.* New York: Crossroad, 1992.

Preaching

Brueggemann, Walter. *Finally Comes the Poet: Daring Speech for Proclamation.* Minneapolis: Fortress Press, 1989.

Buttrick, David. *Homiletic: Moves and Structures.* Philadelphia: Fortress Press, 1987.

Craddock, Fred B. *As One without Authority: Essays on Inductive Preaching.* Rev. ed. Enid, Okla.: Phillips Univ. Press, 1974.

————. *Overhearing the Gospel: Preaching and Teaching the Faith to Persons Who Have Heard It All Before.* Nashville: Abingdon, 1978.

Eslinger, Richard L. *Narrative and Imagination: Preaching the Worlds That Shape Us.* Minneapolis: Fortress Press, 1995.

Eslinger, Richard L., ed. *Intersections: Post-Critical Studies in Preaching.* Grand Rapids: Eerdmans, 1994.

Farris, Stephen. *Preaching That Matters: The Bible and Our Lives.* Louisville: Westminster John Knox, 1998.

Hughes, Robert H., and Robert Kysar. *Preaching Doctrine in the Twenty-First Century.* FRP. Minneapolis: Fortress Press, 1997.

Jensen, Richard A. *Telling the Story: Variety and Imagination in Preaching.* Minneapolis: Augsburg, 1980.

————. *Thinking in Story: Preaching in a Post-Literate Age.* Lima: C.S.S., 1993.

Kastner, Patricia Wilson. *Imagery for Preaching.* FRP. Minneapolis: Fortress Press, 1989.

Kysar, Robert. "Preaching as Biblical Theology: A Proposal for a Homiletical Method." In *The Promise and Practice of Biblical Theology,* edited by John Reumann, 143–56. Minneapolis: Fortress Press, 1991.

————. "The Renaissance and Demise of the Listener: Empowering the Laity Through Preaching." *Lutheran Partners* 13/6 (1997): 18–21.

Long, Thomas G. *Preaching and the Literary Forms of the Bible.* Philadelphia: Fortress Press, 1989.

Lowry, Eugene L. *The Homiletical Plot: The Sermon as Narrative Art Form.* Atlanta: John Knox, 1980.

————. *How to Preach a Parable: Designs for Narrative Sermons.* Nashville: Abingdon, 1989.

————. *The Sermon: Dancing the Edge of Mystery.* Nashville: Abingdon, 1997.

Ourisman, David. *From Gospel to Sermon: Preaching Synoptic Texts.* St. Louis: Chalice, 1999.

Rose, Lucy Atkinson. *Sharing the Word: Preaching the Roundtable Church.* Louisville: Westminster John Knox, 1997.

Smith, D. Moody. *Interpreting the Gospels for Preaching.* Philadelphia: Fortress Press, 1980.

Tisdale, Leonora Tubbs. *Preaching as Local Theology and Folk Art.* FRP. Minneapolis: Fortress Press, 1997.

Wardlaw, Don M., ed. *Preaching Biblically: Creating Sermons in the Shape of Scripture.* Philadelphia: Westminster, 1983.

Index of Passages in John

Index of Sermons
and Sermon Fragments

Index of Gospel Lessons from John in the Revised Common Lectionary

Year A

Year B

Year C

Years A, B, C